W9-CQN-065

A Compilation of Shorthand Outlines for 33,586 Words;
1,381 Names; 523 Geographical Expressions;
1,396 Frequently Used Phrases; 126 Abbreviations;
and 48 Metric Terms

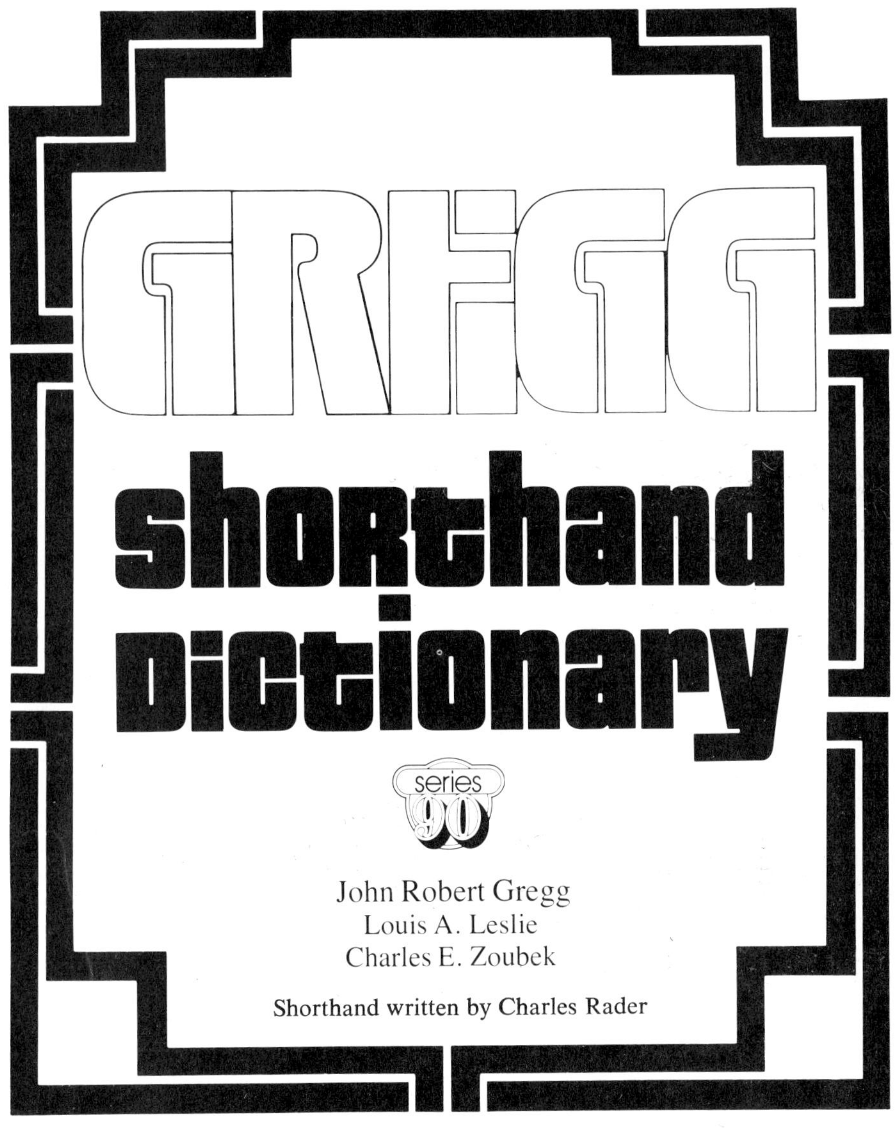

Gregg Shorthand Dictionary

Series 90

John Robert Gregg
Louis A. Leslie
Charles E. Zoubek

Shorthand written by Charles Rader

McGraw-Hill Book Company

New York St. Louis San Francisco Auckland Bogotá
Guatemala Hamburg Lisbon London Madrid
Mexico Montreal New Delhi Panama Paris
San Juan São Paulo Singapore Sydney Tokyo Toronto

Gregg Shorthand Dictionary, Series 90

Copyright © 1978, 1974, 1963, by McGraw-Hill, Inc. All Rights Reserved. Copyright 1949 by McGraw-Hill, Inc. All Rights Reserved. Copyright renewed 1977. Printed in the United States of America. No part of this publication may be reproduced, stored in a retrieval system, or transmitted, in any form or by any means, electronic, mechanical, photocopying, recording or otherwise, without the prior written permission of the publisher.

6789 DOC/DOC 99876543210

ISBN: 0-07-024599-1

First McGraw-Hill Trade Edition, 1983

Library of Congress Cataloging in Publication Data

Gregg, John Robert, 1867-1948.
Gregg shorthand dictionary, series 90.

1. Shorthand–Gregg–Dictionaries. I. Leslie, Louis A., date joint author. II. Zoubek, Charles E., date joint author. III. Title.
Z55.5.G697 1978 653'.427'03 77-855
ISBN 0-07-024599-1

foreword

Gregg Shorthand Dictionary, Series 90, issued on the occasion of the 90th anniversary of the publication of Gregg Shorthand in 1888, is divided into six parts in order to provide maximum usefulness to the writer who wishes an authoritative outline for a word, name, or phrase.

Contents

Part One contains, in alphabetical order, the shorthand outlines for 33,586 words.

Part Two contains 177 common names of women, 189 common names of men, and 1,015 most common surnames in the United States as determined by the records of the Social Security Administration.

Part Three contains 523 American and foreign geographical expressions.

Part Four contains, in alphabetical order, the shorthand outlines for 1,396 phrases frequently used in business.

Part Five contains a list of 126 abbreviations and suggested outlines for them.

Part Six contains a list of 48 metric terms with suggested shortcuts for them.

Shortcuts

It is easily possible to construct shorter outlines for many technical, scientific, and literary terms for which full outlines are given in this dictionary. It is not advisable for average writers to learn shorter outlines for these expressions unless there is a reasonable possibility they will use those shorter outlines with sufficient frequency to justify the effort of learning them. Otherwise, the short, but half-learned, outlines will cause mental hesitation that will result in slower, rather than faster, writing.

Speed of Writing

Research techniques using high-speed motion pictures have proved that most shorthand writers actually write each outline at about the same speed regardless of the speed of the dictation. The 100-word-a-minute writer writes each outline as rapidly as the 200-word-a-minute writer. What, then, is the difference between the two writers? The difference is that the 100-word-a-minute writer is consuming time thinking, pausing, and hesitating. The 200-word-a-minute writer, on the other hand, does not have to stop to think—he or she writes continuously.

The problem of increasing shorthand speed, therefore, is actually a problem of decreasing hesitations in writing—hesitations caused by the struggle of the mind to remember and use abbreviations provided in a shorthand system.

The fewer shortcuts and exceptions the mind must remember and use, the easier it is for the writer to decrease or eliminate hesitations that reduce speed. Therefore, any attempts by writers to manufacture additional shortcuts are more likely to reduce their speed than to increase it unless the new shortcuts are used with such frequency that they become automatized.

"Dictionary" Outlines

There is room for some difference of opinion as to the most appropriate outline for a given word. This dictionary offers outlines that have been discussed and decided upon by experienced writers of Gregg Shorthand. Sometimes an apparently obvious improvement in an outline will actually create the danger of a conflict in reading. More often, an outline different from the one provided in this dictionary would be individually satisfactory but would not be consistent with the outlines for other members of the same word family.

Of one thing the user of this dictionary may be sure—every outline in this dictionary is the result of serious thought and consideration. This dictionary as a whole represents the accumulated experience of all those who have worked with Gregg Shorthand since its publication in 1888.

The publishers are confident that this dictionary will render a valuable service to shorthand writers by placing at their disposal a facile and fluent outline for any word, name, or phrase of interest to them.

The Publishers

part one

Part One of *Gregg Shorthand Dictionary, Series 90,* contains shorthand outlines for 33,586 words arranged in alphabetical order. These words actually represent a far larger vocabulary because many simple derivatives have been omitted—words ending in *ing* and *s,* for example.

More than 500 words that have been added to the language in recent years are included—words such as *astrospace, depollution,* and *software.* A number of words have been added that were rarely used in the past but which, because of changes in the times, are today more frequently used—*racist, sexism, ecology,* for example.

Types of Words Included

The authors have included every word that they feel a shorthand writer might possibly have occasion to wish an outline for. This includes many simple words; it includes many long and technical words.

Many words are included because shorthand students, while still in school, may have occasion to use them in their schoolwork. For this reason, many mathematical, mineralogical, chemical, and physiological expressions are included. For the same reason, many literary words are included—words that usually have very little business value but that the student uses in schoolwork.

Consistency Rather Than Brevity

Consistency, rather than brevity, of outline has been the guiding principle in the recommended outlines in this dictionary. The fastest shorthand outline (within reasonable limits) is the outline that requires the least mental effort. The speed with which an outline may be written is not to be judged solely by its brevity to the eye, nor even by its facility to the hand; it is to be judged by the speed with which it may be constructed by the mind and supplied by the mind to the hand.

It is strongly urged, therefore, that the shorthand outline given in this dictionary be accepted as a normal outline for any expression unless that expression occurs so frequently in a writer's dictation that learning a shorter form for it is justified.

Suggestion. As a famous shorthand reporter of an earlier generation once observed, "The longer I write shorthand, the *longer* I write shorthand." Keep this observation in mind as you work to develop your shorthand speed.

a

a
abacus
abaft
abalone
abandon
abandoned
abandonment
abase
abased
abasement
abash
abatable
abate
abated
abatement
abbess
abbey
abbot
abbreviate
abbreviated
abbreviation
abdicate
abdicated

abdication
abdomen
abdominal
abduct
abduction
abed
aberration
aberrational
abet
abetted
abettor
abeyance
abhor
abhorred
abhorrence
abhorrent
abide
ability
abject
abjuration
abjure
abjured
abjurement

ablative
ablaut
ablaze
able
able-bodied
ablution
ably
abnegation
abnormal
abnormality
abnormity
aboard
abode
abolish
abolished
abolition
abolitionism
abolitionist
abominable
abominably
abominate
abomination
aboriginal

aborigine
abortive
abound
aboundingly
about
above
abrade
abraded
abrasion
abrasive
abreaction
abreast
abridge
abridged
abridgment
abroad
abrogate
abrogated
abrogation
abrogative
abrupt
abruptly
abruptness
abscess
abscessed
abscissa
abscission
abscond
absconded
absconder
absence
absent
absentee

absenteeism
absently
absinthe
absolute
absolutely
absoluteness
absolution
absolutism
absolutist
absolve
absolved
absorb
absorbed
absorbency
absorbent
absorbingly
absorption
absorptive
abstain
abstained
abstainer
abstemious
abstemiously
abstemiousness
abstention
abstinence
abstinent
abstinently
abstract
abstracted
abstractedly
abstraction
abstractionist

abstractly
abstruse
abstruseness
absurd
absurdism
absurdist
absurdity
absurdly
abundance
abundant
abundantly
abuse
abused
abusive
abusively
abusiveness
abut
abutment
abuttal
abutted
abutter
abysm
abysmal
abyss
acacia
academic
academician
academies
academy
Acadian
acanthaster
acanthus
accede

acceded
accelerando
accelerant
accelerate
accelerated
acceleration
accelerative
accelerator
acceleratory
accent
accented
accentuate
accentuated
accentuation
accept
acceptability
acceptable
acceptance
acceptation
accepted
access
accessibility
accessible
accession
accessory
accidence
accident
accidental
accidentally
accipitrine
acclaim
acclaimed
acclamation
acclamatory
acclimate
acclimated
acclimation
acclimatization
acclimatize
acclimatized
acclivity
accolade
accommodate
accommodated
accommodatingly
accommodation
accommodative
accompanied
accompaniment
accompanist
accompany
accomplice
accomplish
accomplished
accomplishment
accord
accordance
accorded
accordingly
accordion
accost
accosted
account
accountability
accountable
accountancy
accountant
accounted
accoutered
accouterment
accredit
accredited
accretion
accrual
accrue
accrued
accumulate
accumulated
accumulates
accumulation
accumulative
accumulator
accuracy
accurate
accurately
accusation
accusative
accusatory
accuse
accused
accuser
accusingly
accustom
accustomed
ace
acerb
acerbic
acerbity
acetate

acetic
acetone
acetylene
ache
ached
achievable
achieve
achieved
achievement
achromatic
achromatically
achromatosis
acid
acidification
acidifier
acidify
acidity
acidless
acidosis
acidproof
acidulate
acidulated
acidulous
acknowledge
acknowledged
acknowledgment
acme
acne
acolyte
aconite
acorn
acoustic
acoustical
acoustically
acoustics
acquaint
acquaintance
acquaintanceship
acquainted
acquiesce
acquiesced
acquiescence
acquiescent
acquire
acquired
acquirement
acquires
acquisition
acquisitive
acquisitiveness
acquit
acquittal
acquitted
acre
acreage
acrid
acridity
acridly
acrimonious
acrimoniously
acrimoniousness
acrimony
acrobat
acrobatic
acrobatically
acrobatics
acrophobe
acropolis
acrosin
across
acrylic
act
acted
actinic
actinium
action
actionable
activate
activated
activation
activator
active
actively
activist
activity
activize
actor
actress
actual
actualities
actuality
actually
actuarial
actuary
actuate
actuated
acuity
acumen
acupuncture

acute
acuteness
adage
adagio
adamant
adamantine
adapt
adaptability
adaptable
adaptation
adapted
adapter
adaptive
add
added
addenda
addendum
adder
addict
addicted
addiction
addition
additional
additionally
additive
addle
addled
address
addressed
addressee
Addressograph
adduce
adduced

adduct
adduction
adductive
adductor
adenoid
adenology
adenoma
adept
adequacy
adequate
adequately
adequateness
adhere
adhered
adherence
adherent
adhesion
adhesive
adhesiveness
adieu
adipose
adiposity
adjacency
adjacent
adjectival
adjective
adjoin
adjoined
adjourn
adjourned
adjournment
adjudge
adjudged

adjudicate
adjudicated
adjudication
adjudicative
adjudicator
adjunct
adjuration
adjuratory
adjure
adjured
adjust
adjustable
adjusted
adjuster
adjustment
adjutancy
adjutant
administer
administered
administration
administrative
administratively
administrator
administratrix
admirable
admirably
admiral
admiralty
admiration
admire
admired
admissibility
admissible

admission
admit
admittance
admitted
admittedly
admixture
admonish
admonition
admonitory
adobe
adolescence
adolescent
adopt
adopted
adoption
adoptive
adorable
adoration
adore
adored
adoringly
adorn
adorned
adornment
adrenal
adrenaline
adrift
adroit
adroitly
adroitness
adsorb
adsorption
adulation

adulatory
adult
adulterant
adulterate
adulterated
adulteration
adulterer
adulterous
adultery
adulthood
adumbrate
adumbrated
adumbration
advance
advanced
advancement
advantage
advantageous
advent
Adventist
adventitious
adventure
adventurer
adventuresome
adventuress
adventurous
adverb
adverbial
adverbially
adversary
adversative
adverse
adversely

adversity
advert
advertise
advertisement
advertiser
advice
advisability
advisable
advise
advised
advisedly
advisee
advisement
advisory
advocacy
advocate
advocated
advowson
adz
aegis
aeolian
aeon
aerate
aerated
aeration
aerator
aerial
aerobics
aeronautical
aeroplankton
aerosol
aerospace
aerotrain

aesthetic
affability
affable
affably
affect
affectation
affected
affectedly
affectingly
affection
affectionate
affectionately
affectivity
affiance
affianced
affiant
affidavit
affiliate
affiliated
affiliation
affinity
affirm
affirmable
affirmation
affirmative
affirmatory
affirmed
affix
affixed
afflatus
afflict
afflicted
affliction
afflictive
affluence
affluent
afford
afforded
afforest
afforestation
affray
affright
affrighted
affront
affronted
afghan
afield
afire
aflame
afloat
afoot
aforesaid
aforethought
aforetime
afoul
afraid
Afro
Afro-American
after
afterbeat
aftercare
afterclap
afterdeck
after-dinner
aftereffect
afterglow
aftergrowth
afterguard
afterhatch
afterheat
afterhold
afterimage
afterlife
aftermath
aftermost
afternoon
afterpart
aftertaste
afterthought
aftertime
afterward
again
against
agape
agate
agateware
agave
age
aged
ageless
agency
agenda
agendum
agent
ageratum
agglomerate
agglomerated
agglomeration
agglomerative

agglutinate
agglutination
agglutinative
aggrandize
aggrandizement
aggravate
aggravated
aggravatingly
aggravation
aggregate
aggregation
aggression
aggressive
aggressor
aggrieve
aggrieved
aghast
agile
agility
agio
agitate
agitated
agitation
agitator
agleam
agnate
agnostic
agnosticism
agog
agonize
agonized
agonizingly
agony

agoraphobic
agrarian
agree
agreeability
agreeable
agreeableness
agreed
agreement
agricultural
agriculture
agrochemicals
agro-industry
agronomy
aground
ague
ahead
ahoy
ahungered
aid
aided
aigrette
aiguillette
ail
ailanthus
ailed
aileron
ailment
aim
aimless
air
airbag
airbrush
airbus

air-dry
aired
airfield
airfreight
airily
airliner
airmail
airman
airmobile
airplane
airport
airship
airsick
airspace
air-taxi
airtight
airway
airworthy
airy
aisle
ajar
akimbo
akin
alabaster
alacrity
alamo
alarm
alarmed
alarmingly
alarmist
alas
albacore
albatross

albino
album
albumin
albuminous
alchemist
alchemy
alcohol
alcoholic
alcoholism
alcoholize
alcove
alder
alderman
aldermanic
Alderney
aleatoric
aleatory
alembic
alembicate
alemite
alert
alertly
alertness
alewife
alexandrite
alfalfa
algebra
algebraic
Algerian
Algol
alias
alibi
alidade
alien
alienability
alienable
alienate
alienated
alienation
alienist
alight
align
alignment
alike
alimentary
alimentation
alimony
aliquant
aliquot
alive
aliveness
alizarin
alkali
alkalinity
all
allay
allayed
allegation
allege
alleged
allegedly
allegiance
allegorical
allegorize
allegory
allegretto
allegro
allergen
allergic
allergy
alleviate
alleviated
alleviation
alley
alleyway
alliance
allied
alligator
alliterate
alliteration
alliterative
alliteratively
allocable
allocate
allocated
allocation
allocution
allograft
allopath
allopathic
allopathy
allot
allotment
allotted
allow
allowable
allowance
allowed
allowedly

alloy
alloyage
alloyed
allspice
allude
alluded
allure
allured
allurement
alluringly
allusion
allusive
allusively
allusiveness
alluvial
alluvium
ally
almanac
almighty
almond
almoner
almost
alms
almshouse
alodium
aloe
aloft
aloha
alone
along
alongside
aloof
aloofly

alopecia
aloud
alpaca
alphabet
alphabetic
alphabetical
alphabetize
alphametic
already
also
altar
altarpiece
alter
alterable
alteration
alterative
altercate
altercation
altered
alternate
alternated
alternation
alternative
alternator
although
altigraph
altimeter
altiplano
altissimo
altitude
alto
altogether
altruism

altruist
altruistic
altruistically
alum
alumina
aluminate
aluminiferous
aluminosis
aluminum
alumna
alumnae
alumni
alumnus
alveolar
alveolus
always
alyssum
am
amalgam
amalgamate
amalgamated
amalgamation
amanuensis
amaranth
amaranthine
amass
amateur
amateurish
amateurism
amative
amativeness
amatory
amaze

amazed
amazement
amazingly
amazon
amazonian
ambassador
ambassadorial
ambassadorially
ambassadress
amber
ambergris
ambidexterity
ambidextrous
ambidextrously
ambidextrousness
ambient
ambiguity
ambiguous
ambiguously
ambiguousness
ambition
ambitious
ambitiously
ambivalence
ambivalent
amble
ambrosia
ambrosial
ambrosially
ambrotype
ambulance
ambulant
ambulatory
ambuscade
ambush
ameliorate
ameliorated
amelioration
ameliorative
amen
amenability
amenable
amend
amended
amendment
amenity
American
Americanization
Americanize
Americanologist
Americanophobe
amethyst
amiability
amiable
amicability
amicable
amidships
amidst
amiss
amity
ammeter
ammonia
ammonium
ammunition
amnesia
amnesty
amoeba
among
amongst
amoral
amorous
amorously
amorousness
amorphous
amortization
amortize
amortized
amount
amounted
amour
amperage
ampere
amphetamine
amphibian
amphibious
amphibiously
amphitheater
amphora
ampicillin
ample
amplification
amplified
amplifier
amplify
amplitude
amply
ampulla
amputate
amputated

amputation
amputative
amputee
Amtrak
amulet
amuse
amused
amusement
amusingly
an
anabolism
anachronism
anachronistic
anachronous
anaconda
anagram
analects
analgesia
analgesic
analogical
analogies
analogous
analogously
analogue
analogy
analyses
analysis
analyst
analytic
analytical
analytically
analyze
analyzed
analyzer
anamnesis
anarchic
anarchical
anarchism
anarchist
anarchy
anastigmatic
anathematize
anatomic
anatomical
anatomist
anatomize
anatomized
anatomy
ancestor
ancestors
ancestral
ancestry
anchor
anchorage
anchored
anchorite
anchovy
ancient
ancillary
and
andante
andiron
anecdotage
anecdote
anemia
anemometer
anemometry
anemone
anent
aneroid
anesthesia
anesthesiology
anesthesis
anesthetic
anesthetization
anesthetize
anesthetized
aneurysm
anew
angel
angelic
Angelus
anger
angered
angle
angled
angler
Anglican
Anglo-Saxon
Angora
angrier
angriest
angrily
angry
anguish
anguished
angular
angularity
angulation

anhydrous
aniline
animadversion
animal
animate
animated
animatedly
animation
animator
animism
animist
animistic
animosity
animus
anise
aniseroot
ankle
anklebone
anklet
ankylosis
annalist
annals
anneal
annealed
annex
annexation
annexationist
annexed
annihilate
annihilated
annihilation
anniversary
annotate

annotated
annotation
announce
announced
announcement
announcer
annoy
annoyance
annoyed
annoyingly
annual
annually
annuitant
annuity
annul
annular
annulled
annulment
annunciation
annunciator
anode
anodyne
anoint
anointed
anomalies
anomalous
anomalously
anomaly
anon
anonymity
anonymous
anonymously
anopheles

another
answer
answerable
answered
ant
antacid
antagonism
antagonist
antagonistic
antagonistically
antagonize
antagonized
antarctic
ante
anteater
antecedent
antechamber
antedate
antedated
antelope
antenatal
antenna
anterior
anteroom
anthem
anthologies
anthologist
anthologize
anthology
anthracite
anthrax
anthropoid
anthropological

anthropology
antibody
antic
Antichrist
anticipate
anticipated
anticipation
anticipatory
anticlimax
anticline
antidote
antidumping
antifertility
antigen
antihero
antiknock
antimony
antinomy
antipathies
antipathy
antiphonal
antipodes
antipollution
antipoverty
antiquarian
antiquary
antiquated
antique
antiqued
antiquity
antiscience
antisepsis
antiseptic

antiseptically
antismog
antisocial
antitank
antitheses
antithesis
antithetical
antitoxin
antitrust
antler
antlered
antonym
antrum
anvil
anxiety
anxious
any
anybody
anyhow
anyone
anything
anyway
anywhere
aorta
aortic
apace
apart
apartheid
apartment
apathetic
apathetically
apathy
aperient

aperitive
aperture
apex
apexes
aphasia
aphid
aphonia
aphorism
aphoristic
apiarist
apiary
apical
apices
apiece
apocalypse
apogee
Apollo
apologetic
apologetical
apologies
apologist
apologize
apologized
apology
apoplectic
apoplexy
apostasy
apostate
apostle
apostolic
apostolical
apostrophe
apostrophize

apothecary
apothegm
apotheosis
appall
appalled
appallingly
appanage
apparatus
apparatuses
apparel
appareled
apparent
apparition
appeal
appealed
appealingly
appear
appearance
appeared
appeasable
appease
appeased
appeasement
appeasingly
appellant
appellate
appellation
appellee
append
appendage
appendectomy
appended
appendicitis

appendix
appendixes
apperceive
apperceived
apperception
apperceptive
appertain
appertained
appetite
appetizer
appetizingly
applaud
applauded
applause
apple
applejack
applenut
applesauce
appliance
applicability
applicable
applicant
application
applicator
applied
appliqué
apply
appoint
appointed
appointee
appointive
appointment
apportion

apportioned
apportionment
apposite
apposition
appraisal
appraise
appraised
appraiser
appraisingly
appreciable
appreciably
appreciate
appreciated
appreciation
appreciative
appreciatively
apprehend
apprehended
apprehendingly
apprehension
apprehensive
apprehensively
apprehensiveness
apprentice
apprenticed
apprenticeship
apprise
apprised
approach
approachable
approached
approbation
approbative

approbativeness
appropriate
appropriated
appropriately
appropriateness
appropriation
approval
approve
approved
approvingly
approximate
approximated
approximately
approximation
appurtenance
appurtenant
apricot
April
apron
apropos
apse
apsis
apt
aptitude
aptly
aptness
aquafarm
aquamarine
aquanaut
aquarelle
aquarium
aquascutum
aquatic
aquatint
aqueduct
aqueous
aquiline
Arab
arabesque
Arabian
Arabic
arability
Arabist
arable
arachnid
arachnoid
aragonite
Aramaic
arbalest
arbiter
arbitrable
arbitrage
arbitrament
arbitrarily
arbitrariness
arbitrary
arbitrate
arbitrated
arbitration
arbitrative
arbitrator
arbor
arboreal
arboreous
arboretum
arbutus
arc
arcade
arcaded
arcadia
arcanum
arch
archaeologist
archaeology
archaic
archangel
archangelic
archbishop
archdeacon
archdiocese
archducal
archduchess
archduchy
archduke
archer
archerfish
archery
archetypal
archetype
archfiend
archipelago
architect
architectonic
architectural
architecturally
architecture
architrave
archives
archivist

archly
archness
archway
arcology
arctic
ardent
ardently
ardor
arduous
arduously
are
area
arena
argent
argentiferous
argon
argonaut
argot
arguable
argue
argued
argument
argumentation
argumentative
Argyrol
aria
arid
aridity
aright
arise
arisen
aristocracy
aristocrat

aristocratic
arithmetic
arithmetical
ark
arm
armada
armadillo
armament
armature
armchair
armed
Armenian
armful
armhole
armistice
armlet
armor
armored
armorial
armory
armpit
armrest
armscye
army
arnica
aroma
aromatic
around
arouse
arpeggio
arraign
arraigned
arraignment

arrange
arranged
arrangement
arranger
arras
array
arrayed
arrearage
arrears
arrest
arrester
arrhythmic
arrival
arrive
arrived
arrogance
arrogant
arrogantly
arrogate
arrogated
arrogation
arrow
arrowhead
arrowheaded
arrowwood
arrowy
arroyo
arsenal
arsenate
arsenic
arsenical
arsenide
arsenite

arson
arsonist
art
arterial
artery
artful
artfully
arthritic
arthritical
arthritis
arthroplasty
artichoke
article
articled
articulate
articulated
articulation
articulative
artifact
artifice
artificer
artificial
artificiality
artificially
artillerist
artillery
artisan
artist
artistic
artistry
artless
Aryan
as

asafetida
asbestos
ascend
ascendancy
ascendant
ascender
ascension
ascent
ascertain
ascertainment
ascetic
asceticism
ascites
ascorbic
ascot
ascribe
ascribed
ascription
asepsis
aseptic
ash
ashamed
ashen
ashes
ashlar
ashore
ashpit
ashram
ashwort
ashy
Asian
Asiatic
aside

asinine
asininity
ask
askance
askew
aslant
asleep
asp
asparagus
aspect
aspen
asperity
asperse
aspersed
aspersion
asphalt
asphaltic
asphodel
asphyxia
asphyxiate
asphyxiation
aspic
aspirant
aspirate
aspirated
aspiration
aspirator
aspire
aspired
aspirin
assagai
assail
assailant

assailed
assassin
assassinate
assassinated
assassination
assault
assaulted
assay
assayed
assayer
assemblage
assemble
assembled
assembler
assembly
assent
assented
assentingly
assert
asserted
assertion
assertive
assertively
assess
assessable
assessed
assessment
assessor
assessorship
asset
asseverate
asseveration
assiduity
assiduous
assiduously
assign
assignable
assignation
assigned
assignee
assignment
assignor
assimilable
assimilate
assimilated
assimilation
assimilative
assimilatory
assist
assistance
assistant
assisted
assists
assize
associate
associated
association
associative
assonance
assonant
assort
assorted
assortment
assuage
assuaged
assumable
assumably
assume
assumed
assumedly
assumpsit
assumption
assurance
assure
assured
assuredly
assuredness
assurer
Assyrian
aster
asterisk
astern
asteroid
asthenia
asthenic
asthma
asthmatic
astigmatic
astigmatism
astonish
astonishingly
astonishment
astound
astounded
astoundingly
astraddle
astragalus
astrakhan
astral

astray
astride
astringency
astringent
astrodome
astrodynamics
astrologer
astrology
astronaut
astronautics
astronomer
astronomical
astronomy
astrophotographer
astrophysical
astrophysicist
astrophysics
astrospace
astroturf
astutely
astuteness
asunder
asylum
asymmetric
asymmetrical
asymmetry
at
ataraxia
atavism
atavistic
atheism
atheist
atheistic

athenaeum
Athenian
athlete
athletic
athletics
athwart
atmosphere
atmospheric
atoll
atom
atomatic
atomic
atomistic
atomize
atomized
atomizer
atonal
atonality
atone
atoned
atonement
atrazine
atrium
atrocious
atrociously
atrocity
atrophied
atrophy
atropine
attach
attaché
attached
attachment

attack
attacker
attain
attainable
attainder
attained
attainment
attar
attempt
attempted
attend
attendance
attendant
attention
attentive
attentively
attentiveness
attenuate
attenuated
attenuation
attest
attestation
attests
attic
attire
attired
attitude
attitudinize
attorney
attorneys
attract
attracted
attraction

attractive
attractively
attribute
attributed
attribution
attributive
attrition
attune
attuned
atwitter
atypical
auburn
auction
auctioned
auctioneer
audacious
audaciously
audacity
audibility
audible
audibly
audience
audio
audiolingual
audiometer
audiotape
audiotyping
audiovisual
audited
audition
auditor
auditorium
auditory

auger
aught
augment
augmentation
augmentative
augmented
augur
augured
augury
august
August
aunt
au pair
aura
aural
aureole
auricle
auricular
auriferous
aurora
auroral
auscultate
auscultation
auspice
auspices
auspicious
austere
austerely
austerity
Australian
Austrian
authentic
authenticate

authenticated
authentication
authenticity
author
authoritarian
authoritative
authoritatively
authority
authorization
authorize
authorized
authorship
autobahn
autobiographical
autobiography
autochthonous
autocide
autoclave
autocracy
autocrat
autocratic
autocratically
autodrome
autograph
autoimmune
autointoxication
automatic
automation
automatize
automaton
automobile
autonomize
autonomous

autonomy
autopsies
autopsy
autosuggestion
autumn
autumnal
auxiliary
avail
availability
available
availed
avalanche
avarice
avaricious
avariciously
avatar
avenge
avenged
avenue
aver
average
averaged
averment
averred
averse

aversion
avert
averted
aviary
aviation
aviator
avid
avidity
avidly
avigation
avocado
avocation
avoid
avoidable
avoided
avowal
avowedly
avuncular
await
awaited
awake
awaken
awakened
award
awarded

aware
awareness
awash
away
awe
awesome
awful
awfully
awkward
awkwardly
awkwardness
awl
awning
awoke
awry
ax
axiom
axiomatic
axis
axle
azalea
azimuth
Aztec
azure
azurite

b

babbitt
babble
baboon
baby
Babylonian
baccalaureate
bacchanal
bacchanalian
bachelor
bachelorhood
bacillus
back
backache
backboard
backbone
backbreaker
backdrop
backer
backfire
backgammon
background
backhand
backhanded

backlash
backlog
backsaw
backslide
backslider
backspin
backstage
backstamp
backstitch
backstop
backstroke
backtrack
backup
backward
backwardness
backwash
backwater
backwoods
bacon
bacteria
bacterial
bactericidal
bactericide

bacteriological
bacteriology
bacterium
bad
badge
badger
badinage
badlands
badly
badminton
badness
baffle
baffled
bag
bagasse
bagatelle
baggage
bagged
bagpipe
bail
bailed
bailee
bailiff

bailiwick
bailment
bailout
bait
baize
bake
Bakelite
baker
bakery
balance
balanced
balboa
balbriggan
balcony
bald
baldachin
balderdash
baldness
baldric
bale
baled
baleful
balk
ball
ballad
ballast
balled
ballerina
ballet
balletomane
ballistics
balloon
balloonist

ballot
ballplayer
ballroom
ballute
balm
balsa
balsam
balsamiferous
baluster
balustrade
bamboo
bamboozle
bamboozled
ban
banal
banality
banalize
banana
band
bandage
bandanna
bandbox
bandeau
banded
banderole
bandicoot
bandit
bandmaster
bandolier
bandstand
bandy
baneful
bang

bangboard
banged
bangle
banish
banishment
banister
banjo
bank
bankbook
banked
banker
bankrupt
bankruptcy
banned
banner
banns
banquet
banqueted
banshee
bantam
banter
bantered
banteringly
banyan
banzai
baptism
baptismal
baptist
baptize
baptized
baptizement
bar
barb

barbarian
barbaric
barbarism
barbarity
barbarous
barbecue
barbed
barber
barberry
barbette
barbiturate
bard
bare
bareback
bared
barefaced
barefoot
bareheaded
barely
bareness
bargain
bargained
barge
bargeman
bariatrician
bariatrics
baritone
barium
bark
barley
barmaid
barn
barnacle

barnyard
barococo
barogram
barograph
barometer
barometric
baron
baronage
baroness
baronet
baronetcy
baronial
barony
baroque
baroquerie
barrack
barracuda
barrage
barratry
barrel
barren
barrenness
barricade
barricaded
barrier
barrister
barrow
barter
bartered
basal
basalt
bascule
base

baseboard
based
baseless
basely
basement
baseness
baser
basest
bashful
basic
basically
basilica
basilisk
basin
basis
bask
basket
basketball
basketwork
bas-relief
bass
bassinet
basso
bassoon
basswood
basted
bastinado
bastion
bat
batch
bath
bathe
bathed

bather
bathhouse
bathos
bathrobe
bathroom
batiste
baton
battalion
batten
battened
batter
battered
battery
battle
battled
battlement
battleship
bawl
bawled
bayberry
bayonet
bayoneted
bayou
bazaar
be
beach
beached
beachcomber
beacon
bead
beaded
beadle
beadwork
beagle
beak
beaker
beam
beamed
bean
bear
bearable
beard
bearded
bearer
bearish
bearskin
beast
beastliness
beastly
beat
beaten
beater
beatific
beatification
beatify
beatings
beatnik
beauteous
beautiful
beautifully
beautify
beauty
beaver
becalm
becalmed
became
because
beckon
beckoned
becloud
become
becomingly
becomingness
bed
bedaub
bedbug
bedchamber
bedclothes
bedded
bedeck
bedevil
bedeviled
bedfellow
bedizen
bedlam
bedpost
bedridden
bedrock
bedroll
bedroom
bedside
bedspread
bedspring
bedstead
bedtime
bee
beech
beef
beefsteak

beeline
been
beer
beeswax
beetle
befall
befell
befit
befog
before
beforehand
befriend
befuddle
befuddled
beg
beget
beggar
begged
begin
begone
begonia
begot
begrime
beguile
beguiled
begum
begun
behalf
behave
behavior
behavioral
behaviorism
behead

beheadings
beheld
behemoth
behest
behind
behold
beholden
beholder
behoove
beige
bejewel
bejeweled
belabor
belated
belatedly
belch
beleaguer
beleaguered
belfry
Belgian
belie
belief
believable
believe
belittle
belittled
bell
belladonna
bellbird
bellboy
bellicose
bellicosity
belligerence

belligerency
belligerent
belligerently
bellowed
bellows
belong
belonged
belongings
beloved
below
belt
belted
belvedere
bemoan
bemoaned
bemused
bench
bend
bended
beneath
benediction
benefaction
benefactor
benefactress
beneficent
beneficial
beneficiary
benefit
benefited
benevolence
benevolent
benighted
benign

benignancy
benignant
benignity
bent
benzene
bequeath
bequest
berate
berated
bereave
bereaved
bereavement
berry
berth
beryl
beseech
beseeched
beseechingly
beset
beside
besides
besiege
besieged
besmirch
besotted
bespangle
bespeak
Bessemer
best
bestial
bestiality
bestow
bestowed
bestride
bet
betake
betide
betimes
betoken
betray
betrayal
betrayer
betroth
betrothal
better
bettered
betterment
between
betwixt
bevel
beveled
beverage
bevy
bewail
bewailed
beware
bewilder
bewildered
bewilderingly
bewilderment
bewitch
bewitchingly
beyond
bezel
biannual
biannually
bias
biased
bibelot
bible
biblical
bibliographical
bibliography
bibulous
bicameral
bicarbonate
bicentenary
biceps
bichloride
bichromate
bicuspid
bicycle
bid
bidder
bide
biennial
biennium
bier
bifocal
big
bigamist
bigamous
bigamy
bigger
biggest
bighorn
bight
bigot
bigoted

bigotry
bijou
biker
bikeway
bilateral
bile
bilge
biliary
bilingual
bilious
bilk
bill
billboard
billed
billet
billeted
billfish
billfold
billhead
billiards
billings
billion
billionaire
billow
billposter
billsticker
bimetallic
bimetallism
bimetallist
bimonthly
bin
binary
binaural

bind
binder
bindery
bindingly
bindings
bindweed
bingo
binnacle
binocular
binomial
biodegradability
biodegradable
biodegradation
bioengineer
biofeedback
biographer
biographic
biographical
biographically
biography
biological
biologically
biologist
biology
biomathematician
biomedicine
biomorphism
bionics
biopsy
biorhythm
bioscience
bioscientific
biotelemetric

bipartite
biped
biplane
bipolar
birch
bird
birdlime
birdman
birth
birthday
birthmark
birthplace
birthright
biscuit
bisect
bishop
bishopric
bismuth
bison
bisque
bit
bite
biter
bitingly
bitten
bitter
bitterest
bitterly
bittern
bitterness
bitters
bitterweed
bitumen

bituminous
bivouac
bizarre
black
blackball
blackberry
blackbird
blackboard
blacken
blacker
blackest
blackfish
blackguard
blackhead
blackish
blackjack
blackleg
blackmail
blackmailer
blackness
blacksmith
blackstrap
blackthorn
bladder
blade
blame
blamed
blameless
blamelessly
blamelessness
blameworthy
blanch
blancmange

bland
blandish
blandishingly
blandishment
blandly
blandness
blank
blanked
blanker
blankest
blanket
blankly
blare
blared
blarney
blaspheme
blasphemed
blasphemer
blasphemous
blasphemy
blast
blasted
blast-off
blaze
blazed
blazer
blazon
blazoned
bleach
bleached
bleacher
bleak
bleat

bleed
bleeder
blemish
blench
blend
blended
blendings
bless
blessedness
blessings
blew
blight
blighted
blimp
blind
blinded
blinder
blindfold
blindly
blindness
blink
blinked
blinker
blip
bliss
blissful
blissfully
blister
blistered
blisteringly
blistery
blithe
blithely

blithesome
blizzard
bloat
bloated
block
blockade
blockaded
blockader
blockbuster
blockhead
blockhouse
blond
blood
blooded
bloodhound
bloodiest
bloodless
bloodletting
bloodline
bloodroot
bloodshed
bloodshot
bloodstain
bloodwood
bloody
bloom
bloomed
bloomer
blossom
blossomed
blot
blotch
blotter

blouse
blow
blower
blowfish
blowfly
blowgun
blowhard
blowhole
blown
blow off
blowout
blowpipe
blowtorch
blowy
blubber
bludgeon
bludgeoned
blue
bluefish
bluegrass
bluenose
bluestocking
bluff
bluffed
bluffer
blunder
blundered
blunderbuss
blunderer
blunderingly
blunt
blunted
bluntly

bluntness
blur
blurb
blurred
blurt
blush
blushed
blushingly
bluster
blustered
blusteringly
blustery
boa
board
boarded
boarder
boast
boasted
boaster
boastful
boastfully
boat
boatload
boatman
boatswain
bobbin
bobcat
bobolink
bobtail
bode
bodice
bodily
bodkin

body
bodyguard
bodymaker
bodysuit
bog
bogey
boggle
boggled
bogus
bogwood
Bohemian
boil
boiled
boiler
boisterous
boisterously
bola
bold
bolder
boldest
boldface
boldly
boldness
bolero
boleweed
Bolivia
boliviano
boll
bolo
bolometer
Bolshevik
bolster
bolstered

bolt
bolted
bolthead
bolus
bomb
bombard
bombarded
bombardier
bombardment
bombast
bombastic
bombed
bomber
bombproof
bombshell
bonanza
bonbon
bond
bondage
bonded
bondholder
bondman
bondslave
bondsman
bone
boned
bonefish
boneless
boneset
bonfire
bongo
bonito
bonnet

bonneted
bonus
bony
booby
boodle
book
bookbinder
booked
bookings
bookish
bookkeeper
bookkeeping
booklet
booklets
bookmaker
bookman
bookmark
bookplate
bookrack
bookrest
bookseller
bookshelf
bookstall
bookstand
bookworm
boom
boomed
boomerang
boon
boor
boorish
boost
boosted

booster
boot
bootblack
booted
bootee
bootery
booth
bootjack
bootleg
bootlegger
bootless
bootstrap
booty
booze
boracic
borate
borax
Bordeaux
border
bordereau
bordered
bore
bored
boreal
borealis
boredom
borer
boresome
boric
borine
borings
born
boron

borough
borrow
borrowed
borrower
borrowings
borsch
bosky
Bosnian
bosom
boss
bossed
bossism
bossy
botanic
botanical
botanist
botanize
botanized
botany
botch
botched
botfly
both
bother
bothered
bothersome
Bothnian
bottle
bottlebird
bottled
bottlehead
bottleholder
bottleneck

bottlenose
bottom
bottomless
bottomry
botulism
boudoir
bough
boughed
bought
bouillabaisse
bouillon
boulder
boulevard
bounce
bounced
bouncer
bound
boundary
bounded
bounden
bounder
boundless
bounteous
bounteously
bountiful
bounty
bouquet
bourgeois
bourgeoisie
bourse
bout
boutique
bovarysm

bovine
bow
bow
bowdlerize
bowed
bowed
bowel
bower
bowerbird
bowfin
bowie
bowknot
bowl
bowled
bowlegged
bowler
bowman
bowshot
bowsprit
bowstring
box
boxboard
boxcar
boxed
boxer
boxwood
boy
boycott
boyhood
boyish
boyishness
brace
braced

bracelet
bracken
bracket
bracketed
brackish
bradawl
brag
bragged
braggadocio
braggart
Brahman
braid
braided
braille
brain
brained
brainfag
brainless
brainsick
brainwork
brainy
braise
braised
brake
brakeage
braked
brakeman
bramble
bran
branch
branched
branchling
brand

branded
brandied
brandish
brandished
brand-new
brandy
brash
brass
brassard
brassbound
brassie
brassiness
brassy
brat
bratling
bravado
brave
bravely
braver
bravery
bravest
bravo
bravura
brawl
brawled
brawler
brawn
brawny
bray
brayed
braze
brazed
brazen

brazened
brazier
brazilite
brazilwood
breach
breached
bread
breadbasket
breadboard
breadboarding
breaded
breadfruit
breadroot
breadstuff
breadth
breadwinner
break
breakable
breakage
breakdown
breaker
breakfast
breakneck
break off
breakout
breakover
breakthrough
breakup
breakwater
breast
breastband
breastbone
breasted

breast-fed
breastmark
breastpin
breastplate
breastweed
breastwork
breath
breathed
breathless
bred
breech
breed
breeder
breeze
breezed
breezy
brethren
breve
brevet
breviary
brevier
brevity
brew
brewed
brewer
brewery
brewhouse
bribe
bribed
bribery
bric-a-brac
brick
brickbat

bricked
bricklayer
brickmason
brickyard
bridal
bride
bridegroom
bridesmaid
bridge
bridged
bridgehead
bridgework
bridle
bridled
brief
briefer
briefest
briefly
briefness
brier
brig
brigade
brigadier
brigand
brigandage
brigantine
bright
brighten
brighter
brightest
brightly
brightness
brightwork

brilliance
brilliancy
brilliant
brilliantine
brilliantly
brilliantness
brim
brimful
brimmed
brimstone
brindled
brine
bring
brink
briny
brioche
briquette
brisk
brisken
brisket
briskly
briskness
bristle
bristled
bristlier
bristliest
bristly
Britannia
Britannic
Briticism
British
Britisher
Briton

brittle
brittleness
broach
broached
broad
broadax
broadbill
broadbrim
broadcast
broadcaster
broaden
broader
broadest
broadleaf
broadloom
broadly
broadside
broadway
broadwise
brocade
brocaded
brocatel
broccoli
brochette
brochure
brogan
brogue
broil
broiled
broiler
broke
broken
brokenly

broker
brokerage
bromate
bromide
bromidic
bromine
bronchial
bronchitis
bronchoscope
bronchus
bronco
bronze
bronzed
brooch
brood
brooded
brooder
broodling
brook
brooklet
broom
broomweed
broomwood
broth
brother
brotherhood
brother-in-law
brotherliness
brotherly
brougham
brought
brow
brown

browner
brownest
brownout
browse
browsed
bruin
bruise
bruised
bruit
brummagem
brunch
brunet
brunt
brush
brushed
brushful
brushless
brushwood
brushwork
brusque
brutal
brutality
brutalization
brutalize
brutalized
brutally
brute
brutish
brutishly
brutishness
bubble
bubbled
bubbletop

bubbly
bubonic
buccal
buccaneer
buck
buckboard
bucked
bucket
bucketed
bucketful
buckle
buckled
buckler
buckram
bucksaw
buckshot
buckskin
buckwheat
bucolic
bud
budded
buddy
budge
budged
budget
budgetary
budgeted
budwood
budworm
buff
buffalo
buffer
buffered

buffet
buffet
buffeted
buffoon
buffoonery
bug
bugbear
bugging
buggy
bugle
bugler
bugleweed
bugproof
bugweed
build
builded
builder
building
buildings
built
bulb
bulbous
bulge
bulged
bulk
bulkhead
bulkier
bulkiest
bulky
bull
bulldoze
bulldozed
bulldozer

bullet
bulletin
bulletproof
bullfight
bullfinch
bullfrog
bullhead
bullion
bullish
bullock
bullweed
bully
bullyrag
bulrush
bulwark
bum
bump
bumper
bumpier
bumpiest
bumpkin
bumpy
buna
bunch
bunched
bundle
bundled
bung
bungalow
bungle
bungled
bungler
bunion

bunker
bunkhouse
bunt
buoy
buoyant
buoyantly
burden
burdened
burdensome
bureau
bureaucracy
bureaucrat
burette
burgee
burgeon
burgeoned
burgess
burglar
burial
burin
burlap
burlesque
burlesqued
burly
burn
burned
burner
burnish
burnisher
burnout
burnt
burr
burro

burrow
burrowed
bursar
bursitis
burst
bury
bus
buses
bush
bushed
bushel
busheler
bushings
busily
business
businesses
businesslike
buskin
bust
bustard
bustle
bustled
busy
busybody
but
butcher
butchered
butchery
butler
butt
butter
butterball
buttercup

buttered
butterfat
butterfish
butterfly
butternut
butterscotch
buttery
button
buttoned
buttonhole
buttonholed

buttons
buttonwood
buttress
buttressed
buxom
buy
buyer
buzz
buzzard
buzzed
buzzer

by
bygone
bypass
bypath
byplay
by-product
Byronic
bystander
byway
byword

C

cab
cabal
cabbage
cabin
cabinet
cable
cabled
cablegram
caboose
cabriolet
cacao
cachalot
cache
cachet
cachinnation
cackle
cackled
cacophonous
cacophony
cacti
cactoid
cactus
cactuses

cadaver
cadaverous
caddie
cadence
cadenza
cadet
cadmium
Cadmus
cadre
caduceus
cadweed
Caesarean
caesura
café
cafeteria
caffeine
cage
caged
cairn
caisson
caissoned
caitiff
cajole

cajoled
cajolery
cake
cakewalk
calabash
calamine
calamitous
calamitously
calamity
calcareous
calcification
calcify
calcimine
calcine
calcined
calcium
calculate
calculated
calculation
calculator
caldron
calefaction
calendar

calender
calendered
calf
calfskin
caliber
calibrate
calibrated
calibration
calico
caliper
caliph
calisthenics
calk
calked
calker
call
calla
callable
called
caller
calligraphy
calliope
callosity
callous
calloused
callously
callow
callowly
callus
calm
calmed
calmer
calmest

calmly
calmness
calomel
caloric
calorie
calumet
calumniate
calumniated
calumniation
calumniator
calumny
calvary
calved
calypso
calyx
camaraderie
camber
cambium
cambric
came
camel
cameleer
Camelot
Camembert
cameo
camera
cameraman
camisole
camomile
camouflage
camp
campaign
campanile

camper
campfire
camphor
camphorate
camphorated
campus
can
canal
canalization
canary
cancan
cancel
canceled
cancellation
cancer
cancerous
cancerweed
candelabrum
candid
candidacy
candidate
candidly
candied
candle
candled
candlefish
candlelight
candlenut
candlestick
candor
candy
candymaker
cane

canebrake
canine
canister
canker
cankered
cankerous
cankerweed
cankerworm
canned
canner
cannery
cannibal
cannibalism
cannily
cannon
cannonade
cannoneer
canny
canoe
canon
canonical
canonicals
canonization
canonize
canopy
cant
can't
cantaloupe
cantankerous
cantata
canteen
canter
cantered
canticle
canticles
cantilever
cantle
canto
canton
cantonment
cantor
canvas
canvased
canvass
canvassed
canvasser
canyon
caoutchouc
capabilities
capability
capable
capably
capacious
capacitance
capacitate
capacitated
capacitor
capacity
cape
caper
capered
caperings
capillarity
capillary
capital
capitalism
capitalist
capitalistic
capitalists
capitalization
capitalize
capitalized
capitol
capitulate
capitulated
capitulates
capitulation
capon
capped
caprice
capricious
capsize
capsized
capstan
capsule
captain
captaincy
caption
captious
captiously
captiousness
captivate
captivated
captivation
captive
captivity
capture
captured
car

carabao
carabineer
caracal
caracole
carafe
caramel
caramelize
carapace
carat
caravan
caravansary
caravel
caraway
carbide
carbine
carbohydrate
carbolic
carbon
carbonate
carbonated
carbonic
carboniferous
carbonization
carbonize
carbonized
carborundum
carboy
carbuncle
carburetor
carcass
carcinogenic
carcinogenicity
carcinoma

card
cardboard
carded
cardiac
cardigan
cardinal
cardinalate
cardiogram
cardiograph
cardiology
care
cared
careen
careened
career
carefree
careful
carefully
careless
carelessly
carelessness
caress
caressed
caressingly
caret
carfare
cargo
caribou
caricature
caries
carillon
carloadings
carminative

carmine
carnage
carnal
carnally
carnation
carnelian
carnival
carnivorous
carol
caroled
carom
caromed
carotid
carousal
carouse
caroused
carp
carpal
carpenter
carpet
carpeted
carport
carriage
carried
carrier
carrion
carrot
carrotty
carry
carrying
cartage
carted
cartel

cartilage
cartilaginous
cartography
carton
cartoon
cartouche
cartridge
carve
carved
carver
carvings
caryatid
casaba
cascade
cascaded
cascara
case
casein
casement
casework
cash
cashbook
cashbox
cashed
cashew
cashier
cashiered
cashmere
cashomat
casino
cask
casket
cassation

cassava
casserole
cassette
cassino
cassock
cast
castanet
caste
caster
castigate
castigated
castigation
castle
castoff
castor
castrametation
casual
casually
casualty
casuist
casuistry
catabolism
cataclysm
catacomb
catafalque
catalepsy
cataleptic
catalog
cataloged
catalpa
catalysis
catalyst
catalytic

catalyze
catamount
catapult
cataract
catarrh
catarrhal
catastrophe
catastrophic
catastrophically
catatonic
Catawba
catbird
catboat
catcall
catch
catcher
catchweed
catchword
catchy
catechesis
catechetical
catechism
catechize
categorical
categorize
category
catenary
cater
catered
caterer
caterpillar
catfish
catgut

catharsis
cathartic
cathead
cathedral
catheter
catheterize
cathode
catholic
catholicism
catholicity
catholicize
catkin
catlike
catnip
cattail
cattle
catwalk
caucus
caucused
caudal
caught
cauliflower
causal
causality
causation
causative
cause
caused
causeless
causerie
causeway
caustic
cauterization

cauterize
cauterized
cautery
caution
cautionary
cautioned
cautious
cavalcade
cavalier
cavalry
cavatina
cave
caveat
cavern
cavernous
caviar
cavil
cavity
cavort
cayenne
cease
ceased
ceaseless
ceaselessly
cecum
cedar
cedarbird
cede
ceded
cedilla
ceding
ceilings
celebrant

celebrate
celebrated
celebration
celebrity
celerity
celery
celesta
celestial
celestially
celibacy
celibate
cell
cellar
cellarer
cellaret
cellist
cello
cellophane
cellular
cellularized
cellulitis
celluloid
cellulose
Celtic
cement
cementation
cemetery
cenacle
cenobite
cenotaph
censer
censor
censored

censorial
censorious
censorship
censurable
censure
censured
census
cent
centaur
centenarian
centenary
centennial
center
centerboard
centered
centerfold
centerpiece
centigrade
centimeter
centipede
central
centralization
centralize
centralized
centrifugal
centrifuge
centripetal
centrism
centrist
centurion
century
cephalic
ceramic

cereal
cerebellum
cerebral
cerebration
cerebrum
cerement
ceremonial
ceremonially
ceremonious
ceremoniously
ceremoniousness
ceremony
cerise
cerium
certain
certainly
certainty
certificate
certificated
certification
certified
certify
certiorari
certitude
cervical
cervix
cesium
cessation
cession
cesspool
cestus
cetacean
chafe

chaffer
chaffered
chaffinch
chaffweed
chagrin
chagrined
chain
chained
chainwork
chair
chairman
chairperson
chaise
chalcedony
chalet
chalice
chalk
chalkiness
challenge
challenged
chamber
chambered
chamberlain
chambermaid
chameleon
chamois
champagne
champerty
champion
championship
chance
chanced
chancel

chancellery
chancellor
chancery
chandelier
chandler
chandlery
change
changeable
changed
changeless
changeling
channel
channeled
chant
chanted
chaos
chaotic
chaotically
chaparral
chapel
chaperon
chaplain
chaplet
chapter
char
character
characteristic
characteristically
characterization
characterize
characterized
charade
charbroil

charcoal
charge
chargeable
charged
charger
charily
chariness
chariot
charioteer
charisma
charitable
charitably
charity
charlatan
charm
charmed
charmingly
charnel
charred
charrette
chart
charted
charter
chartered
chartreuse
chary
chase
chased
chasm
chassis
chaste
chasten
chastened

chasteningly
chastise
chastised
chastisement
chastity
chasuble
château
chatelaine
chattel
chatter
chattered
chatterer
chatty
chauffeur
chauvinism
chauvinist
cheap
cheapen
cheapened
cheaper
cheapest
cheaply
cheapness
cheat
cheated
cheater
check
checkbook
checked
checker
checkerboard
checkered
checkmate

checkmated
checkoff
checkrein
cheeky
cheer
cheered
cheerful
cheerfully
cheerfulness
cheerily
cheerless
cheerlessly
cheery
cheese
cheesecake
cheesecloth
chef
chemical
chemically
chemise
chemist
chemistry
chenille
cherish
cheroot
cherry
cherub
cherubic
cherubim
chervil
chess
chessboard
chessman

chest
chesterfield
chestnut
chevron
chew
chic
chicanery
chickadee
chicken
chickweed
chicle
chicory
chide
chief
chiefly
chieftain
chiffon
chiffonier
chigger
chilblain
child
childhood
childish
childishly
childishness
childless
childlike
childproof
children
chili
chill
chilled
chillier

chilliest
chillingly
chilly
chime
chimed
chimera
chimerical
chimney
chimpanzee
chin
china
chinch
chinchilla
chine
Chinese
chink
chintz
chip
chipmunk
chipped
chipper
chirography
chiropodist
chiropractor
chirp
chisel
chiseled
chitchat
chitterling
chivalric
chivalrous
chivalry
chive

chloral
chlorate
chloride
chlorinate
chlorine
chlorite
chloroform
chlorophyll
chlorosis
chocolate
choice
choir
choirboy
choke
choker
choler
cholera
choleric
choose
chop
chophouse
chopped
chopper
choral
chord
chorea
choreography
chorister
chortle
chorus
chose
chosen
chow
chowder
chrism
christen
Christendom
christened
christenings
Christian
Christianity
Christmas
chromate
chromatics
chrome
chromic
chromite
chromium
chromosome
chronic
chronically
chronicle
chronicled
chronicler
chronicles
chronograph
chronological
chronologically
chronology
chronometer
chronometric
chrysalis
chrysanthemum
chrysolite
chubbiness
chubby
chuck
chuckle
chuckled
chucklehead
chucklingly
chum
chummy
chump
chunk
chunkiness
chunky
church
churchman
churl
churlish
churlishly
churlishness
churn
churned
chute
chutney
chyle
cicada
cicatrix
cider
cigar
cigarette
cinch
cincture
cinctured
cinder
cinema
cinematograph

cinnabar
cinnamon
cinquefoil
cion
cipher
ciphered
circadian
circannual
circle
circled
circuit
circuitous
circuitously
circuitry
circular
circularization
circularize
circulate
circulated
circulation
circulatory
circumambient
circumference
circumferential
circumflex
circumlocution
circumlocutory
circumnavigate
circumscribe
circumscribed
circumspect
circumspection
circumspectly
circumspectness
circumstance
circumstances
circumstantial
circumstantiality
circumstantiate
circumstantiated
circumstellar
circumvent
circumvented
circumvention
circus
cirrhosis
cirrhotic
cirrus
cistern
citadel
citation
cite
cited
citizen
citizenry
citizenship
citrate
citric
citron
city
civic
civil
civilian
civility
civilization
civilize
civilized
civilly
clack
claim
claimant
claimed
clairvoyance
clairvoyant
clamant
clambake
clamber
clambered
clammy
clamor
clamored
clamorous
clamp
clamshell
clan
clandestine
clang
clanged
clangor
clank
clanked
clannish
clanship
clansman
clap
clapped
clapper
claptrap
claque

claret
clarification
clarified
clarify
clarinet
clarion
clarity
clash
clasp
class
classic
classical
classicalism
classicalist
classically
classicist
classification
classified
classifier
classify
classmate
classroom
classwork
clatter
clattered
clause
claustrophobia
claustrophobic
clavichord
clavicle
claw
clay
claymore

clean
cleaned
cleaner
cleanest
cleanliness
cleanly
cleanness
cleanse
cleanser
cleanup
clear
clearance
cleared
clearer
clearest
clearheaded
clearinghouse
clearly
clearness
cleat
cleated
cleavage
cleave
cleaver
clef
cleft
clematis
clemency
clement
clench
clerestory
clergy
clergyman

clerical
clericalism
clerk
clever
cleverer
cleverest
cleverness
clew
cliché
click
client
clientele
cliff
climacteric
climactic
climate
climatic
climax
climb
climbed
climber
clinch
clincher
cling
clingingly
clinic
clinical
clinician
clink
clinked
clinker
clip
clipper

clippings
clique
cloak
clock
clocked
clockwise
clod
clog
cloisonné
cloister
cloistered
clone
clonic
close
closed
closely
closeness
closer
closest
closet
closeted
closure
clot
cloth
clothed
clothes
clothespin
clothier
clotted
cloud
cloudier
cloudiest
cloudiness
cloudless
cloudy
clout
clouted
clove
cloven
clover
clown
clowned
clownish
cloy
cloyed
club
clubbed
clubhouse
clubman
cluck
clump
clumsier
clumsiest
clumsily
clumsiness
clumsy
cluster
clustered
clutch
clutter
cluttered
coach
coachman
coadjutor
coagulate
coagulated
coagulates
coagulation
coagulative
coal
coalesce
coalesced
coalescence
coalescent
coalition
coalsack
coarse
coarsen
coarsened
coarser
coarsest
coast
coastal
coaster
coastwise
coat
coated
coatings
coattails
coauthor
coax
coaxed
coaxial
coaxingly
cobalt
cobble
cobbled
Cobol
cobweb

cocaine
coccyx
cochineal
cockade
cockatoo
cockle
cockleshell
cockney
cockpit
cockroach
cocksure
cocksureness
cocktail
cocoa
coconut
cocoon
coda
code
coded
codefendant
codeine
codex
codfish
codicil
codification
codify
coed
coeducation
coefficient
coerce
coerced
coercion
coercive

coeval
coexecutor
coffee
coffer
coffin
cog
cogency
cogent
cogitate
cogitated
cogitation
cogitative
cognac
cognate
cognition
cognizance
cognizant
cognomen
cohabit
cohere
cohered
coherence
coherent
coherently
coherer
cohesion
cohesive
cohort
coif
coiffure
coign
coil
coiled

coin
coinage
coincide
coincided
coincidence
coincidental
coined
coiner
coinsurance
coinsure
coinsurer
coke
colander
cold
colder
coldest
coldly
coleslaw
colic
coliseum
colitis
collaborate
collaborated
collaboration
collage
collapse
collapsed
collapsible
collar
collarband
collarbone
collate
collated

collateral
collation
collator
colleague
collect
collected
collectible
collection
collective
collectivism
collectivist
collector
collectorship
college
collegiality
collegiate
collide
collided
collie
collier
collision
collocation
collodion
colloid
colloidal
colloquial
colloquy
collotype
collusion
collusive
cologne
colon
colonel

colonial
colonist
colonization
colonize
colonized
colonnade
colony
colophon
color
coloration
coloratura
colored
colorless
colossal
colosseum
colossus
colporteur
colt
columbine
column
columnar
coma
comatose
comb
combat
combatant
combative
combativeness
combed
combination
combine
combined
combings

combust
combustible
combustion
come
comedian
comedy
comeliness
comely
comestible
comet
comfit
comfort
comfortable
comfortably
comforted
comforter
comfortless
comic
comical
comings
comma
command
commandant
commanded
commandeer
commander
commandery
commandingly
commandment
commando
commemorate
commemorated
commemoration

commemorative
commence
commenced
commencement
commend
commendable
commendation
commendatory
commended
commensurable
commensurate
comment
commentary
commentator
commented
commerce
commercial
commercialism
commercialization
commercialize
comminatory
commingle
commingled
comminute
comminuted
comminution
commiserate
commiseration
commissar
commissariat
commissary
commission
commissioned

commissioner
commit
commitment
committed
committee
commodious
commodity
commodore
common
commonalty
commoner
commonest
commonly
commonplace
commonwealth
commotion
communal
commune
communicable
communicant
communicate
communicated
communication
communicative
communion
communiqué
communism
communist
communistic
community
communization
communize
commutation

commutator
commute
commuted
commuter
compact
companion
companionable
companionship
companionway
company
comparability
comparable
comparative
compare
compared
comparison
compartment
compass
compassion
compassionate
compassionately
compatibility
compatible
compatriot
compeer
compel
compelled
compellingly
compend
compendious
compendium
compensate
compensated

compensation
compensator
compensatory
compete
competed
competence
competency
competently
competition
competitive
competitor
compilation
compile
compiled
compiler
complacence
complacency
complacent
complain
complainant
complained
complainingly
complaint
complaisance
complaisant
complement
complemental
complementary
complemented
complete
completed
completion
completist
complex
complexion
complexity
compliance
compliant
complicate
complicated
complication
complicity
complied
compliment
complimentary
complin
comply
component
comport
compose
composed
composer
composite
composition
compositor
compost
composure
compote
compound
comprehend
comprehended
comprehensibility
comprehensible
comprehension
comprehensive
compress
compressibility
compressible
compression
compressor
comprise
compromise
compromisingly
Comptometer
comptroller
compulsion
compulsive
compulsory
compunction
computation
compute
computer
computerese
computerizable
computerization
computerized
comrade
concave
concavity
conceal
concealed
concealment
concede
conceded
conceit
conceited
conceitedly
conceivable
conceivably

conceive
conceived
concelebrant
concentrate
concentrated
concentration
concentric
concept
conception
conceptual
concern
concerned
concert
concerted
concertina
concession
concessionaire
conch
conciliate
conciliated
conciliation
conciliatory
concise
conciseness
conclave
conclude
concluded
conclusion
conclusive
conclusively
concoct
concocted
concoction
concomitant
concord
concordance
concourse
concrete
concur
concurred
concurrence
concurrent
concussion
condemn
condemnation
condemnatory
condemned
condensation
condense
condensed
condenser
condescend
condescendingly
condescension
condign
condiment
condition
conditional
conditionally
conditioned
condole
condolence
condominium
condonation
condone
condoned
condor
conducive
conduct
conducted
conduction
conductivity
conductor
conduit
condyle
cone
confection
confectioner
confectionery
confederacy
confederate
confederation
confer
conferee
conference
conferred
confess
confessedly
confession
confessional
confessor
confide
confided
confidence
confident
confidential
confidentially
confidently
confidingly

configuration
confine
confined
confinement
confirm
confirmation
confirmed
confiscate
confiscated
confiscation
confiscatory
conflagration
conflict
conflicted
confliction
confluence
confluent
conform
conformable
conformation
conformational
conformed
conformer
conformity
confound
confounded
confrere
confront
confrontation
confronted
confuse
confused
confusedly

confusingly
confusion
confutation
confute
confuted
congeal
congealed
congelation
congener
congenial
congeniality
congenital
congest
congested
congestion
conglomeracy
conglomerate
conglomeration
congratulate
congratulated
congratulates
congratulation
congratulatory
congregate
congregated
congregation
congregational
congress
congressional
congruence
congruity
congruous
conic

conical
conifer
coniferous
conjectural
conjecture
conjectured
conjugal
conjugate
conjugated
conjugation
conjunction
conjunctive
conjunctivitis
conjuration
conjure
conjured
conjurer
connect
connectedly
connection
connective
connector
connivance
connive
connived
connoisseur
connotation
connote
connoted
connubial
conquer
conquered
conqueror

conquest
consanguinity
conscience
conscientious
conscientiously
conscious
consciously
consciousness
conscript
conscription
consecrate
consecrated
consecration
consecrative
consecutive
consensus
consent
consented
consequence
consequent
consequential
consequently
conservation
conservatism
conservative
conservatory
conserve
conserved
consider
considerable
considerate
consideration
considered

consign
consigned
consignee
consignment
consignor
consist
consistency
consistent
consistory
consolation
console
consoled
consolidate
consolidated
consolidation
consolingly
consols
consommé
consonance
consonant
consonantal
consort
consorted
conspicuous
conspicuously
conspiracy
conspirator
conspiratorial
conspire
conspired
constable
constabulary
constancy

constant
constantly
constellation
consternation
constipation
constituency
constituent
constitute
constituted
constitution
constitutional
constitutionality
constitutionally
constrain
constrained
constraint
constrict
constricted
constriction
construct
constructed
constructive
construe
construed
consul
consular
consulate
consulates
consult
consultant
consultation
consultative
consulted

consumable
consume
consumed
consumerism
consummate
consummation
consumption
consumptive
contact
contagion
contagious
contain
contained
containerization
containerize
contaminate
contaminated
contamination
contemplate
contemplated
contemplation
contemplative
contemporaneous
contemporary
contempt
contemptible
contemptuous
contend
contended
contender
content
contented
contention

contentious
contentment
contest
contestant
contestation
context
contextual
contiguity
contiguous
continence
continent
continental
contingency
contingent
continual
continually
continuance
continuant
continuation
continue
continued
continuity
continuous
continuously
continuum
contort
contorted
contortion
contortionist
contour
contraband
contrabass
contract

contracted
contractile
contraction
contractor
contractual
contradict
contradiction
contradictory
contradistinction
contraindicate
contraindication
contralto
contraption
contrarily
contrariness
contrariwise
contrary
contrast
contravene
contravention
contribute
contribution
contributive
contributor
contributory
contrite
contritely
contrition
contrivance
contrive
control
controllable
controlled

controller
controversial
controversy
controvert
contumacious
contumacy
contumelious
contumely
contuse
contused
contusion
conundrum
convalesce
convalescence
convalescent
convection
convene
convened
convenience
conveniences
convenient
conveniently
convent
convention
conventional
conventionality
conventionalize
conventionally
conventual
conventually
converge
converged
convergence

convergent
conversant
conversation
conversational
conversationalist
converse
conversion
convert
converted
convertibility
convertible
convex
convexity
convey
conveyance
conveyed
conveyer
convict
convicted
conviction
convince
convincingly
convivial
conviviality
convivially
convocation
convoke
convoked
convolute
convoluted
convolution
convoy
convoyed

convulse
convulsion
convulsive
cookbook
cooker
cookery
cookhouse
cool
cooled
cooler
coolest
coolheaded
coolhouse
coolie
coolly
coolness
coop
co-op
cooperage
cooperate
cooperated
cooperation
cooperative
co-opt
co-opted
coordinate
coordinated
coordination
coordinator
coot
copal
copartner
copartnership

cope
coped
Copernican
copied
copier
coping
copious
copiously
copiousness
copper
copperhead
copperplate
coppersmith
coppice
copra
copy
copyholder
copyist
copyreader
copyright
coquetry
coquette
coquettish
coracle
coracoid
coral
coralline
cord
cordage
corded
cordial
cordiality
cordially
cordite
cordon
cordovan
corduroy
cordwood
core
cored
corespondent
coriander
Corinthian
cork
corkage
corkscrew
corkwood
cormorant
corn
cornea
corner
cornered
cornerstone
cornet
cornfield
cornflower
cornice
cornstalk
cornucopia
corollary
corona
coronary
coronation
coroner
coronet
corporal
corporate
corporately
corporation
corporative
corporeal
corps
corpse
corpulence
corpulent
corpus
corpuscle
corpuscular
corral
correct
corrected
correction
correctional
corrective
correctly
correctness
corrector
correlate
correlated
correlation
correlative
correspond
corresponded
correspondence
correspondent
correspondingly
corresponds
corridor
corroborate

corroboration
corroborative
corroboratory
corrode
corroded
corrosible
corrosion
corrosive
corrugate
corrugated
corrugation
corrupt
corrupted
corruptibility
corruptible
corruption
corruptly
corsage
corsair
corselet
corset
cortege
cortex
cortical
corundum
coruscate
coruscated
coruscation
corvette
coryza
cosignatory
cosigner
cosily

cosine
cosmetic
cosmetician
cosmeticize
cosmic
cosmogony
cosmology
cosmonaut
cosmopolitan
cosmopolite
cosmos
cossack
cost
costal
costive
costliness
costly
costume
costumer
cosy
cot
coterie
coterminous
cotillion
cottage
cotter
cotton
cottontail
cottonwood
couch
cougar
cough
could

council
councilor
counsel
counseled
count
countdown
countenance
counter
counteract
counterattack
counterbalance
counterblast
counterchange
countercheck
counterclaim
counter-clockwise
countered
counterfeit
counterfeiter
counterfoil
counterirritant
countermand
countermarch
countermine
counteroffensive
counterpane
counterpart
counterplot
counterpoint
countershaft
countersign
countersink
countervail

counterweight
countess
countless
country
countryman
countryside
county
coup
coupé
couple
coupler
couplet
coupling
coupon
courage
courageous
courier
course
coursed
courser
court
courted
courteous
courtesy
courthouse
courtier
courtliness
courtly
court-martial
courtship
courtyard
cousin
cove

covenant
cover
coverage
covered
coverlet
covert
covet
coveted
covetous
covey
coward
cowardice
cowardly
cowbell
cowboy
cowcatcher
cower
cowl
cowlick
co-worker
cowslip
coxcomb
coxswain
coy
coyly
coyness
coyote
cozen
cozier
coziest
cozily
coziness
cozy

crab
crack
cracked
cracker
crackle
crackled
cradle
cradled
craft
craftier
craftiest
craftily
craftiness
craftsman
crafty
crag
cram
crammed
cramp
crampon
cranberry
crane
craned
cranial
craniometry
craniotomy
cranium
crank
crankcase
cranked
crankily
crankiness
cranky

cranny
crape
crash
crashworthiness
crashworthy
crass
crassly
crassness
crate
crated
crater
cravat
crave
craved
craven
cravenette
cravings
crawfish
crawl
crawled
crawlway
crayfish
crayon
craze
crazier
craziest
crazily
craziness
crazy
creak
creakingly
cream
creamed
creamery
creamier
creamiest
creamy
crease
create
created
creation
creative
creatively
creativeness
creativity
creator
creature
crèche
credence
credential
credenza
credibility
credible
credit
creditability
creditable
credited
creditor
credo
credulity
credulous
credulousness
creed
creek
creel
creep
creeper
creepiness
cremains
cremate
cremated
cremation
crematory
Cremona
creole
creosote
crepe
crepitant
crepitate
crepitation
crescendo
crescent
crest
crested
crestfallen
cretin
cretinism
cretinoid
cretinous
cretonne
crevasse
crevice
crew
crewel
crib
cribbage
cribwork
cricket
crime

criminal
criminality
criminalization
criminalize
criminally
criminologist
criminology
crimp
crimson
cringe
cringed
crinkle
crinkled
crinoline
cripple
crippled
crises
crisis
crisp
crisper
crispest
crisply
crispness
crisscross
criteria
criterion
critic
critical
critically
criticism
criticize
criticized
critique

croak
croaked
croaker
croakingly
crochet
crock
crockery
crocodile
crocus
crook
crooked
crookedness
croon
crooned
crooner
crop
croquet
croquette
crosier
cross
crossbar
crossbow
crossbowman
crossbred
crossbusing
crosscut
crosshatch
crossings
crossover
crossroad
crosswalk
crosswise
crossword

crotchet
crouch
crouched
croup
croupier
crow
crowbar
crowd
crowded
crown
crowned
crownwork
crucial
crucially
crucible
crucified
crucifix
crucifixion
cruciform
crucify
crude
cruder
crudest
crudity
cruel
cruelly
cruelty
cruet
cruise
cruiser
cruller
crumb
crumble

crumbled
crump
crumpet
crumple
crumpled
crunch
crupper
crusade
crusader
cruse
crush
crushed
crusher
crushingly
crust
crusted
crustier
crustiest
crusty
crutch
crux
cry
cryobiology
cryolite
cryonics
cryoprobe
cryosurgeon
crypt
cryptic
cryptical
cryptically
cryptogram
cryptograph
cryptography
crystal
crystalline
crystallization
crystallize
crystallized
crystalloid
cub
cubbyhole
cube
cubeb
cubic
cubicle
cubism
cubit
cuckoo
cucumber
cuddle
cuddled
cudgel
cudgeled
cue
cuff
cuffed
cuirass
cuisine
culinary
cull
culled
culminate
culminated
culmination
culotte
culpability
culpable
culprit
cult
cultivate
cultivated
cultivation
cultivator
cultural
culturalization
culturally
culture
cultured
culvert
cumber
cumbered
cumbersome
cumbrous
cummerbund
cumulative
cumulus
cuneiform
cunning
cunningly
cup
cupboard
cupcake
cupel
cupellation
cupful
Cupid
cupidity
cupola

cupped
cupric
cuprous
cur
curable
curaçao
curacy
curare
curate
curative
curator
curb
curbed
curd
cure
cured
curettage
curette
curfew
curie
curio
curiosities
curiosity
curious
curiously
curl
curled
curler
curlew
curlicue
curly
curmudgeon
currant

currency
current
currently
curricula
curricular
curriculum
curry
curse
cursed
cursive
cursory
curt
curtail
curtailed
curtain
curtesy
curtly
curvature
curve
curved
curvilinear
cushion
cushioned
cusp
cuspidor
cussedness
custard
custodial
custodian
custody
custom
customarily
customary

customer
cut
cutaneous
cutaway
cutback
cute
cuticle
cutlass
cutlery
cutlet
cutoff
cutout
cutpurse
cutter
cuttings
cuttlefish
cutweed
cutworm
cyanate
cyanic
cyanide
cyanite
cyanogen
cyanosis
cybernated
cybernation
cybernetics
cyclamate
cycle
cyclic
cycloid
cyclometer
cyclone

cyclonic
cyclopedic
cyclops
cyclorama
cygnet
cylinder
cylindric
cylindrical

cymbal
cynic
cynical
cynically
cynicism
cynosure
cypress
Cyrillic

cyst
cystitis
cystoid
cystolith
czar
Czech

d

dabble
dachshund
dacoit
daedal
daemon
daffodil
daft
dagger
daguerreotype
dahlia
daily
daintier
daintiest
daintily
daintiness
dainty
dairy
dairymaid
dairyman
dais
daisy
dalliance
dally

dalmation
dam
damage
damaged
damascene
damascened
damascus
damask
dammed
damnable
damnation
damp
dampen
dampened
damper
dampest
dampness
damsel
dance
dancer
dandelion
dandle
dandled

dandruff
dandy
danger
dangerous
dangerously
dangle
dangled
Danish
dank
dapper
dapple
dappled
dare
dared
daringly
dark
darken
darker
darkest
darkly
darkness
darling
darned

dart
darted
dash
dashboard
dashed
dashiki
dashingly
dastardly
data
dataphone
date
dated
dative
datum
daub
daubed
daughter
daughter-in-law
daunt
daunted
dauntless
dauphin
davenport
davit
dawdle
dawdled
dawn
dawned
day
daybook
daybreak
daydream
daylight

daytime
dazzle
dazzled
deacon
dead
deaden
deadened
deadfall
deadhead
deadlight
deadliness
deadlock
deadly
deadwood
deaf
deafen
deafened
deafeningly
deafer
deafest
deal
dealer
dealings
dean
deanery
dear
dearer
dearest
dearly
dearness
dearth
death
deathbed

deathblow
deathless
deathlike
deathly
debacle
debar
debark
debarred
debase
debased
debasement
debatable
debate
debated
debater
debauch
debauched
debauchery
debenture
debilitate
debilitated
debility
debit
debited
debris
debt
debtor
debugging
debut
debutante
decade
decadence
decadent

decalcomania
decametric
decamp
decant
decanter
decapacitate
decapacitation
decapitate
decapitation
decarbonize
decathlete
decathlon
decay
decayed
decease
deceased
decedent
deceit
deceitful
deceitfulness
deceive
deceived
deceleration
December
decency
decennial
decent
decently
decentralization
decentralize
deception
deceptive
deceptively
deceptiveness
decide
decidedly
deciduous
decimal
decimate
decimated
decimation
decipher
decipherable
deciphered
decision
decisive
decisively
decisiveness
deck
decked
deckhouse
deckle
declaim
declaimed
declamation
declamatory
declaration
declarative
declaratory
declare
declared
declension
declination
decline
declined
declivity
decoction
décolletage
décolleté
decompensate
decompensation
decompose
decomposed
decomposition
decontaminate
decorate
decorated
decoration
decorative
decorator
decorous
decorously
decorousness
decorum
decoy
decrease
decreased
decreasingly
decree
decreed
decrement
decrepit
decrepitude
decretal
decried
decry
dedicate
dedicated
dedication

dedicatory
deduce
deduced
deducible
deduct
deducted
deductible
deduction
deductively
deed
deeded
deem
deemed
deep
deepen
deepened
deeper
deepest
deeply
deepness
deer
deerhound
deerskin
deerstalker
deerweed
de-escalate
de-escalation
de-escalatory
deface
defaced
defalcate
defalcated
defalcation

defamation
defamatory
defame
defamed
default
defaulted
defaulter
defeasible
defeat
defeated
defeatism
defect
defection
defective
defectology
defector
defend
defendant
defended
defender
defense
defensible
defensive
defensively
defensiveness
defer
deference
deferential
deferentially
deferment
deferral
deferred
defiance

defiant
defiantly
deficiency
deficient
deficit
defied
defilade
defiladed
defile
defiled
defilement
definable
define
defined
definite
definitely
definiteness
definition
definitive
definitively
definitiveness
definitize
deflate
deflated
deflation
deflationary
deflect
deflected
deflection
deforestation
deform
deformation
deformed

deformity
defraud
defrauded
defray
defrayed
defrost
deft
deftly
deftness
defunct
defuse
defy
degeneracy
degenerate
degenerated
degeneration
degradability
degradable
degradation
degrade
degraded
degradingly
degree
dehire
dehydrate
dehydrated
deification
deified
deify
deign
deigned
deism
deist

deity
dejected
dejectedly
dejection
delay
delayed
delectability
delectable
delectation
delegate
delegated
delegation
delete
deleted
deleterious
deleteriously
deletion
delftware
deliberate
deliberated
deliberation
deliberative
delicacy
delicate
delicately
delicatessen
delicious
deliciously
delight
delighted
delightful
delightfully
delimit

delimitation
delineate
delineated
delineation
delineative
delineator
delinquency
delinquent
deliquesce
deliquescence
deliquescent
delirious
delirium
deliver
deliverance
delivered
deliverer
delivery
delphinium
delta
deltoid
delude
deluded
deluge
deluged
delusion
delusive
deluxe
delve
demagnetize
demagogic
demagogue
demand

demanded
demandingly
demarcation
demean
demeaned
demeanor
demented
dementia
demerit
demigod
demilitarize
demise
demiworld
demo
demobilization
demobilize
demobilized
democracy
democrat
democratic
democratically
democratization
democratize
demolish
demolished
demolition
demon
demonetization
demonetize
demoniacal
demonology
demonstrable
demonstrate
demonstrated
demonstration
demonstrative
demonstrator
demoralization
demoralize
demoralized
demotic
demountable
demur
demure
demurely
demurrage
demurred
demurrer
den
denature
denatured
dendrology
denial
denied
denigrate
denizen
denominate
denominated
denomination
denominational
denominator
denotation
denote
denoted
denouement
denounce
denounced
dense
denser
densest
density
dent
dental
dentalgia
dented
dentifrice
dentine
dentist
dentistry
dentition
denuclearization
denuclearize
denucleation
denudation
denude
denunciation
denunciatory
deny
deodorant
deodorize
deodorized
depart
departed
department
departmental
departmentalize
departure
depend
depended

dependency
dependent
depersonalize
depict
depicted
depiction
depilatory
deplete
depleted
depletion
deplorable
deplore
deplored
deploy
deployed
deployment
depolarization
depolarize
depollute
depollution
deponent
depopulate
depopulated
deport
deportation
deported
deportment
depose
deposed
deposit
depositary
deposited
deposition
depositor
depository
depot
depravation
deprave
depraved
depravity
deprecate
deprecated
deprecation
deprecatory
depreciate
depreciated
depreciation
depredation
depress
depressant
depressed
depressingly
depression
depressive
depressurization
depressurize
deprivation
deprive
deprived
depth
deputation
depute
deputed
deputize
deputized
deputy
derail
derailed
derailment
derange
deranged
derangement
derby
derelict
dereliction
deride
derided
derision
derisive
derivable
derivation
derivative
derive
derived
dermal
dermatitis
dermatology
dermatosis
derogate
derogated
derogation
derogatory
derrick
dervish
descant
descend
descendant
descent
describe

described
description
descriptive
descry
desecrate
desecrated
desecration
desensitize
desensitizer
desert
deserted
deserter
desertion
deserve
deserved
desiccant
desiccate
desiccated
desiccation
desiccative
desiderata
desideratum
design
designate
designated
designation
designed
designedly
designer
desirability
desirable
desire
desired

desires
desirous
desist
desists
desk
desolate
desolated
desolately
desolation
despair
despaired
despairingly
desperado
desperate
desperately
desperation
despicable
despin
despise
despised
despite
despoil
despoiled
despondency
despondent
despondingly
despot
despotic
despotism
desquamation
dessert
destination
destine

destined
destiny
destitute
destitution
destroy
destroyed
destroyer
destructible
destruction
destructive
desuetude
desultorily
desultory
detach
detachable
detached
detachment
detail
detailed
detain
detained
detect
detected
detection
detective
detector
detention
deter
detergent
deteriorate
deteriorated
deterioration
determinable

determinant
determination
determinative
determine
determined
determinism
deterred
deterrent
detest
detestable
detestation
detested
dethrone
dethroned
detonate
detonated
detonation
detonator
detour
detoured
detract
detracted
detraction
detractor
detriment
detrimental
detritus
devaluate
devaluated
devaluation
devaluationist
devastate
devastated
devastatingly
devastation
develop
developed
development
developmental
deviate
deviated
deviation
device
devil
deviltry
devious
deviousness
devise
devised
devitalize
devoid
devolve
devolved
devote
devoted
devotedly
devotee
devotion
devotional
devour
devoured
devoutly
dew
dewy
dexter
dexterity
dexterous
dexterously
dextrose
diabetes
diabetic
diabolic
diabolical
diaconal
diacritical
diadem
diaeresis
diagnose
diagnosed
diagnoses
diagnosis
diagnostic
diagnostician
diagonal
diagonally
diagram
dial
dialect
dialectic
dialed
dialogue
dialysis
diameter
diametric
diametrically
diamond
diapason
diaper
diaphanous

diaphragm
diarist
diary
diaspora
diastole
diastolic
diathermic
diatom
diatomic
diatribe
dice
dichotomous
dichotomy
Dictaphone
dictate
dictated
dictation
dictator
dictatorial
dictatorship
diction
dictionary
Dictograph
dictum
did
didactic
didn't
die
died
diesel
diestock
diet
dietary
dietetics
differ
differed
difference
different
differential
differentiate
differentiated
differentiation
difficult
difficulty
diffidence
diffident
diffract
diffraction
diffuse
diffused
diffusion
dig
digest
digested
digestible
digestion
digestive
diggings
digit
digitalis
dignified
dignify
dignitary
dignity
digress
digression
dike
dilapidate
dilapidated
dilapidation
dilatation
dilate
dilated
dilation
dilatory
dilemma
dilettante
diligence
diligent
diligently
dilute
diluted
dilution
dim
dime
dimension
dimensional
diminish
diminuendo
diminution
diminutive
dimity
dimly
dimmed
dimmer
dimmest
dimness
dimple
dine

dined
diner
dingy
dinner
dinosaur
dint
diocesan
diocese
diorama
diphtheria
diphthong
diploma
diplomacy
diplomat
diplomatic
diplomatically
diplomatist
diplopia
dipper
dipsomania
dipsomaniac
direct
directed
direction
directional
directive
directly
directness
director
directory
direful
direst
dirge
dirigible
dirt
dirtily
dirty
disability
disable
disabled
disabuse
disadvantage
disadvantaged
disadvantageous
disaffection
disaffirm
disaffirmed
disagree
disagreeable
disagreement
disallow
disallowed
disambiguate
disappear
disappearance
disappeared
disappoint
disappointment
disapprobation
disapproval
disapprove
disarm
disarmament
disarmed
disarmingly
disarrange
disarranged
disarray
disarticulate
disassociation
disaster
disastrous
disavow
disavowal
disband
disbanded
disbar
disbarment
disbarred
disbelieve
disbelieved
disbeliever
disbelievingly
disburse
disbursement
disc
discard
discarded
discern
discerned
discernible
discerningly
discernment
discharge
discharged
disciple
discipleship
disciplinary
discipline

disciplined
disclaim
disclaimed
disclose
disclosure
discolor
discoloration
discolored
discomfit
discomfiture
discomfort
discompose
discomposed
discomposure
disconcert
disconnect
disconnected
disconsolate
discontent
discontented
discontinuance
discontinue
discontinued
discord
discordance
discordant
discotheque
discount
discounted
discountenance
discourage
discouraged
discouragement
discouragingly
discourse
discourteous
discourtesy
discover
discovered
discoverer
discovery
discredit
discreditable
discredited
discreet
discrepancy
discrete
discretion
discretionary
discriminate
discriminated
discrimination
discriminative
discriminatory
discursive
discus
discuss
discussion
disdain
disdained
disdainful
disease
diseased
disembarkation
disembarrass
disembody
disemplane
disenchant
disengage
disestablish
disesteem
disfavor
disfeature
disfigure
disfigured
disfigurement
disfranchise
disgorge
disgrace
disgraceful
disgruntle
disguise
disgust
disgusted
disgustedly
disgustingly
dish
dishabille
disharmony
dishearten
dishevel
disheveled
dishonest
dishonestly
dishonor
dishonorable
dishonored
disillusion
disinclination

disincline
disinclined
disinfect
disinfectant
disingenuous
disinherit
disintegrant
disintegrate
disintegration
disinterested
disintermediation
disjoin
disjoined
disjoinings
disjointed
disjunction
disjunctive
disk
dislike
dislocate
dislocated
dislocation
dislodge
disloyal
disloyalty
dismal
dismally
dismantle
dismantled
dismast
dismasted
dismay
dismayed

dismember
dismembered
dismemberment
dismiss
dismissal
dismount
dismounted
disobedience
disobedient
disobey
disobeyed
disoblige
disobligingly
disorder
disordered
disorderly
disorganize
disorganized
disown
disparage
disparagement
disparagingly
disparate
disparity
dispassionate
dispatch
dispatched
dispatcher
dispel
dispelled
dispensable
dispensary
dispensation

dispense
dispensed
dispersal
disperse
dispersed
dispersion
dispirited
displace
displacement
display
displease
displeasure
disport
disposable
disposal
dispose
disposed
disposition
dispossess
dispossessed
disposure
dispraise
disproof
disproportion
disproportionate
disputable
disputant
disputation
disputatious
dispute
disputed
disqualification
disqualify

disquieted
disquietude
disquisition
disregard
disrepair
disreputable
disrepute
disrespect
disrespectful
disrobe
disroot
disrupt
disruption
disruptive
dissatisfaction
dissatisfied
dissect
dissected
dissemble
disseminate
disseminated
dissemination
dissension
dissent
dissenter
dissentient
dissertation
disservice
dissidence
dissident
dissimilar
dissimilarity
dissimulate

dissimulated
dissimulation
dissipate
dissipated
dissipation
dissociate
dissociated
dissociation
dissolute
dissolution
dissolvableness
dissolve
dissolved
dissonance
dissonant
dissuade
dissuasion
distaff
distal
distance
distant
distaste
distasteful
distemper
distend
distensible
distill
distillate
distillation
distilled
distiller
distillery
distinct

distinction
distinctive
distinctly
distinctness
distinguish
distinguished
distort
distorted
distortion
distract
distractingly
distraction
distrain
distrained
distraught
distress
distribute
distribution
distributive
distributor
district
distrust
distrustful
disturb
disturbance
disturbed
disturber
disunion
disunite
disuse
ditch
ditched
dithyrambic

ditto
ditty
diurnal
divagate
divan
dive
dived
diver
diverge
diverged
divergence
divergent
divergingly
diverse
diversification
diversify
diversion
diversionary
diversity
divert
divest
divide
divided
dividend
divider
divine
divined
divinely
divinity
divisibility
divisible
division
divisor

divorce
divorcee
divorcement
divulge
divulged
dizzier
dizziest
dizzily
dizziness
dizzy
do
docile
docility
dock
docket
dockyard
doctor
doctorate
doctrinaire
doctrinal
doctrine
document
documentary
documentation
documented
dodder
dodge
dodged
dodo
doe
doeskin
doesn't
doff

dog
dogcart
doge
dogged
doggerel
dogma
dogmatic
dogmatism
dogmatize
dogtrot
dogwood
doily
doings
doldrums
dole
doled
doleful
doll
dollar
dolman
dolphin
dolt
domain
dome
domed
domestic
domestically
domesticate
domesticated
domesticity
domicile
domiciliary
dominance

dominant
dominate
dominated
domination
domineer
domineered
domineeringly
dominie
dominion
domino
donate
donated
donation
donative
done
donkey
donor
don't
doom
doomed
door
doorbell
doorframe
doorknob
doornail
doorsill
doorstop
doorway
dooryard
dope
dormant
dormer
dormitory
dormouse
dorsal
dory
dosage
dose
dossier
dot
dotage
dotard
dote
dotingly
dotted
double
doubled
doubleknit
doubt
doubted
doubtful
doubtfully
doubtingly
doubtless
dough
doughboy
doughnut
doughty
doughy
dour
dove
dove
dovecot
dovetail
dowager
dowdier
dowdiest
dowdily
dowdy
dowel
doweled
dower
down
downcast
downfall
downhearted
downhill
downpour
downright
downstairs
downtown
downward
downy
dowry
dowser
doxology
doze
dozen
drab
drachma
draft
drafted
draftee
draftier
draftiest
draftily
drafty
drag
draggle

draggled
dragnet
dragon
dragonfly
dragoon
dragooned
drain
drainage
drained
drainer
drake
drama
dramatic
dramatically
dramatics
dramatist
dramatization
dramatize
dramatized
dramaturgy
drank
drape
draper
drapery
drastic
draught
draw
drawback
drawbar
drawbridge
drawee
drawer
drawings

drawl
drawled
drawn
drawplate
drawstring
dray
drayage
drayman
dread
dreaded
dreadful
dream
dreamed
dreamer
dreamier
dreamiest
dreamily
dreaminess
dreamland
dreamless
dreamlike
dreamy
drearier
dreariest
drearily
dreariness
dreary
dredge
dredged
dreg
drench
drenched
dress

dressed
dresser
dressings
dressmaker
dressy
drew
dribble
dribbled
dried
drier
driest
drift
driftwood
drill
drilled
driller
drink
drinkable
drinker
drip
drippings
drive
drivel
driven
driver
driveway
drizzle
drizzled
droll
drollery
dromedary
drone
droningly

drool
droolings
droop
drop
dropout
dropper
droppings
dropsical
dropsy
dross
drought
drove
drown
drowned
drownings
drowse
drowsily
drowsiness
drowsy
drudge
drudgery
drug
druggist
drugstore
druid
druidical
drum
drumhead
drummed
drummer
drumstick
drunk
drunkard
drunken
dry
dryly
dryness
dual
dualism
dualistic
duality
dubiety
dubious
ducal
ducat
duchess
duchy
duck
duckling
duckpin
duckweed
duct
ductile
ductility
dudgeon
due
duel
duelist
duenna
duet
duffel
duffer
dug
dugong
dugout
duke
dukedom
dulcet
dulcimer
dull
dullard
duller
dullest
dullness
duly
dumb
dumbbell
dummy
dump
dumping
dumpling
dun
dunce
dune
dungaree
dungeon
dunnage
dunned
dupe
duplex
duplicate
duplicated
duplication
duplicator
duplicity
durability
durable
duralumin
durance

duration
duress
during
dusky
dust
dusted
duster
dustier
dustiest
dusty
duteous
duties

dutiful
duty
dwarf
dwarfish
dwell
dwellings
dwelt
dwindle
dwindled
dyad
dynamic
dynamism

dynamite
dynamited
dynamo
dynasty
dysentery
dysfunction
dyslexic
dyspepsia
dyspeptic
dystrophication
dystrophy

each
eager
eagerly
eagerness
eagle
eaglet
ear
earache
earl
earldom
earlier
earliest
early
earmark
earn
earned
earner
earnest
earnestly
earnestness
earnings
earring
earrings
earshot
earth
earthen
earthenware
earthliness
earthly
earthmen
earthquake
earthward
earthwork
earthworm
earwax
earwig
ease
eased
easel
easement
easier
easiest
easily
easiness
east
Easter
easterly
eastern
easterner
eastward
eastwardly
easy
easygoing
eat
eatable
eaten
eater
eavesdrop
ebb
ebbed
ebonize
ebonized
ebony
ebullience
ebullient
ebullition
eccentric
eccentricity
ecchymosis

ecclesiastic
ecclesiastical
echelon
echo
echoed
éclair
éclat
eclectic
eclecticism
eclipse
ecocatastrophe
ecocidal
ecological
ecology
economic
economical
economically
economist
economize
economized
economy
ecru
ecstasy
ecstatic
ecstatically
eczema
eddy
edelweiss
edema
edge
edged
edger
edgeways

edgewise
edibility
edible
edict
edification
edifice
edified
edify
edit
edited
edition
editor
editorial
editorialize
editorially
educable
educate
educated
education
educational
educationally
educator
educe
eel
eelpot
eelworm
eerie
efface
effacement
effect
effected
effective
effectual

effectually
effectuate
effeminacy
effeminate
efferent
effervesce
effervescence
effervescent
effete
efficacious
efficacy
efficiency
efficient
effigies
effigy
effloresce
efflorescence
efflorescent
effluvia
effluvium
efflux
effort
effortless
effrontery
effulgence
effulgent
effusion
effusive
effusively
effusiveness
egalitarian
eggnog
eggplant

eggshell
eglantine
ego
egocentric
egocentricity
egoism
egoistic
egotism
egotistic
egotistical
egregious
egress
egret
Egyptian
eider
either
ejaculate
ejaculation
eject
ejection
ejectment
ejector
elaborate
elaborately
elaboration
elapse
elapsed
elastic
elasticity
elated
elation
elbow
elbowed

elbowroom
elder
elderberry
elderly
eldest
elect
elected
election
electioneer
elective
elector
electoral
electorate
electric
electrical
electrically
electrician
electricity
electrification
electrify
electrocute
electrocution
electrode
electrolier
electrolysis
electrolytic
electrolytical
electrolyze
electromagnet
electrometer
electromotive
electron
electronic

electroplate
electropositive
electroscope
electrotype
electrotyper
eleemosynary
elegance
elegant
elegy
element
elemental
elementally
elementary
elephant
elephantiasis
elephantine
elevate
elevated
elevation
elevator
elfin
elicit
elicited
elide
eligibility
eligible
eliminate
eliminated
elimination
eliminative
elision
elite
elixir

Elizabethan
elk
ellipsis
ellipsoid
elliptic
elliptical
elm
elocution
elocutionist
elongate
elongated
elongation
elope
elopement
eloquence
eloquent
eloquently
else
elsewhere
elsewise
elucidate
elucidated
elucidation
elude
eluded
elusive
elusiveness
elusory
emaciate
emaciated
emaciation
emanate
emanated
emancipate
emancipated
emancipation
emancipator
emasculate
emasculation
embalm
embalmed
embalmer
embankment
embargo
embargoed
embark
embarkation
embarrass
embarrassed
embarrassment
embassy
embattle
embattled
embellish
embellished
embellishment
ember
embezzle
embezzled
embezzlement
embezzler
embitter
embittered
emblazon
emblem
emblematic
emblematical
embodied
embodiment
embody
embolden
emboldened
embolism
embolus
emboss
embossed
embrace
embraced
embrasure
embrocate
embrocation
embroider
embroidered
embroidery
embroil
embroiled
embryo
embryology
embryonic
emend
emendation
emended
emerald
emerge
emerged
emergence
emergency
emergent
emeritus

emery
emetic
emigrant
emigrate
emigrated
emigration
eminence
eminent
emissary
emission
emit
emitted
emollient
emolument
emotion
emotional
emotionally
empanel
emperor
emphases
emphasis
emphasize
emphasized
emphatic
emphatically
empire
empiric
empirical
empiricism
emplacement
employ
employed
employee

employer
employment
emporium
empower
empowered
empress
emptied
emptily
emptiness
empty
empyrean
emu
emulate
emulated
emulates
emulation
emulative
emulatory
emulous
emulsification
emulsifier
emulsify
emulsion
enable
enabled
enact
enacted
enactment
enamel
enameled
enamored
encamp
encampment

encapsulate
encaustic
encephalic
encephalitis
enchant
enchanted
enchantingly
enchantment
encircle
encircled
encirclement
enclave
enclose
enclosed
enclosure
encomia
encomiastic
encomium
encompass
encore
encounter
encountered
encourage
encouraged
encouragement
encouragingly
encroach
encroached
encroachment
encumber
encumbered
encumbrance
encyclical

encyclopedia
encyclopedic
encyst
encysted
end
endanger
endangered
endear
endeared
endeavor
endeavored
ended
endemic
endings
endive
endless
endlessly
endlong
endocrine
endocrinology
endoderm
endogenous
endorse
endorsement
endow
endowed
endowment
endue
endued
endurable
endurance
endure
endured

enduringly
endways
endwise
enemy
energetic
energize
energy
enervate
enervation
enfeeble
enfeebled
enfilade
enfold
enforce
enforceable
enforced
enforcement
enforcer
enfranchise
enfranchised
engage
engaged
engagement
engagingly
engender
engendered
engine
engineer
English
Englishman
engorge
engorgement
engrain

engrained
engrave
engraved
engraver
engross
engrossed
engrosser
engulf
enhance
enhanced
enhancement
enharmonic
enigma
enigmatic
enigmatical
enjoin
enjoined
enjoy
enjoyable
enjoyed
enjoyment
enlarge
enlarged
enlargement
enlarger
enlighten
enlightened
enlighteningly
enlightenment
enlist
enlisted
enlistment
enliven

enlivened
enmesh
enmity
ennoble
ennobled
enormity
enormous
enough
enrage
enraged
enrapture
enraptured
enrich
enriched
enrichment
enroll
enrolled
enrollment
ensemble
enshrine
enshrined
ensign
ensilage
enslave
enslavement
ensue
ensued
ensure
ensured
entablature
entail
entailed
entangle

entangled
entanglement
enter
entered
enteritis
enterprise
entertain
entertained
entertainer
entertainingly
entertainment
enthrall
enthralled
enthrone
enthroned
enthusiasm
enthusiast
enthusiastic
enthusiastically
entice
enticed
enticement
enticingly
entire
entirely
entirety
entitle
entitled
entity
entomb
entombed
entombment
entomologist

entomology
entrails
entrance
entrancingly
entrant
entrap
entreat
entreated
entreaty
entrench
entrust
entry
entryway
entwine
enucleate
enucleation
enumerate
enumerated
enumeration
enumerator
enunciate
enunciated
enunciation
enunciator
envelop
envelope
envenom
enviable
envious
environment
environmental
environmentalist
environmentally

environs
envisage
envisaged
envoy
envoys
envy
enzyme
eon
ephemeral
epic
epicure
epicurean
epidemic
epidermal
epidermic
epidermis
epidermoid
epigastric
epiglottis
epigram
epigrammatic
epigraph
epilepsy
epileptic
epileptoid
epilogue
epiphysis
episcopacy
episcopal
episcopalian
episcopate
episode
episodic
epistemology
epistle
epistolary
epistolatory
epitaph
epithalamium
epithelium
epithet
epitome
epitomize
epizootic
epoch
epochal
eponym
epoxy
equable
equably
equal
equaled
equalitarian
equality
equalization
equalize
equalized
equalizer
equally
equanimity
equate
equated
equation
equator
equatorial
equerry
equestrian
equestrienne
equiangular
equidistance
equidistant
equilateral
equilibrium
equine
equinoctial
equinox
equip
equipage
equipment
equipoise
equitable
equitation
equity
equivalence
equivalency
equivalent
equivocal
equivocally
equivocate
equivocation
era
eradicate
eradicated
eradication
erase
erased
eraser
erasure
erect

erected
erectile
erection
erectness
erg
ergo
ergophobia
ergot
ermine
erode
erosion
erotic
erotologist
err
errand
errata
erratic
erratically
erratum
erred
erroneous
error
erstwhile
erudite
erudition
erupt
eruption
eruptive
erysipelas
escalade
escalator
escapade
escape
escapement
escapist
escarpment
escheat
eschew
escort
escorted
escritoire
escrow
escutcheon
Eskimo
esophagus
esoteric
esparto
especial
especially
Esperanto
espionage
esplanade
espousal
espouse
esprit
espy
esquire
essay
essayed
essayist
essence
essential
essentially
establish
established
establishment
establishmentarian
estate
esteem
esteemed
ester
esthetic
estimable
estimate
estimated
estimation
estimator
estivate
estoppel
estrange
estranged
estrangement
estuary
esurient
etch
etcher
etchings
eternal
eternally
eternity
ethane
ether
ethereal
ethereally
ethical
ethics
ethnic
ethnology
ethyl

etiology
etiquette
etude
etymological
etymology
eucalyptus
Eucharist
euchre
euclidean
eugenics
eulogistic
eulogize
eulogy
euphemism
euphemistic
euphonious
euphony
Eurasian
eureka
Eurodollar
European
eustachian
eutectic
euthanasia
eutrophicate
eutrophication
eutrophied
evacuate
evacuated
evacuation
evade
evaded
evaluate
evaluation
evanesce
evanescence
evanescent
evangelical
evangelist
evaporate
evaporated
evaporation
evaporator
evasion
evasive
evasively
evasiveness
even
evening
evenings
evenly
evenness
event
eventful
eventfully
eventual
eventuality
eventually
eventuate
ever
everglade
evergreen
everlasting
everlastingly
every
everybody
everyday
everyone
everything
everywhere
evict
evicted
eviction
evidence
evident
evidential
evidentially
evil
evilly
evince
evinced
eviscerate
evocation
evocative
evoke
evoked
evolution
evolutionary
evolutionist
evolve
ewe
ewer
exacerbate
exacerbation
exact
exacta
exacted
exaction
exactitude

exactly
exactness
exaggerate
exaggerated
exaggeration
exalt
exaltation
exalted
examen
examination
examine
examined
examiner
example
exasperate
exasperated
exasperation
excavate
excavated
excavation
excavator
exceed
exceeded
exceedingly
excel
excelled
excellence
excellency
excellent
excelsior
except
excepted
exception

exceptional
exceptionally
excerpt
excess
excesses
excessive
excessively
exchange
exchangeable
exchequer
excipient
excise
excision
excitability
excitable
excitant
excitation
excite
excitedly
excitement
exclaim
exclaimed
exclamation
exclamatory
exclude
excluded
exclusion
exclusive
excommunicate
excommunication
excoriate
excoriated
excoriation

excrescence
excrescent
excrete
excreted
excretion
excretory
excruciate
excruciatingly
excruciation
exculpate
exculpated
exculpation
excursion
excusable
excuse
excused
excuses
execrable
execrate
execrated
execration
executant
execute
executed
execution
executioner
executive
executor
executrix
exegesis
exemplar
exemplary
exemplification

exemplify
exempt
exempted
exemption
exequatur
exercise
exercised
exerciser
exert
exerted
exertion
exhalation
exhale
exhaled
exhaust
exhaustion
exhaustive
exhaustless
exhibit
exhibited
exhibition
exhibitor
exhilarate
exhilarated
exhilaration
exhort
exhortation
exhorted
exhumation
exhume
exhumed
exigency
exigent

exiguous
exile
exiled
exist
existed
existence
existent
exit
exobiology
exodus
exonerate
exonerated
exoneration
exorbitant
exorbitantly
exorcise
exorcised
exorcism
exordium
exoteric
exotic
exoticism
expand
expanded
expanse
expansion
expansive
expatiate
expatiated
expatriate
expatriation
expect
expectancy

expectant
expectation
expected
expectorant
expectorate
expectoration
expediency
expedient
expedite
expedited
expedition
expeditionary
expeditious
expeditiously
expel
expelled
expend
expended
expenditure
expense
expensively
experience
experienced
experiences
experiment
experimental
experimentally
experimentation
experimenter
expert
expertise
expertly
expertness

expiate
expiation
expiration
expire
expired
explain
explained
explanation
explanatory
expletive
explicable
explicate
explicit
explicitly
explode
exploded
exploit
exploitation
exploited
exploration
exploratory
explore
explored
explorer
exploringly
explosion
explosive
exponent
exponential
export
exportation
expose
exposed

exposition
expository
expostulate
expostulated
expostulation
exposure
expound
express
expression
expressive
expressively
expressly
expressman
expropriate
expropriation
expulsion
expunge
expunged
expurgate
expurgated
expurgation
exquisite
extant
extemporaneous
extemporary
extempore
extemporization
extemporize
extend
extended
extensible
extension
extensive

extent
extenuate
extenuated
extenuation
exterior
exterminate
exterminated
extermination
exterminator
external
externalization
externally
extinct
extinction
extinguish
extinguished
extinguisher
extirpate
extirpated
extirpation
extol
extolled
extort
extorted
extortion
extortionate
extra
extract
extracted
extraction
extractive
extracurricular
extradite

extradited
extradition
extraneous
extraordinarily
extraordinary
extrapolate
extraterritoriality
extravagance
extravagant
extravaganza
extravasate
extravasation
extreme
extremist
extremity
extricate
extricated

extrication
extrinsic
extroversion
extrovert
extrude
extruded
extrusion
exuberance
exuberant
exudate
exudation
exude
exuded
exult
exultant
exultation
exulted

exultingly
eye
eyeball
eyebrow
eyecup
eyed
eyelash
eyelet
eyelid
eyepiece
eyes
eyeshot
eyesight
eyestrain
eyetooth
eyewash
eyewitness

f

Fabian
fable
fabled
fabric
fabricate
fabricated
fabrication
fabulous
façade
face
faced
facedown
facet
facetious
facial
facile
facilitate
facilitated
facility
facings
facsimile
fact
faction

factional
factious
factitious
factor
factory
factotum
factual
factually
facultative
faculty
faddist
fade
faded
fadingly
Fahrenheit
fail
failed
failingly
failings
faille
failure
faint
fainted

fainthearted
faintly
faintness
fair
fairer
fairest
fairly
fairness
fairway
fairy
fairyland
faith
faithful
faithless
faithlessly
fake
faker
falcon
fall
fallacious
fallacy
fallen
fallibility

fallible
fallout
false
falsehood
falsely
falseness
falsetto
falsification
falsifier
falsify
falsity
falter
faltered
falteringly
fame
famed
familial
familiar
familiarity
familiarize
familiarly
families
family
famine
famish
famous
famously
fanatic
fanatical
fanaticism
fancied
fancier
fanciest

fanciful
fancy
fanfare
fang
fanged
fanlight
fanned
fantail
fantasia
fantastic
fantasy
far
farad
farce
farcial
farcical
farcy
fare
fared
farewell
farfetched
farina
farinaceous
farm
farmed
farmer
farmhouse
farmyard
faro
farrier
farseeing
farsighted
farther

farthest
farthing
fascinate
fascinated
fascination
fascinatingly
fascinator
fascism
fascist
fashion
fashionable
fashioned
fast
fastback
fasten
fastened
fastenings
faster
fastest
fastidious
fastness
fat
fatal
fatalism
fatalist
fatalistic
fatality
fatally
fate
fated
fateful
father
fathered

fatherhood
father-in-law
fatherland
fatherless
fatherliness
fatherly
fathom
fathomed
fathomless
fatigue
fatness
fatten
fattened
fatter
fattest
fatty
fatuity
fatuous
faucet
fault
faultily
faultless
faultlessly
faulty
fauna
favor
favorable
favored
favorite
favoritism
fawn
fawned
fealty

fear
feared
fearful
fearless
fearlessly
fearsome
feasibility
feasible
feast
feat
feather
feathered
featheredge
featherweight
feathery
feature
featured
febrile
February
fecund
fecundate
fecundity
federal
federalism
federalist
federalization
federalize
federalized
federate
federated
federation
federative
fedora

fee
feeble
feebleness
feeblest
feebly
feed
feedback
feedforward
feedings
feel
feeler
feelingly
feelings
feer
feered
feet
feign
feigned
feint
feldspar
felicitate
felicitated
felicitation
felicitous
felicitously
felicity
feline
fellow
fellowship
felon
felonious
felony
felt

felucca
female
feminine
femininity
feminism
feminist
femoral
femur
fen
fence
fencer
fend
fended
fender
fenestrated
fenestration
Fenian
fennel
feral
ferment
fermentation
fermented
fern
ferocious
ferociously
ferocity
ferret
ferreted
ferric
ferrochrome
ferrotype
ferrous
ferrule

ferry
ferryboat
fertile
fertility
fertilization
fertilize
fertilized
fertilizer
ferule
fervent
fervently
fervid
fervidly
fervor
fescue
festal
fester
festered
festival
festive
festivity
festoon
festooned
fetch
fetid
fetish
fetishism
fetlock
fetology
fetter
fettered
fettle
feud

feudal
feudalism
feudatory
fever
feverish
feverishly
few
fewer
fewest
fez
fiasco
fiat
fib
fiber
fibroid
fibula
fiche
fickle
fiction
fictional
fictitious
fiddle
fiddled
fiddler
fidelity
fidget
fiduciary
fief
field
fielded
fieldpiece
fiend
fiendish

fiendishly
fierce
fierceness
fiercer
fiercest
fiery
fife
fig
fight
figment
figuration
figurative
figuratively
figure
figured
figurehead
figurine
filament
filariasis
filature
filbert
filch
filched
file
filed
filial
filibuster
filigree
filings
fill
filled
filler
fillet

fillings
film
filmed
filmstrip
filter
filtered
filth
filthier
filthiest
filthiness
filthy
filtrate
filtration
fin
final
finalist
finality
finally
finance
financial
financially
financier
finch
find
finder
findings
fine
fined
finely
fineness
finer
finery
finespun

finesse
finest
finger
fingered
fingerprint
finial
finis
finish
finished
finisher
finite
fiord
fir
fire
firearm
fireboat
firebomb
firebox
firebrand
firebreak
firebrick
fired
firefly
fireman
fireplace
fireproof
fireside
fireweed
firewood
fireworks
firkin
firm
firmament

firmer
firmest
firmly
firmness
first
firstly
firth
fiscal
fish
fisherman
fishery
fishhook
fishwife
fishy
fissile
fission
fissure
fist
fistic
fisticuffs
fistula
fit
fitful
fitfully
fitness
fitted
fitter
fittingly
fittings
fix
fixation
fixative
fixed
fixer
fixings
fixity
fixture
fizzle
fizzled
flabbier
flabbiest
flabbiness
flabby
flaccid
flag
flagellant
flagellate
flagellation
flageolet
flageolets
flagitious
flagon
flagpole
flagrance
flagrant
flagrantly
flagship
flagstaff
flagstone
flail
flailed
flair
flak
flake
flakiness
flaky
flambeau
flamboyant
flame
flamed
flamenco
flameproof
flamingly
flamingo
flan
flange
flanged
flank
flanked
flannel
flannelette
flap
flapjack
flare
flareback
flared
flash
flashback
flashboard
flashcube
flasher
flashily
flashiness
flashingly
flashlight
flashy
flask
flat
flatboat

flat-footed
flathead
flatiron
flatly
flatness
flatten
flattened
flatter
flattered
flatterer
flatteringly
flattery
flattest
flatulence
flatulent
flatware
flatwise
flatwork
flatworm
flaunt
flaunted
flauntingly
flautist
flavor
flavored
flavorings
flavors
flaw
flawed
flax
flaxen
flaxseed
flay

flea
fleabite
fleck
fledge
fledgling
flee
fleece
fleeced
fleeciness
fleecy
fleet
fleetingly
Flemish
flesh
fleshiness
fleshings
fleshpot
fleshy
fleur-de-lis
flew
flex
flexed
flexibility
flexible
flexure
flick
flicked
flicker
flickeringly
flier
flight
flightiness
flightworthy

flighty
flimsier
flimsiest
flimsily
flimsiness
flimsy
flinch
flinched
flinchingly
fling
flint
flintiness
flintlock
flinty
flippancy
flippant
flippantly
flipper
flirt
flirtation
flirtatious
flirted
flit
flitch
flivver
float
floated
floater
flocculence
flocculent
flock
floe
flog

flogged
floggings
flood
flooded
floodgate
floodlight
floodwater
floor
floorwalker
floppiness
floppy
floral
Florentine
floret
floriculture
florid
floridity
floridly
florin
florist
floss
flossier
flossiest
flossy
flotation
flotilla
flotsam
flounce
flounder
floundered
flounderingly
flour
flourish
flourishingly
floury
flout
flouted
flow
flowed
flower
flowered
floweriness
flowerpot
flowery
flowingly
flown
fluctuate
fluctuated
fluctuation
flue
fluency
fluent
fluently
fluff
fluffiness
fluffy
fluid
fluidly
fluidextract
fluidity
fluke
flume
flung
flunk
flunked
flunky
fluorescence
fluorescent
fluoric
fluoridate
fluoridation
fluoride
fluorinate
fluorine
fluoroscope
fluoroscopy
flurry
flush
flushed
fluster
flustered
flute
fluted
flutings
flutist
flutter
fluttered
flutteringly
fluttery
flux
fluxion
fly
flyer
flyleaf
flytrap
flywheel
foal
foaled
foam

foamed
foamier
foamiest
foaminess
foamy
fob
fobbed
focal
focalization
focalize
focalized
focus
focused
fodder
foe
foeman
fog
foggier
foggiest
foggy
foghorn
foible
foil
foiled
foist
foisted
fold
folded
folder
foliage
foliate
foliation
folio
folk
folkway
follicle
follicular
follow
followed
follower
folly
foment
fomentation
fomented
fond
fondant
fonder
fondest
fondle
fondled
fondly
fondness
fondue
font
food
fool
fooled
foolhardiness
foolhardy
foolish
foolishly
foolishness
foolproof
foolscap
foot
footage
football
footboard
footbridge
footed
footfall
footgear
foothill
foothold
footings
footless
footlights
footloose
footman
footmark
footnote
footpace
footpad
footpath
footprint
footrest
footsore
footstep
footstool
footwear
footwork
footworn
foozle
foozled
foppery
foppish
for
forage
foramen

forasmuch
foray
forbear
forbearance
forbid
forbidden
forbiddingly
force
forceful
forcemeat
forceps
forcible
ford
forded
forearm
forebear
forebode
forebodingly
forebodings
forebore
forecast
forecastle
foreclose
foreclosed
foreclosure
foredeck
foredoom
foredoomed
forefather
forefinger
forefoot
forefront
foregone

foreground
forehanded
forehead
foreign
foreigner
foreignism
foreknowledge
foreleg
forelock
foreman
foremast
foremost
forename
forenoon
forensic
foreordain
foreordained
forequarter
forerunner
foresaw
foresee
foreseeingly
foreshadow
foreshore
foreshorten
foresight
foresightedness
forest
forestall
forestalled
forestation
forested
forester

forestry
foretaste
foretell
forethought
foretold
forever
forewarn
forewarned
forewoman
foreword
forfeit
forfeited
forfeiture
forgather
forgave
forge
forged
forger
forgery
forget
forgetful
forgetfully
forgetfulness
forgive
forgiven
forgiveness
forgivingly
forgo
forgot
forgotten
fork
forked
forlorn

form
formal
formaldehyde
formalism
formality
formalization
formalize
formally
format
formation
formative
formed
former
formerly
formic
formidable
formless
formula
formulary
formulate
formulated
formulation
forsake
forsaken
forsook
forsooth
forswear
forsythia
fort
fortalice
forte
forte
forth

forthcoming
forthright
forthrightness
forthwith
fortification
fortify
fortissimo
fortitude
fortnight
fortnightly
Fortran
fortuitous
fortuity
fortunate
fortune
fortuneteller
forum
forward
forwarded
forwarder
forwardness
fossil
fossiliferous
fossilization
fossilize
fossilized
foster
fostered
fought
foul
foulard
fouler
foulest

foully
foulness
found
foundation
founded
founder
foundling
foundlings
foundry
fount
fountain
fountainhead
foursome
foursquare
fourth
fowl
fox
foxes
foxglove
foxier
foxiest
foxy
fracas
fraction
fractional
fractionally
fractionate
fractionation
fractious
fracturation
fracture
fractured
fragile

fragilely
fragility
fragment
fragmentarily
fragmentary
fragmentation
fragmented
fragrance
fragrant
fragrantly
frail
frailer
frailest
frailty
frame
framed
framework
franc
franchise
franchisee
Franciscan
frank
franker
frankest
frankfurter
frankly
frankness
frantic
frappé
fraternal
fraternally
fraternity
fraternization
fraternize
fraternized
fratricidal
fratricide
fraud
fraudulent
fraught
fray
frazzle
frazzled
freak
freakish
freckle
freckled
free
freebie
freeboard
freeborn
freedom
freehand
freehold
freely
freeman
freemason
freemasonry
freer
freest
freestone
freethinker
freewheeling
freeze
freezer
freight
freighter
French
frenzied
frenzy
frequency
frequent
frequently
fresco
fresh
freshen
freshener
fresher
freshest
freshly
freshman
freshness
fret
fretful
fretted
fretwork
friability
friable
friar
fricassee
friction
frictional
Friday
fried
friend
friendless
friendlier
friendliest
friendliness

friendly
friendship
frieze
frigate
fright
frighten
frightened
frighteningly
frightful
frightfully
frightfulness
frigid
Frigidaire
frigidity
frigidly
frill
frilled
frilliness
frilly
fringe
fringed
frippery
frisbee
frisk
fritter
frittered
frivolity
frivolous
frivolously
frizziness
frizzle
frizzled
frock

frog
frogfish
frolic
frolicked
from
frond
fronded
front
frontage
frontal
fronted
frontier
frontispiece
frontlash
frost
frostbite
frostbitten
frosted
frostfish
frostier
frostiest
frostily
frostiness
frostwork
frosty
froth
frothed
frothy
froward
frown
frowned
frowningly
frowzily

frowzy
froze
frozen
fructiferous
fructify
frug
frugal
frugality
frugally
fruit
fruiterer
fruitful
fruitfully
fruitiness
fruition
fruitless
fruitlessly
fruitlessness
fruitworm
fruity
frump
frustrate
frustration
fry
fryer
fuchsia
fuddle
fuddled
fudge
fuel
fueled
fugacious
fugitive

fugue
fulcrum
fulfill
fulfilled
fulfillment
full
fuller
fullest
fullness
fully
fulminate
fulminated
fulmination
fulsome
fumble
fumbled
fume
fumed
fumigate
fumigated
fumigation
fumigator
fun
function
functional
functionally
functionary
fund
fundamental
fundamentally
funded
funeral
funereal
funereally
fungi
fungible
fungicide
fungoid
fungus
funicular
funnel
funnier
funniest
funny
fur
furbelow
furbish
furious
furiously
furl
furled
furlong
furlough
furloughed
furnace
furnish
furnished
furnishings
furniture
furor
furrier
furriest
furrow
furrowed
furry
further
furtherance
furthermore
furthest
furtive
furtively
furuncle
fury
furze
fuse
fused
fusel
fuselage
fuses
fusibility
fusible
fusillade
fusion
fuss
fussed
fussier
fussy
fustigate
futile
futilely
futility
future
futuristic
futurity
fuzz
fuzzily
fuzziness

g

gabardine
gable
gadfly
gadget
gadolinium
gadroon
gaff
gag
gage
gagged
gaggle
gaiety
gaily
gain
gained
gainer
gainful
gainfully
gainsay
gaited
gaiter
gala
galantine

galaxy
gale
galena
gall
gallant
gallantry
galled
gallery
galley
Gallic
gallingly
gallium
gallon
gallop
gallows
gallstone
galore
galvanism
galvanization
galvanize
galvanized
galvanometer
gambit

gamble
gambled
gambler
gamboge
gambol
gambrel
game
gameness
gammon
gamut
gander
gang
ganged
ganglia
ganglion
gangplank
gangrene
gangrenous
gangster
gangway
gantry
gap
gaped

garage
garb
garbage
garble
garden
gardener
gardenia
gargle
gargoyle
garish
garland
garlic
garment
garner
garnered
garnet
garnish
garnished
garnishee
garnisher
garnishment
garniture
garret
garrison
garrisoned
garrulous
garter
gas
gaseous
gash
gashed
gashouse
gasket
gasoline
gasp
gastight
gastral
gastric
gastritis
gastronomic
gastronomy
gate
gatehouse
gatepost
gateway
gather
gathered
gatherer
gaucherie
gaudier
gaudiest
gaudy
gauge
gauged
gauntlet
gauze
gave
gavel
gavotte
gawky
gay
gayety
gayly
gayness
gaze
gazebo
gazelle
gazette
gazetted
gazetteer
gear
geared
gearshift
geisha
gelatin
gelatinize
gelatinoid
gelatinous
gem
gemstone
gender
gene
genealogical
genealogist
genealogy
general
generalissimo
generalist
generality
generalization
generalize
generalized
generally
generalship
generate
generated
generation
generative
generator

generic
generosity
generous
generously
genesis
genetics
genial
geniality
genially
genitive
genius
genteel
genteelly
gentian
gentile
gentility
gentle
gentleman
gentlemen
gentleness
gentler
gentlest
gently
gentry
genuflect
genuflection
genuine
genuinely
genuineness
genus
geodesy
geodetic
geographer

geography
geological
geologist
geology
geometric
geometrical
geometry
geranium
gerent
geriatrician
geriatrics
germ
German
germane
germicide
germinal
germinant
germinate
germinated
germination
germinative
gerund
gerundial
gerundive
gesso
gestalt
gesticulate
gesticulation
gesture
gestured
get
gewgaw
geyser

ghastliness
ghastly
gherkin
ghetto
ghost
ghostliness
ghostly
ghoul
giant
giantism
gibber
gibberish
gibbet
gibbon
gibe
giblet
giddily
giddiness
giddy
gift
gifted
gig
gigantic
gigantically
gigantism
giggle
giggled
gild
gilded
gilder
gill
gill
gilt

gimbals
gimcrack
gimlet
gin
ginger
gingerly
gingham
gingivitis
giraffe
girandole
gird
girder
girdle
girdled
girdler
girl
girlhood
girlish
girt
girth
gist
give
given
giver
gizzard
glacial
glacier
glad
gladden
gladdened
glade
gladiator
gladiatorial

gladiolus
gladly
gladness
gladstone
glamorous
glamour
glance
gland
glandered
glanders
glandular
glare
glared
glaringly
glass
glassful
glasshouse
glassily
glassiness
glassware
glassy
glaucoma
glaze
glazed
glazier
gleam
gleamed
glean
gleaner
gleanings
gleeful
glib
glibly

glide
glided
glider
glimmer
glimmered
glimmerings
glimpse
glimpsed
glint
glinted
glioma
glissando
glisten
glistened
glister
glitter
glittered
gloat
gloated
global
globally
globe
globular
globule
glockenspiel
gloom
gloomily
gloominess
glorification
glorify
glorious
glory
gloss

glossal
glossary
glossily
glossiness
glossitis
glossy
glottis
glove
glover
glow
glowed
glower
glowered
glowingly
glowworm
glucinum
glucose
glue
glued
gluey
glum
glut
glutted
glutton
gluttonize
gluttonous
gluttony
glycerin
gnarl
gnarled
gnash
gnashed
gnat
gnathic
gnaw
gnawed
gnawings
gneiss
gnome
gnomic
gnomon
gnu
go
goad
goal
goat
goatfish
goatherd
goatskin
goatweed
gobble
gobbled
goblet
goblin
gocart
god
godchild
goddess
godfather
godhead
godhood
godless
godlike
godliness
godly
godmother
godparent
godsend
godson
goggle
goings
goiter
gold
golden
goldenrod
goldfinch
goldsmith
goldweed
golf
golfer
gondola
gondolier
gone
gong
goober
good
good-by
goodly
good-natured
goodness
goodwill
goose
gooseberry
gooseneck
gopher
Gordian
gore
gored
gorge

gorgeous
gorget
gorgon
gorilla
goshawk
gosling
gospel
gossamer
gossip
got
Gothic
gotten
gouache
gouge
gouged
goulash
gourd
gourmand
gourmet
gout
govern
governance
governed
governess
government
governmental
governor
gown
grab
grabbed
grace
graceful
graceless

gracious
graciously
grackle
gradation
grade
graded
gradient
gradual
gradually
graduate
graduated
graduation
graffiti
grafted
grafter
grail
grain
grained
grainfield
grammar
grammarian
grammatical
grammatically
grampus
granary
grand
grandchild
grandee
grandeur
grandfather
grandiloquence
grandiloquent
grandiose

grandly
grandmother
grandness
grandparent
grandsire
grandson
grandstand
grange
granite
granitoid
granivorous
grant
granted
grantsmanship
granular
granulate
granulated
granulation
granule
grape
grapeshot
graph
graphic
graphics
graphite
grapnel
grapple
grappled
grasp
graspingly
grass
grasshopper
grassplot

grate
grated
grateful
grater
gratification
gratify
gratifyingly
gratinate
gratings
gratis
gratitude
gratuitous
gratuity
gravamen
grave
gravedigger
gravel
gravelly
graven
graver
gravest
gravestone
graveyard
gravitate
gravitated
gravitation
gravitational
gravity
gravure
gravy
gray
graybeard
grayish

grayness
graze
grazed
grazier
grease
greased
greasewood
greasier
greasiest
greasily
greasiness
greasy
great
greater
greatest
greatly
greatness
greed
greedier
greediest
greedily
greediness
greedy
Greek
green
greenback
greener
greenery
greenest
greenhorn
greenhouse
greenish
greenness

greenroom
greenstick
greensward
greenwood
greet
greeted
greetings
gregarious
Gregorian
grenade
grenadier
grenadine
grew
greyhound
grid
griddle
gridiron
grief
grievance
grieve
grieved
grievous
grievously
griffin
grill
grilled
grim
grimace
grime
grimier
grimiest
grimily
griminess

grimy
grin
grind
grinder
grindingly
grindstone
grinned
grip
gripe
gripper
grisly
grist
gristle
gristmill
grit
grittiness
gritty
grizzle
grizzled
groan
groaned
groaner
groaningly
grocer
grocery
grog
groggy
groin
grommet
groom
groomed
groove
grooved

grope
gropingly
grosbeak
grosgrain
gross
grosser
grossest
grossly
grossness
grotesque
grotesquely
grotto
grouch
grouchily
grouchy
ground
grounded
groundless
groundlings
groundwork
group
groupings
grouse
grout
grouted
grove
grovel
groveled
grow
grower
growl
growled
grown

growth
grub
grubbed
grubbiness
grubby
grudge
grudgingly
gruel
gruesome
gruff
gruffer
gruffest
gruffly
grumble
grumbled
grumpily
grumpiness
grumpy
grunt
grunted
guarantee
guarantor
guaranty
guard
guarded
guardian
guardianship
guardroom
guardsman
guava
gubernatorial
gudgeon
guerdon

guerrilla
guess
guesswork
guest
guidance
guide
guidebook
guided
guideline
guidon
guild
guile
guileful
guileless
guillotine
guilt
guiltier
guiltiest
guiltily
guiltiness
guilty
guinea
guise
guises
guitar
gulch
gulden
gulf
gull
gullet
gullibility
gullible
gully

gulp
gum
gumbo
gumboil
gummed
gummosis
gummy
gumption
gumshoe
gumweed
gumwood
gun
gunboat
guncotton
gunfire
gunlock
gunman
gunner
gunnery
gunny
gunpaper
gunpowder
gunrunning
gunship
gunshot
gunsmith
gunstock
gunwale
gurgle
guru
gush
gusher
gushy

gusset
gust
gustatory
gustily
gusto
gusty
gutter
guttersnipe
guttural
gutturally
guy
guzzle
guzzled
guzzler
gymkhana
gymnasium
gymnast
gymnastic
gynecologist
gynecology
gypsum
gypsy
gyrate
gyrated
gyration
gyratory
gyrfalcon
gyro
gyrocompass
gyroscope
gyrostat
gyves

h

haberdasher
haberdashery
habiliment
habit
habitable
habitant
habitat
habitation
habited
habitual
habitually
habituate
habituated
habitude
hack
hackle
hackman
hackney
hackneyed
hacksaw
had
haddock
hadn't

haft
hag
haggard
haggle
haggled
hail
hailed
hailstone
hailstorm
hair
hairbreadth
hairbrush
haircut
hairline
hairpin
hairsplitter
hairspring
hairy
hake
halation
halberd
halcyon
hale

half
halfhearted
halftone
halfway
half-witted
halibut
halide
halite
halitosis
hall
hallmark
hallow
hallowed
Halloween
hallucination
hallucinatory
hallucinosis
halo
halogen
halt
halted
halter
haltingly

halves
halyard
ham
hamlet
hammer
hammered
hammerhead
hammerless
hammock
hamper
hampered
hamster
hamstring
hamstrung
hand
handbag
handball
handbill
handbook
handcuff
handed
handful
handicap
handicapped
handicraft
handier
handiest
handily
handiwork
handkerchief
handle
handled
handrail
handset
handshake
handsome
handspring
handwork
handwriting
handy
hang
hangar
hanged
hanger
hangings
hangman
hangup
hanker
hankered
hansom
haphazard
hapless
haploid
happen
happened
happenings
happier
happiest
happily
happiness
happy
harangue
harangued
harass
harassment
harbinger
harbor
harbored
hard
harden
hardened
hardener
harder
hardest
hardhat
hardheaded
hardihood
hardiness
hardly
hardness
hardpan
hardship
hardware
hardy
hare
harebrained
harelip
harem
hark
harlequin
harlequinade
harm
harmed
harmful
harmfully
harmfulness
harmless
harmlessly
harmlessness

harmonic
harmonica
harmonious
harmoniously
harmoniousness
harmonium
harmonization
harmonize
harmonized
harmony
harness
harnessed
harp
harper
harpist
harpoon
harpooned
harpsichord
harrier
harrow
harsh
harsher
harshest
harshly
harshness
hartebeest
harvest
harvested
harvester
has
hash
hashed
hashish
hasp
hassock
haste
hasten
hastened
hastier
hastiest
hastily
hastiness
hasty
hat
hatband
hatch
hatched
hatchery
hatchet
hatchment
hatchway
hate
hated
hateful
hatefully
hatefulness
hatpin
hatred
hatter
haughtier
haughtiest
haughtily
haughty
haul
haulage
hauled
haunch
haunt
haunted
hauntingly
hautboy
hauteur
have
haven
haven't
haversack
havoc
Hawaiian
hawk
hawker
hawkish
hawkweed
hawse
hawser
hawthorn
hay
haycock
hayfork
hayloft
haymow
hayrack
hayseed
haystack
hazard
hazarded
hazardous
hazardously
haze
hazel

hazelnut
hazier
haziest
hazily
haziness
hazy
he
head
headache
headband
headboard
headcheese
headdress
headed
header
headfirst
headforemost
headgear
headhunt
headhunter
headily
headings
headland
headless
headlight
headline
headlock
headlong
headmaster
headphone
headpiece
headquarters
headsman
headspring
headstone
headstrong
headwater
headway
headwork
heady
heal
healed
healer
health
healthful
healthfulness
healthier
healthiest
healthily
healthy
heap
heaped
hear
heard
hearer
hearings
hearken
hearkened
hearsay
hearse
heart
heartache
heartbeat
heartbreak
heartbroken
heartburn
hearten
heartened
heartfelt
hearth
hearthstone
heartier
heartiest
heartily
heartland
heartless
heartsick
heartsore
heartstring
heartwood
hearty
heat
heated
heater
heath
heathen
heathenish
heathenishly
heather
heatstroke
heave
heaven
heavenly
heavenward
heavier
heaviest
heavily
heaviness
heavy

Hebraic
Hebrew
hecatomb
heckle
heckled
heckler
hectic
hectograph
hedge
hedged
hedgehog
hedgerow
hedonism
heed
heeded
heedfully
heedfulness
heedless
heedlessness
heel
heft
hegemony
hegira
heifer
height
heighten
heightened
heinous
heir
heiress
heirloom
heliborne
helical

helicoid
helicopter
heliotrope
helipad
helium
helix
helm
helmet
helmeted
helmsman
help
helper
helpful
helpfully
helpfulness
helping
helpless
helplessly
helplessness
helpmate
hem
hematite
hemicycle
hemiplegia
hemisphere
hemispherical
hemlock
hemmed
hemorrhage
hemp
hempen
hemstitch
hemstitched

hence
henceforth
henceforward
henchman
henequen
henna
hepatic
hepatica
hepatitis
heptagon
heptameter
her
herald
heralded
heraldic
heraldry
herb
herbaceous
herbage
herbal
herbarium
herbicide
herbivorous
Herculean
herd
herded
here
hereabouts
hereafter
hereby
hereditability
hereditable
hereditably

hereditament
hereditarian
hereditary
heredity
hereinafter
hereinbefore
hereon
heresy
heretic
heretical
hereto
heretofore
hereunto
hereupon
herewith
heritability
heritable
heritably
heritage
hermetic
hermetically
hermit
hermitage
hernia
hero
heroic
heroical
heroine
heroism
heron
herpes
herpetology
herring

herringbone
hers
herself
hesitance
hesitancy
hesitant
hesitate
hesitated
hesitatingly
hesitation
hesitatively
heterodox
heterogeneity
heterogeneous
heteronym
heuristic
hew
hewed
hewer
hewn
hexagon
hexagonal
hexameter
hexangular
hexapod
heyday
hiatus
hibernate
hibernation
hibiscus
hickory
hid
hidden

hide
hidebound
hideous
hideously
hideousness
hierarchy
hieratic
hieroglyphic
hi-fi
high
highborn
highboy
higher
highest
highland
highlander
highly
highness
high-rise
highroad
highway
highwayman
hijack
hijacker
hiker
hilarious
hilarity
hill
hillier
hilliest
hilliness
hillock
hillside

hilt
him
himself
hind
hinder
hindered
hindrance
hinge
hinged
hint
hinted
hinterland
hippodrome
hippopotamus
hire
hired
hireling
hirsute
his
Hispanic
histologist
histology
historian
historic
historical
history
histrionic
hit
hitch
hitched
hitchhike
hither
hitherto

hive
hoar
hoard
hoarded
hoarder
hoarfrost
hoarse
hoarser
hoarsest
hoax
hobbit
hobble
hobbled
hobby
hobgoblin
hobnail
hobnailed
hobnob
hobo
hock
hockey
hod
hoe
hog
hogback
hogfish
hoggish
hogshead
hogweed
hoist
hoisted
hoistway
hokum

hold
holder
holdings
hole
holiday
holily
holiness
Holland
hollow
hollowed
holly
hollyhock
holocaust
hologram
holograph
holographic
holography
holophone
holster
holy
holystone
homage
home
homeland
homelike
homeliness
homely
homeopathic
homeopathy
homesickness
homesite
homespun
homestead

homeward
homework
homicidal
homicide
homiletics
homilies
homily
hominy
homogeneity
homogeneous
homogeneously
homogenize
homologous
homonym
homunculus
hone
honed
honest
honestly
honesty
honey
honeybee
honeycomb
honeydew
honeyed
honeymoon
honeysuckle
honk
honor
honorable
honorably
honorarium
honorary
honored
hood
hooded
hoodlum
hoodoo
hoodwink
hoof
hook
hooked
hooker
hookworm
hoop
Hoosier
hope
hopeful
hopefully
hopefulness
hopeless
hopelessly
hopelessness
hoplite
hopper
hopscotch
horde
horehound
horizon
horizontal
hormone
hormonology
horn
hornbook
horned
hornet
hornpipe
horology
horoscope
horrendous
horrible
horrid
horrification
horrified
horrify
horror
horse
horseback
horse chestnut
horsehair
horseman
horsemanship
horsepower
horseshoe
horseweed
horsewhip
horsewoman
hortative
hortatory
horticulture
hose
hosier
hosiery
hospice
hospitable
hospital
hospitality
hospitalization
hospitalize

host
hostage
hostel
hostess
hostile
hostilely
hostility
hot
hotbed
hotbox
hotel
hotheaded
hothouse
hotly
hotness
hotter
hottest
hound
hounded
hour
hourly
house
housed
housefly
housefurnishings
household
householder
housekeeper
housemaid
houseman
housemother
houseroom
housetop
housewares
housewarming
housewife
housework
housing
hover
hovered
hoveringly
how
however
howitzer
howl
howsoever
hoyden
hub
hubbub
huckleberry
huckster
huddle
huddled
hue
huff
hug
huge
huger
hugest
Huguenot
hulk
hull
hulled
hum
human
humane
humanely
humaneness
humanism
humanist
humanistic
humanitarian
humanitarianism
humanity
humanization
humanize
humanized
humankind
humanly
humble
humbled
humbleness
humbler
humblest
humbly
humbug
humdrum
humerus
humid
humidification
humidified
humidifier
humidify
humidity
humidor
humiliate
humiliated
humiliation
humility

hummed
hummingbird
hummock
humor
humored
humoresque
humorist
humorous
humorousness
hump
humus
hunch
hundred
hundredfold
hundredth
Hungarian
hunger
hungered
hungrier
hungriest
hungry
hunk
hunt
hunted
hunter
huntsman
hurdle
hurdled
hurl
hurled
hurricane
hurry
hurt
hurtful
hurtfully
hurtfulness
hurtle
hurtled
husband
husbandry
hush
hushed
husk
huskily
huskiness
husky
hussy
hustings
hustle
hustled
hustler
hut
hutch
hyacinth
hyaloid
hybrid
hybridism
hybridization
hybridize
hydrangea
hydrant
hydrate
hydraulic
hydrocarbon
hydrochloric
hydrocyanic
hydroelectric
hydrofluoric
hydrofoil
hydrogen
hydrometer
hydronaut
hydrophobia
hydroplane
hydrostatics
hydroxide
hyena
hygiene
hygienic
hygienically
hygienist
hygrometer
hygroscopic
hymn
hymnal
hymnbook
hyperbola
hyperbole
hyperbolic
hypercharged
hypercritical
hyperemia
hyperopia
hypersensitive
hyperthyroid
hypertrophy
hypervelocity
hyphen
hyphenate

hyphenated
hyphenation
hypnopedia
hypnosis
hypnotic
hypnotist
hypnotize
hypnotized
hypochondria

hypochondriac
hypocrisy
hypocrite
hypocritical
hypodermic
hypodermically
hypotenuse
hypothecate
hypothecation

hypotheses
hypothesis
hypothesize
hypothetical
hypothetically
hysteria
hysterical
hysterics
hysteroid

i

I
iambic
Iberian
ibex
ibis
ice
iceberg
iceboat
icebox
icebreaker
icehouse
iceman
ichneumon
ichor
ichthyology
icicle
icier
iciest
icily
iciness
icon
iconize
icy

idea
ideal
idealism
idealist
idealistic
idealization
idealize
ideally
ideas
ideation
ideational
identical
identification
identify
identity
ideological
ideology
idiocy
idiom
idiomatic
idiomatically
idiosyncrasy
idiosyncratic

idiot
idiotic
idiotically
idle
idled
idleness
idler
idlest
idly
idol
idolater
idolatrize
idolatrous
idolatry
idolize
idyl
idyllic
if
igloo
igneous
ignite
ignited
ignition

ignoble
ignominious
ignominy
ignoramus
ignorance
ignorant
ignorantly
ignore
ignored
iguana
ilex
Iliad
ilk
ill
illegal
illegality
illegible
illegibly
illegitimacy
illegitimate
illiberal
illicit
illimitable
illiteracy
illiterate
illness
illogical
illuminant
illuminate
illuminated
illumination
illuminator
illumine
illumined
illusion
illusive
illusory
illustrate
illustrated
illustration
illustrative
illustrator
illustrious
image
imagery
imaginable
imaginary
imagination
imaginative
imagine
imagined
imaginings
imago
imam
imbecile
imbecility
imbibe
imbibed
imbroglio
imbue
imbued
imitable
imitate
imitated
imitation
imitative
imitator
immaculate
immaculately
immanent
immaterial
immature
immaturely
immaturity
immeasurable
immediacy
immediate
immediately
immediateness
immemorial
immense
immensely
immensity
immerse
immersed
immersion
immigrant
immigrate
immigrated
immigration
imminence
imminent
immobile
immobility
immobilization
immobilize
immoderate
immodest
immolate

immolation
immoral
immorality
immorally
immortal
immortality
immortalize
immortally
immortelle
immovability
immovable
immovableness
immovably
immune
immunity
immunization
immunize
immunology
immure
immutability
immutable
imp
impact
impaction
impair
impaired
impairment
impala
impale
impaled
impalement
impalpability
impalpable
impanel
impaneled
impart
imparted
impartial
impartiality
impartially
impassability
impassable
impasse
impassion
impassioned
impassive
impassively
impassivity
impatience
impatient
impeach
impeachment
impeccability
impeccable
impecuniosity
impecunious
impedance
impede
impeded
impediment
impedimenta
impel
impelled
impend
impended
impenetrability
impenetrable
impenitent
imperative
imperceptible
imperceptive
imperfect
imperfection
imperforate
imperial
imperialism
imperialist
imperialistic
imperious
imperishable
impermanent
impermeable
imperscriptible
impersonal
impersonate
impersonated
impersonation
impertinence
impertinent
imperturbable
impervious
impetigo
impetuosity
impetuous
impetuously
impetuousness
impetus
impiety
impinge

impinged
impingement
impious
impiously
impish
implacability
implacable
implant
implanted
implausibility
implausible
implement
implemented
implicate
implicated
implication
implicit
implicitly
implied
imploration
implore
implored
imploringly
implosion
imply
impolite
impolitely
impoliteness
impolitic
imponderable
import
importance
important
importation
importer
importunate
importune
importunity
impose
imposed
imposingly
imposition
impossibility
impossible
impost
impostor
imposture
impotence
impotent
impound
impoverish
impoverishment
impower
impracticable
impracticality
imprecate
imprecation
imprecatory
impregnability
impregnable
impregnate
impregnation
impresario
imprescriptible
impress
impressed
impression
impressionable
impressionism
impressive
imprimatur
imprint
imprinted
imprison
imprisoned
imprisonment
improbability
improbable
improbably
impromptu
improper
impropriety
improvable
improve
improvement
improvidence
improvident
improvisation
improvise
improvised
imprudence
imprudent
imprudently
impudence
impudent
impugn
impugnable
impugned
impugnment

impulse
impulsion
impulsive
impunity
impure
impurely
impurity
imputable
imputation
imputative
impute
imputed
in
inability
inaccessibility
inaccessible
inaccuracy
inaccurate
inaction
inactivate
inactive
inactivity
inadequacy
inadequate
inadmissibility
inadmissible
inadvertence
inadvertent
inadvisability
inadvisable
inalienable
inamorata
inane
inanimate
inanition
inanity
inapplicable
inapposite
inappropriate
inapt
inaptitude
inarticulate
inartistic
inasmuch
inattention
inattentive
inaudibility
inaudible
inaudibly
inaugural
inaugurate
inaugurated
inauguration
inauspicious
inboard
inborn
inbred
incalculable
incandesce
incandescence
incandescent
incantation
incapability
incapable
incapacitant
incapacitate
incapacitated
incapacitation
incapacity
incarcerate
incarcerated
incarceration
incarnate
incarnation
incendiarism
incendiary
incense
incensed
incentive
inception
incertitude
incessant
incessantly
incest
incestuous
inch
inchoate
inchworm
incidence
incident
incidental
incidentally
incinerate
incinerated
incineration
incinerator
incipient
incise
incised

incision
incisive
incisively
incisiveness
incisor
incitation
incite
incitement
incivility
inclemency
inclement
inclination
incline
inclined
inclose
inclosed
inclosure
include
included
inclusive
inclusively
inclusiveness
incognito
incoherence
incoherent
incombustibility
incombustible
income
incommensurable
incommensurate
incommode
incommunicado
incomparable

incomparably
incompatibility
incompatible
incompetence
incompetent
incompetently
incomplete
incomprehensibility
incomprehensible
incompressibility
incompressible
inconceivability
inconceivable
inconclusive
inconclusiveness
incongruity
incongruous
inconsequential
inconsiderable
inconsiderate
inconsiderately
inconsistency
inconsistent
inconsolable
inconspicuous
inconspicuously
inconstancy
inconstant
incontestable
incontinence
incontinent
incontrovertible
inconvenience

inconvenienced
inconvenient
inconveniently
inconversibility
inconvertibility
inconvertible
incorporate
incorporated
incorporation
incorporator
incorrect
incorrigibility
incorrigible
incorruptibility
incorruptible
increase
increased
increasingly
incredibility
incredible
incredulity
incredulous
increment
incremental
incretion
incriminate
incriminated
incrimination
incriminatory
incrustation
incubate
incubated
incubation

incubator
incubus
inculcate
inculcated
inculcation
inculpate
inculpated
inculpation
inculpatory
incumbency
incumbent
incunabula
incur
incurable
incurably
incurred
incursion
indebted
indebtedness
indecency
indecent
indecently
indecision
indecisive
indecisively
indecisiveness
indecorous
indecorum
indeed
indefatigability
indefatigable
indefeasible
indefensible

indefinable
indefinite
indefinitely
indefiniteness
indelibility
indelible
indelibly
indelicacy
indelicate
indelicately
indemnification
indemnified
indemnify
indemnity
indent
indentation
indented
indention
indenture
indentured
independence
independent
indescribable
indestructible
indeterminable
indeterminate
index
indexed
indexer
indexes
Indian
indicate
indicated

indication
indicative
indicator
indicatory
indices
indicia
indict
indictable
indicted
indictment
indifference
indifferent
indifferently
indigence
indigenous
indigent
indigestibility
indigestible
indigestion
indignant
indignantly
indignation
indignity
indigo
indirect
indirection
indirectly
indirectness
indiscreet
indiscreetly
indiscretion
indiscriminate
indiscriminately

indispensability
indispensable
indispose
indisposed
indisposition
indisputable
indissoluble
indissolubly
indistinct
indistinctly
indistinguishable
indite
indited
indium
individual
individualism
individualist
individuality
individualize
individually
indivisibility
indivisible
indoctrinate
indoctrinated
indoctrination
indolence
indolent
indolently
indomitable
indoors
indorse
indorsed
indorsement

indorser
indubitable
induce
induced
inducement
induct
inductance
inducted
induction
inductive
inductor
indue
indued
indulge
indulgence
indulgent
indulgently
indurate
indurated
industrial
industrially
industrialism
industrialist
industrialization
industrialize
industrialized
industrious
industriously
industriousness
industry
inebriate
inebriated
inebriation

inebriety
inedible
ineffable
ineffably
ineffective
ineffectual
ineffectually
inefficacious
inefficiency
inefficient
inefficiently
inelastic
inelasticity
inelegance
inelegant
inelegantly
ineligibility
ineligible
ineluctable
inept
ineptitude
inequality
inequitable
inequity
ineradicable
ineradicably
inerrancy
inerrant
inert
inertia
inertly
inertness
inessential

inestimable
inestimably
inevitability
inevitable
inevitably
inexact
inexactitude
inexcusable
inexcusably
inexhaustible
inexhaustibly
inexorable
inexpedience
inexpediency
inexpedient
inexpensive
inexperience
inexpert
inexplicable
inexplicably
inextricable
infallibility
infallible
infamous
infamy
infancy
infant
infanticide
infantile
infantilism
infantry
infantryman
infarct

infarction
infatuate
infatuated
infatuation
infeasible
infect
infected
infection
infectious
infectiously
infectiousness
infelicitous
infelicity
infer
inference
inferential
inferior
inferiority
infernal
infernally
inferno
inferred
infertile
infertility
infest
infestation
infidel
infidelity
infield
infielder
infiltrate
infiltrated
infiltration

infinite
infinitesimal
infinitesimally
infinitive
infinitude
infinity
infirm
infirmary
infirmity
inflame
inflamed
inflammability
inflammable
inflammably
inflammation
inflammatory
inflatable
inflate
inflated
inflation
inflationary
inflationist
inflect
inflected
inflection
inflexibility
inflexible
inflict
inflicted
infliction
influence
influenced
influential

influentially
influenza
influx
inform
informal
informality
informally
informant
information
informative
informed
informer
informingly
infraction
infrangible
infrared
infrequent
infrequently
infringe
infringed
infringement
infuriate
infuriated
infuse
infused
infuses
infusion
ingenious
ingeniously
ingenuity
ingenuous
ingest
ingested

ingestion
ingestive
inglorious
ingot
ingrain
ingrained
ingrate
ingratiate
ingratiation
ingratiatory
ingratitude
ingredient
ingress
ingrown
inhabit
inhabitable
inhabitance
inhabitant
inhabitation
inhabited
inhalation
inhale
inhaled
inhaler
inharmonious
inhere
inhered
inherence
inherent
inherently
inherit
inheritable
inheritance

inherited
inheritor
inhibit
inhibited
inhibition
inhibitory
inhospitable
inhospitably
inhospitality
inhuman
inhumane
inhumanity
inhumation
inhume
inhumed
inimical
inimitable
inimitably
iniquitous
iniquitously
iniquity
initial
initialed
initialism
initially
initiate
initiated
initiation
initiative
initiator
initiatory
inject
injectable

injected
injection
injector
injudicious
injudiciously
injunction
injunctive
injure
injured
injurious
injury
injustice
injustices
ink
inked
inkhorn
inkling
inklings
inkstand
inkwell
inky
inlaid
inland
inlay
inlet
inmate
inmost
inn
innate
innately
inner
innermost
inning
innings
innkeeper
innocence
innocent
innocently
innocuous
innocuously
innovate
innovation
innovative
innovator
innuendo
innumerable
inobservant
inoculate
inoculated
inoculation
inoffensive
inoperable
inoperative
inopportune
inordinate
inorganic
inpatient
input
inquest
inquietude
inquire
inquired
inquirer
inquires
inquiries
inquiringly
inquiry
inquisition
inquisitive
inquisitor
inquisitorial
inroad
inrush
insane
insanely
insanitary
insanitation
insanity
insatiability
insatiable
inscribe
inscribed
inscriber
inscription
inscrutability
inscrutable
insect
insecticide
insectivorous
insecure
insecurity
insensate
insensibility
insensible
insensitive
insensitiveness
insentience
insentient
inseparable

inseparably
insert
inserted
insertion
inset
inshore
inside
insider
insides
insidious
insidiously
insight
insigne
insignia
insignificance
insignificant
insignificantly
insincere
insincerely
insincerity
insinuate
insinuated
insinuatingly
insinuation
insinuative
insipid
insipidity
insipidly
insist
insisted
insistence
insistent
insistently
insobriety
insole
insolence
insolent
insolently
insolubility
insoluble
insolvable
insolvency
insolvent
insomnia
insomniac
insomuch
insouciance
insouciant
inspect
inspected
inspection
inspector
inspectorate
inspiration
inspirational
inspirationally
inspiratory
inspire
inspired
inspirer
inspiringly
inspiritingly
instability
install
installation
installed
installment
instance
instant
instantaneous
instanter
instantly
instate
instated
instead
instep
instigate
instigated
instigation
instigator
instill
instilled
instinct
instinctive
instinctively
instinctual
institute
instituted
institution
institutional
institutionalize
institutionally
instruct
instructed
instruction
instructional
instructive
instructor
instrument

instrumental
instrumentalist
instrumentality
instrumentally
instrumentation
insubordinate
insubordination
insufferable
insufficiency
insufficient
insular
insularity
insulate
insulated
insulation
insulator
insulin
insult
insulted
insultingly
insuperable
insupportable
insuppressible
insurability
insurable
insurance
insure
insured
insurer
insurgency
insurgent
insurmountable
insurrection
insurrectionary
insurrectionist
intact
intaglio
intake
intangibility
intangible
intarsia
integer
integral
integrally
integrate
integrated
integration
integrity
integument
intellect
intellectual
intellectualism
intellectualize
intellectually
intelligence
intelligent
intelligentsia
intelligibility
intelligible
intemperance
intemperate
intemperately
intend
intendant
intended
intense
intensification
intensifier
intensify
intensity
intensive
intent
intention
intentional
intentionally
intently
intentness
interact
interaction
interborough
interbreed
intercede
interceded
intercept
intercepted
interception
interceptor
intercession
intercessory
interchange
interchangeability
interchangeable
intercollegiate
intercom
intercommunicate
interconnect
intercostal
intercourse
interdenominational

interdepartmental
interdependence
interdependent
interdict
interdiction
interest
interested
interestedly
interestingly
interface
interfere
interfered
interference
interferingly
interim
interior
interject
interjected
interjection
interlace
interlaced
interlard
interleaf
interleave
interline
interlineal
interlinear
interlineation
interlined
interlock
interlocked
interlocutor
interlocutory

interloper
interlude
intermarriage
intermarry
intermediary
intermediate
interment
intermezzo
interminable
interminably
intermingle
intermingled
intermission
intermit
intermittence
intermittent
intermittently
intermixture
intern
internal
internally
international
internationalize
internationally
interne
internecine
interned
internment
interpellate
interpellation
interplanetary
interpolate
interpolated

interpolation
interpose
interposed
interposition
interpret
interpretation
interpretative
interpreted
interpreter
interregnum
interrelation
interrogate
interrogation
interrogative
interrogatory
interrupt
interruptedly
interruption
interscapular
interscholastic
intersect
intersected
intersperse
interspersed
interstate
interstellar
interstice
interstices
interstitial
interstitially
intertwine
intertwined
Intertype

interurban
interval
intervene
intervened
intervention
interventionist
intervertebral
interview
interviewed
interviewer
interweave
interwoven
intestacy
intestate
intestinal
intestine
intimacy
intimate
intimated
intimately
intimation
intimidate
intimidated
intimidation
into
intolerable
intolerance
intolerant
intonation
intone
intoned
intoxicate
intoxicated

intoxicatingly
intoxication
intracellular
intractability
intractable
intragovernmental
intramural
intransigence
intransigent
intransitive
intraoffice
intrapsychic
intrastate
intravenous
intrazonal
intrenchment
intrepid
intrepidity
intrepidly
intricacies
intricacy
intricate
intricately
intrigue
intrigued
intrinsic
intrinsical
intrinsically
introduce
introduced
introduction
introductory
introit

introjection
introspect
introspection
introspective
introversion
introvert
introverted
intrude
intruded
intruder
intrusion
intrusive
intrusively
intuition
intuitional
intuitive
intuitively
intumesce
intumescence
intumescent
inunction
inundate
inundated
inundation
inure
inured
inuredness
inurn
invade
invaded
invalid
invalidate
invalidated

invalidation
invalidity
invaluable
Invar
invariability
invariable
invariableness
invasion
invasive
invective
inveigh
inveigle
inveigled
invent
invented
invention
inventive
inventively
inventiveness
inventor
inventory
inverse
inversion
invert
inverted
invertible
invest
invested
investigate
investigated
investigation
investigative
investigator
investiture
investment
investor
inveterate
invidious
invidiously
invigilate
invigorate
invigorated
invigoratingly
invigoration
invigorative
invincibility
invincible
inviolability
inviolable
inviolate
invisibility
invisible
invisibly
invitation
invitational
invite
invited
invitingly
invocation
invoice
invoiced
invoices
invoke
invoked
involuntarily
involuntary
involute
involution
involve
involvement
invulnerability
invulnerable
inward
inwardly
inwardness
iodate
iodic
iodide
iodine
iodize
iodoform
ion
Ionic
ionization
ionize
iota
ipecac
Iranian
irascibility
irascible
irate
irately
ire
iridescence
iridescent
iridium
iris
Irish
Irishman

iritis
irk
irked
irksome
iron
ironbound
ironclad
ironed
ironic
ironical
ironically
ironings
ironside
ironware
ironweed
ironwood
ironwork
ironworker
irony
Iroquois
irradiate
irradiated
irradiation
irrational
irrationality
irrationally
irreclaimable
irreconcilable
irreconciliability
irreconciliable
irrecoverable
irredeemable
irredenta
irreducible
irrefragable
irrefrangible
irrefutable
irregular
irregularity
irregularly
irrelevance
irrelevant
irreligious
irremediable
irremissible
irremovable
irreparable
irreplaceable
irrepressible
irreproachable
irresistible
irresolute
irresolution
irresolvable
irrespective
irresponsibility
irresponsible
irresponsibly
irretraceable
irretrievable
irreverence
irreverent
irreversible
irrevocable
irrigable
irrigate
irrigated
irrigation
irritability
irritable
irritant
irritate
irritated
irritation
irritative
irruption
irruptive
is
ischium
isinglass
Islam
island
islander
isle
islet
isn't
isobar
isolate
isolated
isolation
isolationism
isolationist
isomer
isomeric
isomorphic
isosceles
isotherm
isotope
issuance

issue
issued
issues
isthmian
isthmus
it
Italian
Italianate
italic
italicize

itch
itched
itchier
itchiest
itchy
item
itemize
itemized
iterate
iteration

iterative
itineracy
itinerancy
itinerant
itinerary
itinerate
its
itself
ivory
ivy

j

jabber
jabberingly
jabot
jack
jackal
jackanapes
jackdaw
jacket
jacketed
jackknife
jackstone
jackstraw
jack-up
jackweed
Jacobean
jade
jaded
jadeite
jagged
jaguar
jail
jailed
jailer

jalousie
jam
jamboree
jammed
jangle
janitor
janitress
January
Japan
Japanese
japanned
jar
jargon
jarred
jasmine
jasper
jaundice
jaunt
jauntier
jauntiest
jauntily
jauntiness
jaunty

javelin
jaw
jawbone
jazz
jazzy
jealous
jealousy
jeer
jeered
jeeringly
Jehovah
jejune
jejunum
jellied
jelly
jellyfish
jennet
jeopardize
jeopardy
jeremiad
jerk
jerked
jerkily

jerkin
jerky
jersey
jest
jester
jestingly
Jesuit
Jesus
jet
jetborne
jetliner
jetport
jetsam
jettison
jeweled
jeweler
jewelry
Jewish
Jewry
jibe
jig
jigger
jiggle
jiggled
jigsaw
jingle
jingled
jingo
jingoism
jinrikisha
jinx
jitney
jitters
jittery
job
jobber
jockey
jocose
jocosely
jocosity
jocular
jocularity
jocularly
jocund
jocundity
jodhpurs
jog
jogged
joggle
joggled
join
joinder
joined
joiner
joinings
joint
jointed
jointly
jointure
joist
joke
joker
jokingly
jollier
jolliest
jollification
jollity
jolly
jolt
jolted
jonquil
jostle
jostled
jot
jotted
jounce
journal
journalism
journalist
journalistic
journalize
journalized
journey
journeyed
journeyman
jovial
joviality
jovially
jowl
joy
joyful
joyfully
joyfulness
joyless
joyous
jubilance
jubilant
jubilate
jubilation

jubilee
Judaism
judge
judged
judgeship
judgment
judicative
judicatory
judicature
judicial
judicially
judiciary
judicious
judoist
juggle
juggled
juggler
jugular
juice
juicy
julep
julienne
July
jumble
jumbled
jumbo
jump
jumped
jumper
junction
juncture
June
jungle
junior
juniper
junk
junket
junta
jurat
juridical
jurisconsult
jurisdiction
jurisprudence
jurist
juror
jury
juryman
just
justice
justiciable
justifiable
justification
justificatory
justified
justify
justly
justness
jut
jute
jutted
juvenile
juvenility
juxtaposition

k

kaiser
kale
kaleidoscope
kaleidoscopic
kalsomine
kangaroo
kaolin
kapok
karate
karma
kayak
keel
keen
keener
keenest
keenly
keenness
keep
keeper
keepsake
keg
kelp
kennel
kept
keratin
kerchief
kernel
kerosine
kersey
ketch
ketosis
kettle
key
keyboard
keyed
keyhole
keynote
keystone
khaki
khedive
kibitzer
kibosh
kick
kickback
kicker
kickoff
kickshaw
kid
kidnap
kidnapped
kidney
kidskin
kill
killed
killer
killings
kiln
kilocycle
kilogram
kilometer
kilt
kilted
kin
kind
kinder
kindest
kindergarten
kindhearted
kindle

kindled
kindliness
kindly
kindness
kindred
kine
kinesthetic
kinetic
kineticism
king
kingbird
kingbolt
kingcraft
kingdom
kingfish
kingfisher
kinglet
kingliness
kingly
kingpin
kingship
kink
kinked
kinky
kinship
kinsman
kiosk
kipper
kiss
kissed
kit
kitchen
kitchenette

kite
kith
kitschy
kitten
kleptomania
kleptomaniac
knapsack
knave
knavery
knavish
knead
kneaded
kneecap
kneel
kneeled
knelt
knew
knickers
knickknack
knife
knifed
knight
knighted
knighthood
knightliness
knightly
knit
knitter
knives
knob
knock
knockdown
knocker

knockout
knoll
knot
knothole
knotted
knotty
knotwork
knout
know
knowable
knowingly
knowingness
knowledge
known
knuckle
knuckled
knurl
knurled
knurly
kobold
Kodak
kohlrabi
kooky
kopeck
Koran
Korean
kosher
kraft
kremlin
krypton
kulak
kymograph
kyphosis

L

label
labeled
labial
labor
laboratory
labored
laborer
laborious
laburnum
labyrinth
labyrinthine
lace
laced
lacerate
lacerated
laceration
lacerative
lacewing
lacewood
lacework
laches
lachrymal
lachrymose
lacings
lack
lackadaisical
lackey
lackluster
laconic
lacquer
lacquered
lacrosse
lactase
lactate
lactation
lacteal
lactic
lactose
lacuna
lacunae
ladder
laden
ladle
ladled
lady
ladylike
ladyship
lag
lager
laggard
lagged
lagoon
lair
laird
laity
lake
lambdoid
lambent
lambkin
lamblike
lambrequin
lamé
lame
lamed
lamely
lameness
lament
lamentable
lamentation

lamented
lamina
laminae
laminate
laminated
lamination
lamp
lampblack
lampoon
lampooned
lamprey
lance
lancer
lancet
lancinate
lancinated
lancination
land
landau
landed
landfall
landholder
landlady
landlocked
landlord
landmark
landowner
landscape
landslide
landslip
landsman
landward
language

languid
languish
languor
languorous
lank
lanker
lankest
lanky
lanolin
Lansdowne
lantern
lanthanum
lanyard
lapel
lapful
lapidary
lapidation
lapse
lapsed
lapwing
larboard
larcenous
larceny
larch
lard
larded
larder
large
largely
largeness
larger
largess
largest

lariat
lark
larkspur
larva
larvae
larval
laryngeal
laryngitis
larynx
lasable
lascar
lascivious
laser
lash
lashed
lashings
lass
lassitude
lasso
last
lasted
lastingly
lastly
lasts
latakia
latch
latched
latchkey
latchstring
late
lateen
lately
latency

lateness
latent
later
lateral
laterally
latest
latex
lath
lather
laths
latifundism
Latin
Latinism
latinity
latinization
latinize
latitude
latitudinal
latitudinarian
latter
lattermost
lattice
latticework
laud
laudability
laudable
laudanum
laudation
laudatory
lauded
laugh
laughable
laughingly
laughingstock
laughter
launch
launchings
launder
laundered
launderings
laundress
laundry
laundryman
laureate
laurel
lava
lavaliere
lavatory
lavender
lavish
lavished
lavishness
law
lawbreaker
lawful
lawfully
lawgiver
lawless
lawlessness
lawmaker
lawn
lawsuit
lawyer
lax
laxative
laxity
laxly
laxness
layer
layman
lazaretto
lazier
laziest
lazily
laziness
lazy
leach
leached
lead
leaden
leader
leadership
leadsman
leaf
leaflet
league
leagued
leak
leakage
leakiness
leaky
lean
leaned
leanings
leap
leaped
learn
learned
learnt

lease
leased
leasehold
leaseholder
leash
leashed
least
leather
leathern
leatheroid
leathery
leave
leaven
leavened
leaving
lecithin
lectern
lecture
lectured
lecturer
ledge
ledger
leech
leek
leer
leered
leeringly
leeward
leeway
left
leftfield
left-handed
leftist
leg
legacy
legal
legalism
legalistic
legality
legalization
legalize
legally
legate
legatee
legation
legato
legend
legendary
legerdemain
leggings
legibility
legible
legion
legionary
legislate
legislation
legislative
legislator
legislature
legitimacy
legitimate
legitimately
legitimateness
legitimation
legitimist
legitimize
legume
leguminous
leisure
leisureliness
leisurely
lemmings
lemon
lemonade
lemonweed
lemur
lend
length
lengthen
lengthened
lengthier
lengthiest
lengthily
lengthiness
lengthways
lengthwise
lengthy
lenience
leniency
lenient
leniently
Leninism
lenitive
lenity
lens
lent
Lenten
lenticular
lentil

lentoid
leonine
leopard
leotard
leper
leprechaun
leprosy
leprous
lesion
less
lessee
lessen
lessened
lesser
lesson
lessor
lest
lethal
lethargic
lethargical
lethargy
let's
letter
lettered
letterhead
letterpress
letterspace
lettuce
leucocyte
leucocytosis
leucoderma
leukemia
levant
levee
level
leveled
levelheaded
lever
leverage
levitate
levitated
levitation
levity
levulose
levy
lexicographer
lexicography
lexicon
liability
liable
liaison
liar
lib
libation
libel
libelant
libeled
libelous
liberal
liberalism
liberality
liberalization
liberalize
liberalized
liberally
liberate
liberated
liberation
liberator
libertarian
libertine
liberty
libido
librarian
library
libretto
librium
lice
license
licensee
licentiate
licentious
licentiousness
lichen
lichenoid
licit
lick
licorice
lictor
lie
liege
lien
lieu
lieutenancy
lieutenant
life
lifeguard
lifeless
lifelike

lifelong
lifer
lifetime
lifework
lift
lifted
ligament
ligate
ligation
ligature
ligatured
light
lighted
lighten
lightened
lighter
lighterage
lightest
lightface
lightheaded
lighthearted
lighthouse
lightly
lightness
lightning
lightship
lightweight
ligneous
lignify
lignite
likable
like
liked
likelier
likeliest
likelihood
likely
liken
likeness
likewise
likings
lilac
liliaceous
lilt
liltingly
lily
limb
limber
limbo
lime
limekiln
limelight
limen
limerick
limestone
limewater
liminal
limit
limitable
limitation
limited
limitless
limn
limned
limnology
limousine
limp
limped
limper
limpest
limpet
limpid
limpidity
limpidly
limply
limpness
linage
linden
line
lineage
lineal
lineality
lineament
linear
lined
lineman
linen
liner
linesman
linger
lingered
lingerie
lingeringly
lingo
lingual
linguist
linguistic
linguistically
linguistics

liniment
linings
link
linkage
linked
Linnaean
linnet
linoleum
Linotype
linseed
lint
lintel
lion
lioness
lionize
lipoid
lipoma
liquefacient
liquefaction
liquefactive
liquefiable
liquefied
liquefy
liquescence
liqueur
liquid
liquidate
liquidated
liquidation
liquidator
liquor
lira
lisp
lisped
lispingly
lissome
list
listed
listen
listened
listener
listings
listless
listlessly
listlessness
litany
liter
literacy
literal
literalism
literality
literalize
literally
literary
literate
literature
litharge
lithe
lithesome
lithia
lithium
lithograph
lithographer
lithographic
lithography
lithology
lithotomy
litigable
litigant
litigate
litigated
litigation
litigious
litmus
litter
littered
little
littlest
littoral
liturgical
liturgist
liturgy
livable
live
live
lived
livelier
liveliest
livelihood
liveliness
livelong
lively
liver
livery
liveryman
livid
lividity
livings
lizard

llama
llano
load
loaded
loadings
loaf
loafer
loam
loan
loaned
loathe
loathed
loather
loathful
loathly
loathsome
lobar
lobbied
lobby
lobbyist
lobster
local
localism
locality
localization
localize
localized
locally
locate
located
location
loci
lock
lockage
locker
locket
lockjaw
lockout
locksmith
lockup
locomotion
locomotive
locus
locust
locution
lode
lodestar
lodge
lodged
lodger
lodgings
lodgment
loft
loftily
loftiness
lofty
log
loganberry
logarithm
logbook
loge
loggerheads
loggia
logic
logical
logically
logician
logistics
logorrhea
logotype
logwood
loin
loiter
loitered
loiterer
loll
lolled
lollipop
lone
loneliness
lonely
lonesome
lonesomely
lonesomeness
long
longboat
longed
longer
longest
longevity
longhand
longhorn
longingly
longings
longitude
longitudinal
longshoreman
look
lookout

loom
loomed
loon
loony
loop
loophole
loose
loosely
loosen
loosened
looseness
looser
loosest
loot
looted
lop
lopsided
loquacious
loquaciously
loquacity
lord
lordliness
lordly
lordosis
lordship
lore
lorgnette
lorry
losable
lose
loser
loses
losings

loss
lost
lotion
lottery
lotus
loud
louder
loudest
loudly
loudness
lounge
louse
lout
loutish
louver
lovable
love
loveless
loveliness
lovelorn
lovely
lover
lovesick
lovingly
low
lowborn
lowboy
lowbred
lower
lowered
lowland
lowlier
lowliest

lowliness
lowly
lowmost
loyal
loyalism
loyalist
loyally
loyalty
lozenge
lubricant
lubricate
lubrication
lubricator
lubricity
lucent
lucid
lucidity
lucidly
lucidness
luck
luckily
luckiness
luckless
lucky
lucrative
lucre
lucubration
ludicrous
lug
luggage
lugged
lugger
lugubrious

lukewarm
lull
lullaby
lulled
lumbago
lumber
lumberyard
luminary
luminescence
luminescent
luminiferous
luminosity
luminous
lump
lumpier
lumpiest
lumpy
lunacy
lunar
lunatic
lunch
luncheon
luncheonette
lunchroom
lunette
lung
lunge
lunged
lurch
lurched
lurching
lure
lured
lurid
lurk
lurked
luscious
lush
lust
luster
lustful
lustily
lustiness
lustrous
lustrously
lustrum
lusty
lute
Lutheran
luxuriance
luxuriant
luxuriate
luxuriated
luxurious
luxury
lyceum
lyddite
lymph
lymphatic
lymphoid
lynx
lyonnaise
lyre
lyrebird
lyric
lyrical
lyricism

macabre
macadam
macadamize
macaroni
macaroon
macaw
mace
macerate
macerated
maceration
Mach
machete
machicolation
machinate
machination
machine
machined
machinery
machinist
machismo
macho
mackerel
macrobiotic
macrocosm
macrocyte
macrofouling
macron
maculate
mad
madam
maddeningly
madder
maddest
madhouse
madly
madman
madness
madonna
madrigal
maelstrom
Mafia
mafioso
magazine
magenta
maggot
magi
magic
magical
magically
magician
magisterial
magistracy
magistral
magistrate
magistrature
magnanimity
magnanimous
magnate
magnesia
magnesium
magnet
magnetic
magnetically
magnetism
magnetization
magnetize
magnetized
magneto
magnification

magnificence
magnificent
magnifico
magnifier
magnify
magniloquent
magnitude
magnolia
magnum
magpie
maguey
maharaja
maharani
mahatma
mahogany
maid
maiden
maidenhair
maidenhood
maidenly
maidservant
mail
mailable
mailbag
mailbox
mailed
mailer
mailings
maim
maimed
main
mainland
mainly
mainmast
mainsail
mainsheet
mainspring
mainstay
maintain
maintainable
maintenance
majestic
majesty
majolica
major
majority
majuscule
make
make-believe
maker
makeshift
makings
malachite
maladjusted
maladjustment
maladroit
malady
malapert
malapropism
malapropos
malaria
malarial
malassimilation
Malay
malcontent
male
malediction
maledictory
malefactor
maleficence
maleficent
malevolence
malevolent
malfeasance
malfeasor
malformation
malformed
malice
malicious
maliciously
maliciousness
malign
malignancy
malignant
malignantly
maligned
malignity
malignly
malinger
malingerer
mall
mallard
malleability
malleable
malleolar
malleolus
mallet
mallow
malmsey

malnutrition
malodorous
malposition
malpractice
malt
maltase
Maltese
maltose
maltreat
malversation
mamba
mammal
mammalian
mammary
mammogram
mammography
mammon
mammoplasty
mammoth
man
manacle
manacled
manage
manageable
managed
management
manager
managerial
managerialist
managerially
managership
manatee
mandamus
mandarin
mandate
mandated
mandatory
mandible
mandibular
mandolin
mandrake
mandrel
maneuver
maneuvered
manganate
manganese
mange
manger
mangily
manginess
mangle
mangled
mango
mangrove
mangy
manhole
manhood
mania
maniac
maniacal
manicure
manicurist
manifest
manifestation
manifested
manifesto
manifold
manifolded
manifolder
manikin
manipulate
manipulated
manipulates
manipulation
manipulative
manipulator
manipulatory
mankind
manlike
manliness
manly
manna
manner
mannered
mannerism
mannerly
mannish
manometer
manometric
manor
manorial
mansard
manservant
mansion
manslaughter
manteau
mantel
mantilla
mantis

mantissa
mantle
manual
manually
manufactory
manufacture
manufactured
manufacturer
manumission
manure
manuscript
Manx
many
Maoism
Maori
map
maple
mapped
mar
marabou
maraschino
maraud
marauder
marble
marbled
marcasite
march
marcher
marchioness
marconigram
mare
margarine
margin

marginal
marginalia
marginally
margrave
marigold
marijuana
marimba
marina
marinade
marinate
marinated
marine
mariner
marionette
Marist
marital
maritally
maritime
marjoram
mark
marked
markedly
marker
market
marketability
marketable
markings
marksman
marksmanship
markweed
marl
marlin
marmalade

marmoset
marmot
maroon
marooned
marplot
marquee
marquisette
marred
marriage
marriageable
married
marrow
marrowbone
marrowfat
marrowy
marry
Mars
marshal
marshaled
marshiness
marshmallow
marshy
marsupial
mart
marten
martial
martially
Martian
martinet
martingale
martyr
martyrdom
martyred

marvel
marveled
marvelous
marzipan
mascara
mascot
masculine
masculinist
masculinity
mash
mashed
masher
mashie
mask
masked
masker
mason
masonic
masonry
masquerade
masqueraded
mass
massacre
massage
masseur
massive
mast
master
mastered
masterful
masterfully
masterfulness
masterly

masterpiece
mastership
masterwork
mastery
masthead
mastic
masticate
masticated
mastication
masticator
masticatory
mastiff
mastodon
mastoid
mastoiditis
mat
matador
match
matched
matchless
matchlessly
matchmaker
matchwood
maté
material
materialism
materialist
materialistic
materiality
materialization
materialize
materialized
materially

maternal
maternally
maternity
mathematical
mathematician
mathematics
matin
matinee
matriarch
matriarchy
matrices
matricide
matriculant
matriculate
matriculated
matriculates
matriculation
matrimonial
matrimonially
matrimony
matrix
matron
matronliness
matronly
matte
matted
matter
mattered
mattings
mattock
mattress
maturate
maturated

maturation
maturative
mature
matured
maturely
matureness
maturity
matutinal
maudlin
maul
mauled
maunder
mausoleum
mauve
maverick
mavis
maw
mawkish
maxillary
maxim
maximal
maximize
maximum
may
maybe
mayhem
mayonnaise
mayor
mayoralty
maze
mazurka
me
meadow

meadowland
meager
meal
mealier
mealiest
mealtime
mealy
mealymouthed
mean
meander
meaningful
meaningless
meaningly
meanings
meanly
meanness
meantime
meanwhile
measles
measurable
measurably
measure
measured
measureless
measurement
measurer
meat
meatcutter
meatus
mechanic
mechanical
mechanically
mechanician

mechanics
mechanism
mechanization
mechanize
medal
medalist
medallion
meddle
meddled
meddlesome
media
medial
median
mediate
mediated
mediation
mediative
mediator
medicaid
medical
medically
medicare
medicate
medicated
medication
medicative
medicinal
medicinally
medicine
medieval
medievalist
medievally
mediocre

mediocrity
meditate
meditated
meditation
meditative
medium
medlar
medulla
meek
meeker
meekest
meekly
meekness
meerschaum
meet
meetings
meetinghouse
megabit
megacycle
megahertz
megaphone
megatanker
meiosis
meiotic
melancholia
melancholic
melancholy
melanism
melanosis
meld
meliorate
meliorated
melioration
meliorative
melisma
melismatic
mellifluous
mellow
mellowed
mellower
mellowest
melodeon
melodic
melodion
melodious
melodiously
melodrama
melodramatic
melody
melon
melos
melt
melted
meltingly
member
membership
membrane
membranous
memento
memoir
memorabilia
memorable
memoranda
memorandum
memorandums
memorial
memorialization
memorialize
memorization
memorize
memorized
memory
menace
menaced
menage
menagerie
mend
mendacious
mendacity
mended
Mendelian
mendicancy
mendicant
menfolk
menhaden
menial
menially
meninges
meningitis
meniscus
Mennonite
mensuration
mensurative
mental
mentality
mentally
menthol
mention
mentioned

mentor
menu
mephitic
mercantile
mercenary
mercerize
mercerized
merchandise
merchandiser
merchant
merchantman
merciful
merciless
mercilessly
mercurial
mercury
mercy
merely
merest
meretricious
merge
merged
merger
meridian
meringue
merino
merit
merited
meritocracy
meritorious
meritoriously
merlin
mermaid

merrier
merriest
merrily
merriment
merriness
merry
merrymaking
mesa
mescal
mescaline
mesh
meshwork
mesmerism
meson
mess
message
messenger
messiah
messman
messmate
mestizo
metabolic
metabolism
metacarpal
metacarpus
metal
metallic
metallically
metalloid
metallurgic
metallurgical
metallurgy
metalware

metalwork
metalworker
metamorphose
metamorphoses
metamorphosis
metaphor
metaphoric
metaphorical
metaphorically
metaphysical
metaphysically
metaphysician
metaphysics
metastasis
metastasize
metatarsal
metatarsus
mete
meted
meteor
meteoric
meteorite
meteoroid
meteorology
meter
metered
methadone
methane
methinks
method
methodical
methodically
methodist

methodology
methyl
meticulous
métier
metonymy
metric
metrical
metricate
metrication
metrification
Metroliner
metronome
metropolis
metropolitan
mettle
mettled
mettlesome
Mexican
mezzanine
miasma
miasmal
miasmatic
mica
microbe
microbody
microchip
microcirculation
microcosm
microdot
microfiche
microfile
microfilm
microform
microgram
microlens
micromachining
micrometeoroid
micrometer
micron
microphone
microprogram
microscope
microscopic
microscopy
microslide
microspore
microstructure
microsurgery
microtome
microtomy
Midas
midbrain
midday
middle
middleman
middleweight
midge
midget
midiron
midland
midmost
midnight
midriff
midshipman
midships
midst
midstream
midsummer
midway
midweek
midwife
midwinter
midyear
mien
might
mightily
mightiness
mighty
migraine
migrant
migrate
migrated
migration
migratory
mikado
milch
mild
milder
mildest
mildew
mildly
mildness
mile
mileage
milepost
miler
milestone
militant
militarism

militarist
militaristic
militarize
military
militate
militated
militia
milk
milkmaid
milkman
milkweed
milky
mill
millboard
milled
millenary
millennial
millennium
millepede
miller
millet
milline
milliner
millinery
million
millionaire
millionfold
millionth
millpond
millrace
millstone
millwork
millwright
Miltonic
mime
mimeograph
mimetic
mimic
mimicry
mimosa
minaret
minatory
mince
minced
mincemeat
mincingly
mind
minded
mindful
mindless
mine
miner
mineral
mineralogy
mingle
mingled
miniature
miniaturist
minibus
minidose
minigun
minim
minimal
minimalism
minimax
minimization
minimize
minimum
minipark
minipill
miniskirt
ministate
minister
ministered
ministerial
ministerially
ministration
ministry
minisub
minitanker
miniver
mink
minnow
minor
minority
minster
minstrel
minstrelsy
mint
minted
minuend
minuet
minus
minuscule
minute
minute
minuteness
minutia
minutiae

minx
miracle
miraculous
mirage
mire
mired
mirror
mirrored
mirth
mirthful
mirthfully
mirthless
misadventure
misalliance
misanthrope
misanthropic
misanthropical
misanthropism
misanthropist
misanthropy
misapplication
misapply
misapprehension
misappropriate
misappropriation
misarrange
misbegotten
misbehave
misbehaved
misbehavior
misbeliever
misbrand
miscalculate
miscalculated
miscall
miscarriage
miscarried
miscarry
miscast
miscegenation
miscellanea
miscellaneous
miscellanist
miscellany
mischance
mischief
mischievous
miscible
misconceive
misconception
misconduct
misconstruction
misconstrue
miscount
miscreant
miscue
misdate
misdeal
misdeed
misdemeanor
misdirect
misdirected
misdirection
misdoubt
miser
miserable
miserliness
miserly
misery
misfeasance
misfire
misfired
misfit
misformed
misfortune
misgivings
misgovern
misgoverned
misguide
misguided
mishap
mishmash
misinform
misinformed
misinterpret
misinterpretation
misinterpreted
misjudge
misjudged
mislaid
mislay
mislead
misleadingly
mislike
misliked
mismade
mismanage
mismanagement
mismate

mismated
misname
misnamed
misnomer
misogynist
misplace
misplaced
misprint
misprision
mispronounce
mispronunciation
misquotation
misquote
misread
misremember
misremembrance
misrepresent
misrepresentation
misrule
miss
missal
missed
misshapen
missile
mission
missionary
missioner
missive
misspell
misspelled
misspellings
misspend
misspent
misstate
misstated
misstatement
misstep
mist
mistake
mistaken
mistakenly
mistaught
misteach
mistier
mistiest
mistily
mistiness
mistletoe
mistook
mistreat
mistreatment
mistress
mistrial
mistrust
mistrustful
misty
misunderstand
misunderstandings
misunderstood
misusage
misuse
misused
mite
miter
mitered
mitigable
mitigate
mitigated
mitigation
mitigative
mitigatory
mitosis
mitotic
mitral
mitten
mittened
mix
mixed
mixer
mixture
mizzenmast
mnemonic
moa
moan
moaned
moat
mob
mobcap
mobile
mobility
mobilization
mobilize
mobilized
mobocracy
moccasin
mocha
mock
mockery
mockingly

modal
modality
mode
model
modeled
moderate
moderated
moderately
moderateness
moderation
moderationist
moderator
modern
modernism
modernist
modernistic
modernity
modernization
modernize
modernized
modest
modestly
modesty
modicum
modification
modificationist
modified
modifier
modify
modish
modishly
modishness
modular

modularity
modularize
modulate
modulated
modulation
modulative
modulator
modulatory
module
modulus
mogadore
mogul
mohair
Mohammedan
Mohawk
Moho
moiety
moil
moiled
moiré
moist
moisten
moistened
moistener
moisture
molal
molar
molarity
molasses
mold
moldboard
molded
molder

moldings
moldy
mole
molecular
molecule
molehill
moleskin
molest
molestation
molested
mollification
mollified
mollify
mollusk
mollycoddle
molt
molted
molten
moly
molybdenum
moment
momentarily
momentary
momently
momentous
momentum
monad
monadnock
monarch
monarchial
monarchianism
monarchic
monarchism

monarchist
monarchistic
monarchy
monasterial
monasterially
monastery
monastic
monasticism
monatomic
Monday
monel
monetarism
monetarist
monetary
monetization
monetize
money
moneyed
mongoose
mongrel
monism
monitor
monitored
monitorial
monitory
monk
monkey
monkhood
monkish
monobasic
monocle
monocled
monocular

monody
monogamous
monogamy
monogram
monograph
monolith
monolithic
monologue
monomania
monomaniac
monomaniacal
monomorphic
monoplane
monoplegia
monopolism
monopolist
monopolistic
monopolistically
monopolization
monopolize
monopolized
monopoly
monorail
monosyllabic
monosyllable
monotechnic
monotheism
monotheistic
monotone
monotonous
monotony
monotype
monounsaturated

monoxide
monsignor
monsoon
monster
monstrance
monstrosity
monstrous
month
monthly
monument
monumental
monumentally
mood
moodily
moodiness
moody
moon
moonbeam
mooncraft
moonfaced
moonfish
moonflower
moonlight
moonlighted
moonlighter
moonlighting
moonrise
moonrock
moonshine
moonstone
moonstruck
moonwalk
moor

moorage
moored
moorings
Moorish
moorland
moose
moot
mop
mopped
moppet
moraine
moral
morale
moralist
moralistic
morality
moralization
moralize
moralized
morally
morass
moratorium
moray
morbid
morbidity
morbidly
mordant
more
moreover
mores
morganatic
morgue
moribund

Mormon
morn
morning
mornings
morocco
moron
morose
morosely
morphine
morphinism
morphinize
morphology
morris
morrow
morsel
mortal
mortality
mortally
mortar
mortarboard
mortgage
mortgaged
mortgagee
mortgagor
mortician
mortification
mortified
mortify
mortise
mortmain
mortuary
mosaic
Moslem

mosque
mosquito
moss
mossback
mossiness
mossy
most
mostly
motel
motet
moth
mother
motherhood
mother-in-law
motherland
motherless
motherliness
motherly
mother-of-pearl
motif
motile
motion
motioned
motionless
motivate
motivated
motivation
motivational
motive
motley
motor
motorboat
motorcycle

motored
motorist
motorize
motorman
mottle
mottled
motto
mound
mount
mountain
mountaineer
mountainous
mountainously
mountebank
mounted
mountings
mourn
mourned
mourner
mournful
mournfully
mouse
mouser
mousetrap
mousse
mouth
mouthed
mouthful
mouthpiece
movability
movable
movably
move

moved
movement
mover
movie
movingly
mow
mower
Mr.
Mrs.
Ms.
much
mucilage
mucilaginous
muck
mucker
muckraker
muckweed
muckworm
mucoid
mucosa
mucous
mucus
mud
muddier
muddiest
muddily
muddiness
muddle
muddled
muddle-headed
muddy
mudfish
mudweed

muff
muffin
muffle
muffled
muffler
mufti
mug
mugger
mugging
muggy
mugwump
mulatto
mulberry
mulch
mulched
mulct
mulcted
mule
muleteer
muliebrity
mulish
mull
mulled
mullet
mulligatawny
multichannel
multicompany
multicultural
multidirectional
multiethnic
multifarious
multifold
multiform

multiformity
Multigraph
Multilith
multimarket
multimedia
multimillionaire
multinational
multipack
multiple
multiplex
multiplicand
multiplicate
multiplication
multiplicative
multiplicity
multiplied
multiplier
multiply
multiprocessing
multiprocessor
multiprogramming
multiracialism
multiresistant
multitude
multitudinous
multivalent
multiversity
mumble
mumbled
mummer
mummery
mummification
mummified

mummify
mummy
mumps
munch
munched
mundane
municipal
municipality
municipally
munificence
munificent
muniment
munition
mural
murder
murdered
murderer
murderous
murex
muriatic
murk
murkily
murkiness
murky
murmur
murmured
murmurer
murmurous
muscadine
muscat
muscatel
muscle
muscular

muscularity
muscularly
musculature
muse
mused
musette
museum
mush
mushroom
mushroomed
mushy
music
musical
musicale
musically
musician
musicianly
musk
muskeg
muskellunge
musket
musketeer
musketry
muskmelon
muskrat
Muslim
muslin
muss
mussed
mussel
mussier
mussiest
mussy

must
mustache
mustachio
mustang
mustard
muster
mustered
mustiness
musty
mutability
mutable
mutagenicity
mutate
mutation
mutative
mute
mutely
muted
muteness
mutilate
mutilated
mutilation

mutilator
mutineer
mutinied
mutinous
mutiny
mutism
mutter
muttered
mutterings
mutton
mutual
mutuality
mutually
muzzle
muzzled
my
mycology
mycosis
mydriasis
mydriatic
myeloid
Mylar

myoelectric
myopia
myopic
myriad
myrrh
myrtle
myself
mysterious
mysteriously
mystery
mystic
mystical
mystically
mysticism
mystification
mystified
mystify
myth
mythical
mythological
mythologist
mythology

n

nacelle
nacre
nacreous
Naderism
nadir
naiad
nail
nailed
nailhead
nainsook
naïve
naïveté
naked
nakedly
nakedness
namable
name
named
nameless
namelessly
namely
namesake
nankeen

nanosurgery
nanovolt
nap
napery
naphtha
naphthalene
napkin
napoleon
Napoleonana
Napoleonic
napped
narcissism
narcissus
narcosis
narcotic
narcoticism
narcotize
narcotized
narrate
narrated
narration
narrative
narrator

narrow
narrowed
narrower
narrowest
narrowly
narrowness
narwhal
nasal
nasality
nasalize
nasally
nascent
nastier
nastiest
nastily
nastiness
nasturtium
nasty
natal
natation
natatorium
natatory
nation

national
nationalism
nationalistic
nationality
nationalization
nationalize
nationally
nationwide
native
nativity
natural
naturalism
naturalist
naturalistic
naturalization
naturalize
naturalized
naturally
naturalness
nature
naturistic
naught
naughtily
naughtiness
naughty
nausea
nauseate
nauseated
nauseous
nautical
nautilus
naval
nave

navel
navigable
navigate
navigated
navigation
navigational
navigator
navy
Naxalite
Nazarene
neap
Neapolitan
near
nearby
neared
nearer
nearest
nearly
nearness
nearsighted
neat
neater
neatest
neatherd
neatly
neatness
nebula
nebular
nebulosity
nebulous
nebulously
necessarily
necessary

necessitarian
necessitate
necessitated
necessitous
necessity
neck
neckband
neckcloth
neckerchief
necklace
necktie
neckwear
necrological
necrology
necromancy
necromantic
necrophobia
necropolis
necropsy
necrosis
necrotic
nectar
nectarine
need
needed
needful
needfully
needier
neediest
neediness
needle
needled
needleful

needless
needlessly
needlessness
needlework
needy
nefarious
negate
negated
negation
negative
negatived
negativism
neglect
neglected
neglectful
negligee
negligence
negligent
negligible
negotiability
negotiable
negotiate
negotiated
negotiation
negotiator
negritude
Negro
negrophile
neighbor
neighborhood
neighborliness
neighborly
neither

nematode
nemesis
neocolonial
neofeminist
neoformation
neoglacial
neoglaciation
neoimperial
neoimperialism
neoimperialist
neolithic
neologism
neology
neon
neonationalism
neophilia
neophyte
neoplasm
neopopulism
neorevisionist
nepenthe
nephew
nephrectomy
nephritis
nepotism
nerve
nerveless
nervous
nervously
nervousness
nescience
nescient
nest

nested
nestle
nestled
nestlings
net
nether
nethermost
netsuke
netted
nettings
nettle
nettled
network
neural
neuralgia
neurasthenia
neurasthenic
neuritis
neurobiological
neurobiologist
neurobiology
neurochemical
neurochemist
neurochemistry
neurodepressive
neuroleptic
neuroscience
neuroses
neurosis
neurotic
neuter
neutral
neutralism

neutralist
neutrality
neutralization
neutralize
neutralized
neutralizer
neutrally
neutron
never
nevermore
nevertheless
new
newcomer
newel
newer
newest
newfangled
newly
newness
newsier
newsiest
newsletter
newspaper
newsreel
newsstand
newsy
newt
next
nexus
nibble
nibbled
niblick
nice

nicely
niceness
nicer
nicest
nicety
niche
nick
nicked
nickel
nickeliferous
nickelodeon
nickname
nicknamed
nicotine
nicotinic
niece
niello
niggard
niggardliness
niggardly
niggle
nigglingly
nigh
night
nightcap
nightfall
nightfish
nightgown
nighthawk
nightingale
nightly
nightmare
nightmarish

nightshade
nightshirt
nighttime
nightviewer
nightwear
nightwork
nightworker
nihilism
nihilist
nihilistic
nimble
nimbus
nincompoop
ninepins
nipper
nipple
nippy
nirvana
niter
nitrate
nitric
nitride
nitrification
nitrify
nitrogen
nitrogenous
nitroglycerin
nitrous
nitwit
no
nobility
noble
nobleman

nobler
noblest
nobly
nobody
nocturnal
nocturnally
nocturne
nod
nodded
node
nodule
noel
no-fault
noise
noiseless
noisier
noisiest
noisily
noisiness
noisome
noisy
nomad
nomadic
nomenclature
nominal
nominalism
nominally
nominate
nominated
nomination
nominative
nominee
nonaddict
nonagenarian
nonagon
nonaligned
nonappearance
noncallable
nonce
nonchalance
nonchalant
nonchalantly
noncombatant
noncommissioned
noncommittal
noncommitted
noncommunicant
nonconductor
nonconformism
nonconformist
nonconformity
noncooperation
nondescript
nondisposable
none
nonentity
nonessential
nonesuch
nonethnic
nonexistence
nonfeasance
nonfeasor
nonforfeiture
nongraded
nonintervention
nonmetal
nonmetallic
nonpareil
nonparticipating
nonpartisan
nonpermanent
nonplus
nonplused
nonpolluting
nonproliferation
nonresidence
nonresident
nonresistance
nonresistant
nonsense
nonsensical
nonskid
nonstick
nonstop
nonsubscriber
nonsuit
nonsupport
nonunion
noodle
nook
noon
noonday
noontime
noose
nor
norm
normal
normality
normalize

normalized
normally
Norman
normative
Norse
north
northeast
northeaster
northeasterly
northeastern
northeastward
northeastwardly
northerly
northern
northerner
northland
northward
northwest
northwesterly
northwestern
Norwegian
nose
noseband
nosebleed
nosegay
nosepiece
nosings
nosology
nostalgia
nostalgic
nostril
nostrum
not

notability
notable
notarial
notarially
notary
notation
notch
notched
notchweed
note
notebook
noted
noteworthily
noteworthy
nothing
nothingness
notice
noticeable
noticed
notification
notified
notify
notion
notoriety
notorious
notoriously
notwithstanding
nougat
nougatine
nought
noumenon
noun
nourish

nourished
nourishingly
nourishment
novel
novelette
novelist
novelize
novella
novelty
November
novena
novice
novitiate
Novocain
now
nowadays
nowhere
noxious
noxiousness
nozzle
nuance
nuclear
nucleate
nucleated
nucleation
nuclei
nucleolus
nucleus
nude
nudge
nudged
nudism
nudist

nudity
nugatory
nugget
nuisance
null
nullification
nullificationist
nullified
nullify
nullity
numb
numbed
number
numbered
numberless
numbness
numeral
numerate
numeration
numerator
numeric
numerical
numerous
numismatics
numismatist
numskull
nun
nunciature
nuncio
nunnery
nuptial
nurse
nursed
nursemaid
nursery
nurserymaid
nurseryman
nurslings
nurture
nurtured
nut
nuthatch
nutmeg
nutria
nutrient
nutriment
nutrition
nutritional
nutritionally
nutritionist
nutritious
nutritiously
nutritive
nutritively
nutshell
nuzzle
nuzzled
nyctalopia
nylon
nystagmus

O

oaf
oak
oaken
oakum
oar
oarlock
oarsman
oasis
oaten
oath
oatmeal
obbligato
obduracy
obdurate
obedience
obedient
obeisance
obelisk
obese
obesity
obey
obeyed
obituary

object
objected
objection
objectionable
objective
objectively
objectiveness
objectivity
objector
objurgate
oblate
oblation
obligate
obligated
obligation
obligatory
oblige
obliged
obligingly
oblique
obliquely
obliqueness
obliquity

obliterate
obliterated
obliteration
oblivion
oblivious
obliviously
obliviousness
oblong
obloquy
obnoxious
obnoxiously
oboe
obscene
obscenity
obscure
obscureness
obscurity
obsequious
obsequiously
obsequiousness
obsequy
observable
observance

observant
observation
observatory
observe
observed
observer
observingly
obsess
obsessed
obsession
obsessional
obsessive
obsidian
obsolescence
obsolescent
obsolete
obsoletely
obsoleteness
obstacle
obstetrical
obstetrician
obstetrics
obstinacy
obstinate
obstinately
obstreperous
obstruct
obstructed
obstruction
obstructionism
obstructionist
obstructive
obstructor

obtain
obtainable
obtained
obtrude
obtruded
obtruder
obtrusion
obtrusive
obtuse
obtusely
obtuseness
obverse
obviate
obviated
obviation
obvious
obviously
ocarina
occasion
occasional
occasionally
occasioned
occident
occidental
occidentally
occipital
occiput
occlude
occluded
occlusion
occult
occultation
occultism

occultist
occupancy
occupant
occupation
occupational
occupationally
occupied
occupy
occur
occurred
occurrence
ocean
oceanic
oceanography
ocelot
ocher
ochlocracy
octagon
octagonal
octagonally
octameter
octangular
octave
octavo
octet
October
octogenarian
octopus
ocular
oculist
odd
odder
oddest

oddity
oddly
oddment
oddness
ode
odeum
odious
odiously
odiousness
odium
odometer
odor
odoriferous
odorless
odorous
oenology
of
off
offal
offcast
offend
offended
offense
offensive
offer
offered
offerings
offertory
offhand
office
officer
official
officially

officiate
officiated
officiation
officious
officiously
officiousness
offish
offset
offshoot
offshore
often
oftener
oftenest
oftentimes
ogee
ogive
ogle
ogled
ogre
ohm
ohmage
ohmmeter
oil
oiled
oiler
oilhole
oilier
oiliest
oilily
oiliness
oilman
oilpaper
oilproof

oilseed
oilskin
oilstone
oiltight
oily
ointment
okapi
okra
old
olden
older
oldest
old-fashioned
oldish
oldness
oldster
oleaginous
oleander
oleate
olecranon
oleo
oleomargarine
olfactory
oligarchy
olive
ombudsman
ombudswoman
omega
omelet
omen
omentum
ominous
omission

omit
omitted
omnibus
omnipotence
omnipotent
omnipresent
omniscience
omniscient
omnivorous
on
onager
once
one
oneness
onerous
oneself
onetime
onion
onlooker
only
onomatopoeia
onset
onslaught
onto
ontogeny
ontology
onus
onward
onyx
oölogy
oolong
ooze
oozed

opacity
opal
opalesce
opalescence
opalescent
opaque
open
opened
opener
openings
openly
openness
openwork
opera
operable
operalogue
operand
operate
operated
operatic
operatically
operation
operative
operator
operetta
ophthalmologist
ophthalmology
opiate
opinion
opinionated
opinionative
opium
opossum

opponent
opportune
opportunism
opportunity
opposable
oppose
opposed
opposer
opposing
opposite
opposition
oppress
oppressed
oppression
oppressive
oppressively
oppressiveness
oppressor
opprobrious
opprobriously
opprobriousness
opprobrium
opt
opted
optative
optic
optical
optician
optics
optimism
optimist
optimistic
optimistically

optimum
option
optional
optionally
optoelectronic
optometrist
optometry
opulence
opulent
opus
or
oracle
oracular
oracularly
oral
orally
orange
orangutan
oration
orator
oratorical
oratorio
oratory
orb
orbit
orbital
orbited
orchard
orchestra
orchestral
orchestrate
orchestrated
orchestration

orchid
orchidaceous
ordain
ordained
ordeal
order
ordered
orderliness
orderly
ordinal
ordinance
ordinarily
ordinary
ordination
ordnance
ore
organ
organic
organically
organism
organist
organization
organizational
organize
organized
orgy
oriel
orient
oriental
orientalism
orientalist
orientally
orientate

orientation
oriented
orifice
origin
original
originality
originally
originate
originated
origination
originative
originator
oriole
Orion
orison
orlop
ormolu
ornament
ornamental
ornamentally
ornamentation
ornate
ornately
ornithological
ornithologist
ornithology
orotund
orotundity
orphan
orphanage
orphaned
orphanhood
orpheum

orrery
orthodox
orthoepy
orthography
orthopedic
orthoptic
ortolan
oscillate
oscillated
oscillation
oscillator
oscillatory
oscilloscope
osculate
osculation
osculatory
osier
osmium
osmosis
osmotic
osprey
osseous
ossification
ossified
ossify
ostensible
ostensibly
ostentation
ostentatious
ostentatiously
osteopath
osteopathy
ostracism
ostracize
ostracized
ostrich
other
others
otherwise
otiose
otter
ottoman
ought
ounce
our
ours
ourselves
oust
ouster
out
outcast
outclass
outcome
outcrop
outcry
outcurve
outdistance
outdo
outdoors
outer
outermost
outface
outfield
outfit
outfitter
outflank
outflow
outgo
outgrowth
outgun
outings
outlandish
outlandishness
outlast
outlaw
outlawry
outlay
outlet
outlets
outline
outlined
outlive
outlived
outlook
outlying
outmarch
outmoded
outnumber
output
outrage
outrageous
outrageously
outrageousness
outrank
outranked
outreach
outrider
outrigger
outright

outrun
outset
outside
outsider
outsize
outskirt
outstandingly
outstay
outstrip
outvote
outward
outwardly
outwear
outwit
outwork
oval
ovate
ovation
oven
ovenbird
ovenware
over
overachieve
overage
overage
overalls
overawe
overawed
overbalance
overbear
overbearingly
overbid
overboard
overbook
overbuild
overbuilt
overburden
overcapitalize
overcast
overcentralization
overcharge
overcharged
overclothes
overcoat
overcome
overcompensation
overcorrect
overcount
overdevelop
overdo
overdone
overdose
overdraft
overdraw
overdrawn
overdress
overdrew
overdrive
overdriven
overdub
overdue
overeat
overeducate
overestimate
overexploitation
overexpose
overexposure
overflow
overflowingly
overgrown
overhand
overhang
overhaul
overhead
overheat
overinflated
overissue
overkill
overland
overlap
overlook
overlord
overly
overmark
overmasteringly
overmodulation
overnight
overoccupied
overpass
overpay
overpopulation
overpower
overpowered
overpoweringly
overprescribe
overproduction
overqualified
overrate
overrated

overreach
override
overripe
overrule
overruled
overrun
overseas
oversee
overseer
oversell
overshadow
overshadowed
overshoe
overside
oversight
oversize
overspread
overstate
overstatement
overstay
overstep
overstock
overstrain
overstructured
oversubscribe
oversupply

overt
overtake
overtax
overtaxed
overthrew
overthrow
overthrown
overtime
overtone
overture
overturn
overturned
overvalue
overweeningly
overweight
overwhelm
overwhelmed
overwhelmingly
overwind
overwork
overworked
overwrought
oviduct
oviparous
ovipositor
ovule

ovum
owe
owed
owl
owlet
owlish
own
owned
owner
ownership
ox
oxalate
oxalic
oxidation
oxide
oxidizable
oxidize
oxidized
oxtongue
oxygen
oxygenate
oyster
oystershell
ozone
ozonize
ozonized

p

pabulum
pace
pacemaker
pacer
pachyderm
pachysandra
pacific
pacifically
pacificate
pacification
pacificatory
pacified
pacifier
pacifism
pacifist
pacify
pack
package
packaged
packer
packet
packings
packsack
packsaddle
packthread
pact
pad
padded
paddings
paddle
paddled
paddlefish
paddock
padlock
paean
pagan
paganism
paganize
page
pageant
pageantry
paged
pagination
pagoda
paid
pail
pain
pained
painful
painkiller
painless
painstakingly
paint
painted
painter
paintings
paintpot
pair
paired
pairings
pajama
palace
paladin
palanquin
palatability
palatable
palatal
palatalize
palate

palatial
palatially
palatinate
palatine
palaver
pale
paled
paleography
paler
palest
palette
palfrey
palimpsest
palindrome
palings
palinode
palisade
pall
palladium
pallbearer
palled
pallet
palliate
palliated
palliation
palliative
pallid
pallidity
pallidly
pallium
pallor
palm
palmate

palmed
palmer
palmetto
palmist
palmistry
palpability
palpable
palpate
palpated
palpation
palpatory
palpitant
palpitate
palpitated
palpitatingly
palpitation
palsied
palsy
palter
paltered
paltry
pampas
pamper
pampered
pamphlet
pamphleteer
pamphletize
pan
panacea
panama
Pan-American
Pan-Americanism
pancake

panchromatic
pancreas
pancreatic
panda
pandemic
pandemonium
pander
pandered
pane
panegyric
panegyrical
panegyrize
panegyrized
panel
paneled
pang
pangram
Panhellenic
panic
panicked
panicky
panjandrum
panned
pannier
pannikin
panoply
panorama
panoramic
pansy
pant
pantaloon
panted
pantheism

pantheist
pantheistic
pantheon
panther
pantograph
pantomime
pantry
pantryman
pantyhose
papacy
papal
papaya
paper
paperback
paperboard
papered
paperer
papeterie
papoose
paprika
Papuan
papule
papyrus
par
parable
parabola
parabolic
parabolical
paraboloid
parachute
parade
paraded
paradigm

paradise
paradox
paradoxical
paraffin
paragon
paragraph
paragraphed
parakeet
parallax
parallel
paralleled
parallelism
parallelogram
paralysis
paralytic
paralytically
paralyze
paralyzed
paramedic
parameter
paramount
paranoia
paranoiac
paranoid
parapet
paraphernalia
paraphrase
paraphrased
paraphrastic
paraplegia
paraplegic
paraprofessional
parasite

parasitic
parasitical
parasiticide
parasitism
parasitize
parasol
parathyroid
paratyphoid
paravane
parboil
parboiled
parcel
parceled
parch
parched
parchment
pardon
pardonable
pardoned
pare
pared
paregoric
parenchyma
parent
parentage
parental
parentally
parentheses
parenthesis
parenthesize
parenthetical
parenthetically
parenthood

paresis
parfait
pariah
parietal
parietals
parings
parish
parishioner
parity
park
parka
parked
parkway
parlance
parlando
parlay
parley
parleyed
parliament
parliamentarian
parliamentarily
parliamentary
parlor
parlous
Parmesan
Parnassus
parochial
parochialism
parochially
parody
parole
paronomasia
parotid
paroxysm
paroxysmal
paroxysmally
parquet
parricidal
parricidally
parricide
parried
parrot
parroted
parry
parse
parsed
parsimonious
parsimony
parsley
parsnip
parson
parsonage
part
partake
partaker
parted
parterre
parthenogenesis
Parthenon
Parthian
partial
partiality
partially
participant
participate
participated
participation
participational
participative
participator
participial
participially
participle
particle
particular
particularity
particularize
particularized
particularly
partings
partisan
partisanship
partition
partitioned
partitive
partner
partnership
partridge
party
parvenu
paschal
pasha
pass
passable
passage
passageway
passbook
passed
passenger

passion
passionate
passionately
Passionist
passionless
passive
passiveness
passivism
passivist
passivity
passkey
Passover
passport
password
past
paste
pasteboard
pasted
pastel
pastern
pasteurization
pasteurize
pasteurized
pastiche
pastille
pastime
pastiness
pastor
pastoral
pastorally
pastorate
pastry
pastryman

pasturage
pasture
pastured
pasty
pat
Patagonian
patch
patched
patchouli
patchwork
patchy
patella
patellar
patent
patentable
patented
patentee
paterfamilias
paternal
paternalism
paternalistic
paternally
paternity
path
pathetic
pathetically
pathless
pathologist
pathology
pathos
pathway
patience
patient

patina
patio
patness
patois
patriarch
patriarchal
patriarchate
patriarchy
patrician
patricide
patrimonial
patrimony
patriot
patriotic
patriotically
patriotism
patristic
patrol
patrolled
patrolman
patron
patronage
patroness
patronize
patronized
patronymic
patroon
patted
patten
patter
pattered
pattern
patterned

paucity
Paulist
paunch
paunchiness
pauper
pauperism
pauperization
pauperize
pauperized
pause
paused
pave
paved
pavement
paver
pavillion
paw
pawed
pawl
pawn
pawnbroker
pawned
pawnshop
pay
payable
paycheck
payday
payee
payees
payer
payload
paymaster
payment

payroll
pea
peace
peaceable
peaceably
peaceful
peacekeeper
peacemaker
peach
peacock
peak
peaked
peal
pealed
peanut
pear
pearl
pearlite
pearly
peasant
peasantry
peashooter
peat
peavey
pebble
pebbled
pebbleware
pebbly
pecan
peccadillo
peccancy
peccant
peccary

peck
pectase
pectin
pectoral
peculate
peculated
peculation
peculator
peculiar
peculiarity
peculiarly
pecuniary
pedagogic
pedagogical
pedagogically
pedagogue
pedagogy
pedal
pedaled
pedant
pedantic
pedantical
pedanticism
pedantry
peddle
peddled
peddler
pedestal
pedestrian
pedestrianism
pediatrician
pediatrics
pedicular

pediculosis
pedicure
pedigree
pedigreed
pediment
pedometer
peek
peel
peeled
peelings
peen
peep
peer
peerage
peered
peerless
peevish
peg
Pegasus
pegged
pejorative
pekoe
pelagic
pelf
pelican
pelisse
pellagra
pellet
pellucid
pelota
pelt
pelted
peltry
pelvic
pelvis
pemmican
pen
penal
penalization
penalize
penalized
penalty
penance
penchant
pencil
penciled
pendant
pendency
pending
pendulous
pendulum
penetrability
penetrable
penetrant
penetrate
penetrated
penetratingly
penetration
penetrative
penguin
penholder
penicillin
peninsula
peninsular
penitence
penitent
penitential
penitentially
penitentiary
penitently
penknife
penman
penmanship
pennant
penniless
pennon
penny
pennyroyal
pennyweight
penologist
penology
pension
pensionary
pensioned
pensioner
pensive
penstock
pent
pentagon
pentagonal
pentameter
Pentateuch
pentathlon
pentatonic
Pentecost
penthouse
pentoxide
penult
penultimate

penumbra
penurious
penury
peon
peonage
peony
people
peopled
peplum
pepper
peppered
pepperiness
peppermint
peppery
pepsin
peptic
peptone
peradventure
perambulate
perambulator
perborate
percale
perceivable
perceive
perceived
percent
percentage
percentile
percept
perceptibility
perceptible
perception
perceptive
perceptual
perceptually
perch
perchance
percipiency
percipient
percolate
percolation
percolator
percussion
percussive
perdition
perdu
perdurable
peregrination
peremptorily
peremptoriness
peremptory
perennial
perennially
perfect
perfected
perfectibility
perfectible
perfection
perfectionism
perfectionist
perfectly
perfecto
perfidious
perfidy
perforate
perforated
perforation
perforative
perforator
perforce
perform
performable
performance
performative
performed
performer
perfume
perfumed
perfumer
perfumery
perfunctorily
perfunctoriness
perfunctory
perfuse
perfused
pergola
perhaps
pericardial
pericarditis
pericardium
perigee
peril
perilous
perilously
perimeter
period
periodate
periodic
periodical

periodically
periodicity
periosteum
peripatetic
peripheral
peripherally
periphery
periphrastic
periscope
periscopic
perish
perishable
perished
peristalsis
peristaltic
peristaltically
peristyle
peritoneum
peritonitis
periwinkle
perjure
perjured
perjurer
perjuriously
perjury
perky
permalloy
permanence
permanent
permanently
permanganate
permeability
permeable

permeate
permeated
permeation
permissibility
permissible
permission
permissiveness
permit
permitted
permutation
permute
permuted
pernicious
peroration
peroxide
perpendicular
perpendicularity
perpetrate
perpetrated
perpetration
perpetrator
perpetual
perpetually
perpetuate
perpetuated
perpetuation
perpetuator
perpetuity
perplex
perplexed
perplexedly
perplexingly
perplexity

perquisite
perquisition
persecute
persecuted
persecution
persecutor
perseverance
perseveration
persevere
persevered
persiflage
persimmon
persist
persistence
persistency
persistent
persistingly
person
personable
personage
personal
personality
personalize
personally
personalty
personhood
personification
personified
personify
personnel
perspective
perspicacious
perspicacity

perspicuous
perspiration
perspiratory
perspire
perspired
persuade
persuaded
persuader
persuasion
persuasive
persuasiveness
persulphate
pert
pertain
pertained
pertinacious
pertinacity
pertinence
pertinent
perturb
perturbable
perturbation
perturbed
perusal
peruse
perused
Peruvian
pervade
pervaded
pervadingly
pervasion
pervasive
perverse
perversion
perversity
perversive
pervert
perverted
pervious
pessimism
pessimist
pessimistic
pessimistically
pest
pester
pestered
pesthole
pesthouse
pestiferous
pestilence
pestilent
pestilential
pestilentially
pestle
pet
petal
petard
petite
petition
petitioned
petitioner
petnapper
petrel
petrifaction
petrifactive
petrify
petrol
petrolatum
petroleum
petrology
petted
petticoat
pettier
pettiest
pettifogger
pettily
pettiness
pettish
petty
petulance
petulant
petunia
pew
pewter
phaeton
phagocyte
phalange
phalanstery
phalanx
phantasm
phantasmagoria
phantom
pharaoh
pharmaceutic
pharmaceutical
pharmaceutics
pharmacist
pharmacology
pharmacopoeia

pharmacy
pharyngitis
pharynx
phase
phased
phasedown
pheasant
phenol
phenomena
phenomenal
phenomenology
phenomenon
phial
philander
philanderer
philanthropic
philanthropical
philanthropist
philanthropy
philatelic
philatelist
philately
philharmonic
philippic
Philippine
philistine
philologist
philology
philosopher
philosophic
philosophical
philosophize
philosophy
philter
phlebitis
phlebotomy
phlegm
phlegmatic
phlegmatically
phloem
phlox
phobia
phoenix
phone
phonetic
phonetically
phonetician
phonetics
phonic
phonograph
phosphate
phosphide
phosphite
phosphoresce
phosphorescence
phosphoric
phosphorous
phosphorus
photocopier
photoelectric
photoengraving
photogenic
photograph
photographed
photographer
photographic
photography
photogravure
photolithograph
photomicrograph
photon
photoplay
photosensitize
Photostat
photosynthesis
phrase
phrased
phraseology
phrenetic
phrenic
phrenologist
phrenology
phthisis
phylactery
physic
physical
physically
physician
physicist
physics
physiognomy
physiological
physiologically
physiology
physique
pianissimo
pianist
piano
pianoforte

piazza
pica
picaresque
piccolo
pick
pickax
picked
picker
pickerel
picket
picketed
pickings
pickle
pickled
picklock
pickpocket
pickup
picnic
picnicker
picric
pictograph
pictorial
pictorially
picture
Picturephone
picturesque
pie
piebald
piece
piecemeal
piecework
piecrust
pied

pieplant
pier
pierce
pierced
piety
pig
pigeon
pigeonhole
pigfish
piggery
piggish
pigheaded
piglet
pigment
pigmentary
pigmentation
pigmented
pignut
pigpen
pigskin
pigsticker
pigsty
pigtail
pigweed
pike
piker
pikestaff
pilaster
pilchard
pile
piled
pilework
pileworm

pilfer
pilferage
pilfered
pilferings
pilgrim
pilgrimage
pill
pillage
pillaged
pillar
pillion
pillory
pillow
pillowcase
pillowed
pilot
piloted
pimento
pimpernel
pimple
pin
pinafore
pincers
pinch
pinched
pincushion
pine
pineapple
pined
pinfeather
pinfish
Ping-Pong
pinguid

pinhole
pinion
pink
pinkish
pinkweed
pinkwood
pinnace
pinnacle
pinned
pinochle
pinprick
pint
pinto
pinweed
pinworm
pioneer
pioneered
pious
piously
pip
pipage
pipe
piped
pipeline
piper
pipestem
pipestone
pipette
pipewood
pipingly
pipings
pipit
pipkin

pipsissewa
piquancy
piquant
pique
piqué
piqued
piracy
pirate
pirated
piratic
piratical
pirogue
pirouette
pirouetted
piscatology
piscatorial
piscatorially
pistachio
pistol
pistole
piston
pit
pitch
pitched
pitcher
pitchfork
piteous
piteousness
pitfall
pith
pithily
pithiness
pithy

pitiable
pitiful
pitiless
pitilessly
pitilessness
pittance
pitted
pituitary
pity
pityingly
pivot
pivotal
pivoted
placability
placable
placard
placate
placated
placatively
placatory
place
placebo
placeman
placement
placenta
placer
placid
placidity
placidly
placket
plagiarism
plagiarist
plagiarize

plagiary
plague
plagued
plaid
plain
plainer
plainest
plainly
plainness
plaint
plaintiff
plaintive
plait
plaited
plaitings
plan
planchette
plane
planet
planetarian
planetarium
planetary
planetoid
planetology
plangent
planisphere
plank
planked
plankton
planless
planned
planographic
plant

plantain
plantar
plantation
planted
planter
plantings
plaque
plasma
plaster
plastered
plasterer
plasterwork
plastic
plasticity
plastron
plate
plateau
plated
plateholder
platelet
platen
plater
platform
platina
platinate
platings
platinic
platinize
platinoid
platinum
platitude
platitudinize
platitudinous

platoon
platter
platypus
plaudit
plausibility
plausible
play
playback
playbill
playboy
played
player
playful
playfulness
playground
playings
playmate
playreader
playroom
playscript
plaything
playtime
playwright
plaza
plea
plead
pleaded
pleader
pleadingly
pleadings
pleasant
pleasantly
pleasantness

pleasantry
please
pleased
pleasurable
pleasure
pleat
plebeian
plebiscite
pledge
pledged
pledgee
pledgeor
pledger
pledget
plenarily
plenary
plenipotentiary
plenitude
plenteous
plentiful
plenty
plenum
pleonasm
pleonastic
plethora
plethoric
pleura
pleural
pleurisy
plexus
pliability
pliable
pliancy

pliant
pliers
plight
plighted
plinth
plod
plodded
plodder
ploddingly
plot
plotted
plotter
plough
plover
plow
plowboy
plowings
plowman
plowshare
pluck
plucked
pluckier
pluckiest
pluckily
pluckiness
plucky
plug
plugged
plum
plumage
plumb
plumbago
plumbate

plumbed
plumber
plumbic
plumbous
plume
plumed
plummet
plummeted
plump
plumper
plumpest
plumply
plumpness
plunder
plundered
plunderer
plunge
plunged
plunger
plunk
plunked
plural
pluralism
pluralist
pluralistic
plurality
pluralize
pluralized
plus
plush
plutocracy
plutocrat
plutocratic

plutocratically
plutonic
plutonium
ply
pneumatic
pneumatically
pneumatics
pneumonia
poach
poacher
pocket
pocketbook
pocketknife
pockmark
pod
podagra
podiatry
podium
poem
poesy
poet
poetaster
poetic
poetical
poetry
poi
poignancy
poignant
poinciana
poinsettia
point
pointed
pointedly
pointer
pointless
pointlessly
poise
poised
poison
poisoned
poisoner
poisonous
poke
poked
poker
pokeweed
polar
polarity
polarization
polarize
polarized
polarizer
pole
polecat
polemic
polemical
polemicist
polemics
polestar
police
policed
policeman
policy
polish
polished
polisher
polite
politely
politeness
politic
political
politically
politician
politics
politicization
polka
poll
pollard
pollarded
polled
pollen
pollinate
pollination
pollster
pollute
polluted
pollution
polo
polonaise
polonium
poltroon
polyandrous
polyandry
polychrome
polyclinic
polygamist
polygamous
polygamy
polyglot

polygon
polygonal
polymeric
polymerism
polymerization
polymerize
polynomial
polyp
polyphony
polysyllabic
polytechnic
polyunsaturated
pomade
pomander
pomatum
pomegranate
Pomeranian
pommel
pommeled
pomology
pomp
pompadour
pompano
Pompeian
pompon
pomposity
pompous
poncho
pond
ponder
ponderable
pondered
ponderosa
ponderosity
ponderous
pondfish
pondweed
pongee
poniard
pontiff
pontifical
pontifically
pontificate
pontoon
pony
poodle
pool
pooled
poolroom
poor
poorer
poorest
poorhouse
poorly
poorness
pop
popcorn
popgun
popinjay
poplar
poplin
popover
popped
poppet
poppy
populace
popular
popularist
popularity
popularization
popularize
popularized
populate
populated
population
populous
porcelain
porch
porcupine
pore
pored
porgy
pork
pornography
porosity
porous
porphyry
porpoise
porridge
porringer
port
portable
portage
portal
portcullis
portend
portended
portent
portentous

porter
porterhouse
portfolio
porthole
portico
portiere
portion
portioned
portmanteau
portrait
portraitist
portraiture
portray
portrayal
portrayed
Portuguese
portulaca
pose
posed
position
positive
positivism
positivistic
positron
posse
possess
possessed
possession
possessive
possessor
possessorship
possibility
possible

possibly
possum
post
postage
postal
postbox
postdate
postdated
posted
poster
posterior
posterity
postern
postgraduate
posthaste
posthole
posthumous
postilion
postimpressionism
postings
postlude
postman
postmarital
postmark
postmaster
postmeridian
postmistress
postmortem
postnuptial
postoperative
postpaid
postpone
postponed

postponement
postprandial
postscript
postulant
postulate
postulated
postulation
posture
postured
posturings
posy
pot
potability
potable
potash
potassium
potation
potato
potboiler
potency
potent
potentate
potential
potentiality
potentially
potentiometer
potherb
pothole
pothook
pothouse
potion
potlatch
potluck

potpie
potpourri
potsherd
pottage
potter
pottery
pouch
poult
poulterer
poultice
poulticed
poultry
pounce
pounced
pound
poundage
pound cake
pounded
poundings
pour
poured
pout
pouted
poverty
powder
powdered
powdery
power
powered
powerful
powerfully
powerless
powerlessly

powerlessness
powwow
practicability
practicable
practicably
practical
practicality
practically
practice
practiced
practicum
practitioner
pragmatic
pragmatical
pragmatically
pragmatism
pragmatist
prairie
praise
praised
praiseworthy
praline
prance
pranced
prancingly
prank
prankster
prate
prated
pratings
pratique
prattle
prattlingly

prawn
pray
prayed
prayer
prayerful
prayerfully
preach
preached
preacher
preachment
preachy
preadolescent
preamble
prearrange
prearrangement
prebendary
precanceled
precarious
precaution
precautionary
precede
preceded
precedence
precedent
precept
preceptor
preceptress
precession
prechill
precinct
preciosity
precious
preciously

precipice
precipitancy
precipitant
precipitate
precipitated
precipitately
precipitation
precipitous
précis
precise
précised
precisely
preciseness
precision
precisionist
preclinical
preclude
precluded
preclusion
precocious
precociously
precocity
preconceived
preconception
preconsciousness
precook
precool
precursor
precursory
predaceous
predacity
predate
predation
predative
predator
predatory
predecease
predecessor
predecide
predesignated
predesignation
predestinarian
predestinarianism
predestination
predestine
predestined
predeterminant
predeterminate
predetermination
predetermine
predetermined
prediabetes
prediastolic
predicament
predicate
predicated
predication
predicative
predict
predictable
predicted
prediction
predictional
predictive
predigest
predigested
predigestion
predilection
predisclosure
predispose
predisposed
predisposition
predominance
predominant
predominate
predominated
predominately
predominatingly
predraft
predry
preeminence
preeminent
preempt
preempted
preemption
preemptive
preen
preened
preestimate
preexist
preexistent
preface
prefaced
prefashion
prefatory
prefect
prefecture
prefer
preferable

preferably
preference
preferential
preferentially
preferment
preferred
prefigure
prefigured
prefix
prefixal
prefixed
preform
preformed
pregather
pregnancy
pregnant
preharvest
prehensile
prehensility
prehistoric
preimagine
preinaugural
preincline
preinclined
preinventory
prejudge
prejudged
prejudiced
prejudicial
prejudicially
prelacy
prelate
preliminary
preliterate
prelude
prematernity
premature
premedical
premeditate
premeditated
premeditation
premier
premise
premises
premium
premonition
premonitory
prenatal
prenatally
prenuclear
preoccupation
preoccupied
preoccupy
preoperative
preordain
preordained
prepaid
preparation
preparative
preparatory
prepare
prepared
preparedness
prepay
prepayment
prepense
preponderance
preponderant
preponderate
preponderatingly
preposition
prepositional
prepossess
prepossession
preposterous
preprint
prerelease
prerequisite
prerogative
presage
presaged
presbyter
Presbyterian
presbytery
prescience
prescient
prescribe
prescribed
prescription
prescriptive
presence
present
presentability
presentable
presentation
presented
presentiment
presently
presentment

preservation
preservative
preserve
preserver
preside
presided
presidency
president
presidential
press
pressboard
pressed
pressings
pressman
pressroom
pressure
presswork
prestidigitator
prestige
prestigious
presto
presumable
presume
presumed
presumedly
presumption
presumptive
presumptuous
presuppose
presystolic
pretax
preteen
pretend

pretended
pretender
pretense
pretension
pretentious
pretentiously
pretentiousness
preterit
pretermit
pretermitted
preternatural
pretext
prettier
prettiest
prettily
prettiness
pretty
pretzel
prevail
prevailed
prevailingly
prevalence
prevalent
prevalently
prevaricate
prevaricated
prevarication
prevaricator
prevent
preventability
preventable
prevented
prevention

preventive
preview
previous
prevision
prevocational
prey
price
priced
priceless
prick
pricked
prickle
prickled
prickliness
prickly
pride
prideful
priest
priestess
priesthood
priestly
priggish
prim
primacy
primal
primarily
primary
primate
primateship
prime
primed
primer
primeval

primitive
primitivism
primly
primness
primogeniture
primordial
primrose
prince
princeliness
princeling
princely
princes
princess
principal
principality
principally
principle
principled
print
printable
printed
printer
printings
printout
prior
priority
priory
prism
prismatic
prison
prisoner
pristine
privacy

private
privateer
privately
privateness
privation
privet
privilege
privily
privity
privy
prize
prized
probability
probable
probably
probate
probation
probationary
probe
probity
problem
problematic
proboscis
procedural
procedure
proceed
proceeded
proceedings
process
processed
processes
procession
processor

proclaim
proclaimed
proclamation
proclivity
proconsul
procrastinate
procrastinated
procrastination
procrastinator
procreation
procreative
proctor
procurable
procuration
procurator
procure
procured
procurement
prod
prodded
prodigal
prodigality
prodigally
prodigious
prodigiously
prodigy
produce
produced
producer
product
production
productive
productivity

proem
profanation
profanatory
profane
profaned
profanity
profess
professed
professedly
profession
professional
professionalism
professionalize
professionally
professor
professorial
professorship
proffer
proffered
proficiency
proficient
proficiently
profile
profit
profitable
profitably
profited
profiteer
profitless
profligacy
profligate
profound
profoundness
profundity
profuse
profusely
profuseness
profusion
progenitor
progeny
prognosis
prognostic
prognosticate
prognosticated
program
programmed
programmer
progress
progressed
progression
progressive
prohibit
prohibited
prohibition
prohibitionist
prohibitive
prohibitory
project
projected
projectile
projection
projective
projector
proletarian
proletariat
proliferate
proliferation
prolific
prolification
prolix
prolixity
prologue
prolong
prolongate
prolongation
prolonged
promenade
promenaded
prominence
prominent
promiscuity
promiscuous
promiscuously
promiscuousness
promise
promised
promisingly
promissory
promontory
promote
promoted
promoter
promotion
promotional
prompt
prompted
prompter
promptest
promptitude

promptly
promptness
promulgate
promulgated
promulgation
pronate
pronation
prone
prong
pronghorn
pronominal
pronoun
pronounce
pronounceable
pronounced
pronouncement
pronunciation
proof
proofed
prop
propaganda
propagandist
propagate
propagated
propagation
propel
propellant
propelled
propeller
propensity
proper
properly
property

prophecy
prophesied
prophesy
prophet
prophetic
prophetically
prophylactic
prophylaxis
propinquity
propitiate
propitiated
propitiation
propitiatory
propitious
proponent
proportion
proportionable
proportional
proportionally
proportionate
proportionately
proportioned
proposal
propose
proposed
proposition
propound
propounded
proprietary
proprietor
proprietorial
proprietorially
proprietorship

proprietory
propriety
propulsion
propulsive
prorate
prorated
proration
prorogation
prorogue
prorogued
prosaic
prosaically
proscenium
proscribe
proscribed
proscription
prose
prosecute
prosecuted
prosecution
prosecutor
proselyte
proselyted
proselytize
proselytizer
prosier
prosiest
prosify
prosily
prosiness
prosody
prospect
prospected

prospective
prospector
prospectus
prosper
prospered
prosperity
prosperous
prosperously
prosthesis
prosthetic
prostrate
prostrated
prostration
prosy
protagonist
protean
protect
protected
protectingly
protection
protectionism
protectionist
protective
protectively
protectiveness
protector
protectorate
protégé
protein
protest
protestant
protestation
protested
protesters
prothonotary
protocol
proton
protoplasm
prototype
protoxide
Protozoa
protract
protracted
protractile
protraction
protractive
protractor
protrude
protruded
protrusion
protrusive
protuberance
protuberant
proud
prouder
proudest
proudly
provable
prove
proved
proven
provenance
Provencal
provender
proverb
proverbial
proverbially
provide
provided
providence
provident
providential
providentially
provider
province
provincial
provincialism
provinciality
provincially
provision
provisional
provisionally
proviso
provisory
provocation
provocative
provoke
provoked
provokingly
provost
prow
prowess
prowl
prowled
prowler
proximal
proximally
proximate
proximity

proximo
proxy
prude
prudence
prudent
prudential
prudentially
prudently
prudery
prudish
prune
pruned
prurience
prurient
pruritus
Prussian
pry
pryingly
psalm
psalmbook
psalmist
psalmodist
psalmody
psalter
pseudonym
psoriasis
psychedelia
psychedelic
psychiatric
psychiatrically
psychiatrist
psychiatry
psychic
psychical
psychically
psychoanalysis
psychobiology
psychodynamics
psychogenesis
psychogenetic
psychological
psychologist
psychology
psychopathic
psychopathology
psychopathy
psychosis
psychotic
Ptolemaic
ptomaine
public
publication
publicist
publicity
publicize
publicly
publish
published
publisher
puce
puck
pucker
puckered
puddings
puddle
puddled
puddler
pudency
pudginess
pudgy
pueblo
puerile
puerility
puff
puffin
puffiness
puffy
pug
pugilism
pugilist
pugilistic
pugnaciously
pugnacity
puissance
puissant
pulchritude
pulchritudinous
puling
pulingly
pull
pulled
pullet
pulley
Pullman
pullulate
pulmonary
pulmotor
pulp
pulpier

pulpiest
pulpiness
pulpit
pulpiteer
pulpy
pulsar
pulsate
pulsated
pulsation
pulsator
pulsatory
pulse
pulverization
pulverize
pulverizer
pumice
pump
pumpernickel
pumpkin
pun
punch
punched
puncheon
punchings
punctilio
punctilious
punctiliously
punctiliousness
punctual
punctuality
punctually
punctuate
punctuated
punctuation
puncture
punctured
pundit
pung
pungency
pungent
puniness
punish
punishable
punished
punishment
punitive
punk
punt
puny
pup
pupa
pupae
pupil
puppet
puppeteer
puppetry
puppy
purblind
purchase
purchased
purchaser
pure
purely
purer
purest
purgative
purgatory
purge
purged
purification
purified
purifier
purify
purism
purist
puritan
puritanic
puritanical
puritanism
purity
purl
purlieu
purloin
purple
purplish
purport
purported
purpose
purposeful
purposefully
purposefulness
purposeless
purposely
purposive
purr
purred
purse
pursed
purser

purslane
pursuance
pursuant
pursue
pursued
pursuit
pursuivant
pursy
purulence
purulency
purulent
purvey
purveyance
purveyor
purview
pus
push
pushcart
pusher
pusillanimity
pusillanimous

pussyfoot
pustulant
pustular
pustulate
pustulation
pustule
put
putative
putrefaction
putrefactive
putrefied
putrefy
putrescence
putrescent
putrid
putt
puttee
putter
putty
puzzle
puzzled

puzzler
puzzles
pyemia
pygmy
pyjama
pylon
pylorus
pyorrhea
pyramid
pyramidal
pyre
pyrex
pyrexia
pyrites
pyrography
pyromania
pyrometer
pyrotechnics
pyroxylin
pyrrhic
python

q

quack
quackery
quad
quadrangle
quadrangular
quadrant
quadrat
quadratic
quadratics
quadrature
quadrennial
quadrennially
quadrennium
quadrilateral
quadrille
quadripartite
quadriphonic
quadruped
quadruple
quadruplet
quadruplex
quadruplicate
quaff

quagmire
quahog
quail
quailed
quaint
quaintly
quaintness
quake
quaked
quaker
quakingly
qualification
qualified
qualifier
qualify
qualitative
qualities
quality
qualm
quandary
quantitative
quantities
quantity

quantum
quarantine
quarantined
quark
quarrel
quarreled
quarrelsome
quarrier
quarry
quarryman
quart
quartan
quarter
quarterback
quartered
quarterings
quarterly
quartermaster
quartersaw
quartet
quartile
quarto
quartz

quasar
quash
quasi
quaternary
quatrain
quatrefoil
quaver
quavered
quaveringly
quay
quayage
queasy
queen
queenly
queer
queerer
queerest
quell
quelled
quench
quenched
quenchless
queried
querulous
query
quest
questingly
question
questionable
questioned
questioner
questioningly
questionnaire

queue
quibble
quick
quickchange
quicken
quickened
quicker
quickest
quicklime
quickly
quickness
quicksand
quicksilver
quickstep
quiddity
quiescence
quiet
quieted
quietly
quietness
quietude
quietus
quill
quilled
quillwork
quilt
quilted
quince
quinine
quinquennial
quintal
quintessence
quintessential

quintet
quintuplet
quip
quipu
quire
quirk
quirt
quit
quitclaim
quite
quitrent
quittance
quitter
quiver
quivered
quiveringly
quixotic
quiz
quizmaster
quizzical
quoin
quoit
quondam
quorum
quota
quotable
quotation
quote
quoted
quoth
quotidian
quotient
quoting

r

rabbet
rabbinical
rabbit
rabbitry
rabble
rabid
rabidly
rabies
raccoon
race
raced
racer
raceway
rachitic
rachitis
racial
racially
racily
raciness
racism
racist
racket
racy

radar
radial
radially
radiance
radiant
radiantly
radiate
radiated
radiation
radiator
radical
radicalism
radically
radicular
radii
radio
radioactive
radioactivity
radiogram
radiograph
radiometer
radiophone
radiophotograph

radioscope
radiosensitive
radiosterilization
radiosterilize
radiotelegram
radiotoxic
radish
radium
radius
radiuses
radix
radon
raffia
raffle
raffled
raft
rafter
raftsman
rag
ragamuffin
rage
raged
ragged

raglan
ragout
ragpicker
ragtime
ragweed
raid
rail
railbird
railed
railhead
railingly
railings
raillery
railroad
railroader
railway
raiment
rain
rainbow
raincoat
rained
rainfall
rainspout
rainstorm
rainy
raise
raised
raisin
raja
rake
rakish
rallied
rally

ram
ramble
rambled
rambler
rambunctious
ramekin
ramification
ramified
ramify
rammed
rammer
ramp
rampage
rampant
rampart
ramrod
ramshackle
ranch
rancher
ranchero
ranchman
rancho
rancid
rancidity
rancidly
rancor
rancorous
random
range
ranged
ranger
rank
ranked

rankle
rankled
ranklingly
ransack
ransom
ransomed
rant
ranted
rantingly
rapacious
rapacity
rapid
rapidity
rapidly
rapier
rapine
rapport
rapscallion
rapt
raptorial
rapture
rapturous
rapturously
rapturousness
rare
rarefaction
rarefy
rarely
rareness
rarer
rarest
rarity
rascal

rascality
rascally
rash
rasher
rashest
rashly
rashness
rasp
raspberry
rasped
raspingly
rat
ratable
ratchet
rate
rated
rather
rathskeller
ratification
ratified
ratify
ratings
ratio
ratiocination
ratiocinative
ration
rational
rationalism
rationalist
rationalistic
rationalization
rationalize
rationalized
rationally
rationed
ratline
rattan
ratter
rattle
rattlebrain
rattlebrained
rattled
rattleheaded
rattler
rattlesnake
rattlings
rattly
raucous
ravage
ravaged
rave
raved
ravel
raveled
raven
ravenous
ravenously
ravenousness
ravigote
ravine
ravings
ravioli
ravish
ravished
ravisher
ravishingly
ravishment
raw
rawboned
rawer
rawest
rawhide
rawness
ray
rayless
rayon
raze
razed
razor
razorback
razoredge
reach
reached
reachings
react
reactance
reaction
reactionary
reactivate
reactivation
read
readability
readable
reader
readily
readiness
readings
readjust
readjustable

readjustment
readmission
readmit
readout
ready
reaffirm
reaffirmation
reagent
real
realign
realism
realist
realistic
realistically
reality
realizable
realization
realize
realized
really
realm
Realtor
realty
ream
reamed
reamer
reanimate
reap
reaper
reappear
reappearance
reappoint
reappointment

rear
reared
reargue
rearm
rearmament
rearmed
rearmost
rearrange
rearrangement
rearward
reason
reasonable
reasonableness
reasonably
reasoned
reassemble
reassert
reasserted
reassign
reassume
reassurance
reassure
reassured
rebate
rebated
rebel
rebelled
rebellion
rebellious
rebind
rebirth
reborn
rebound

rebounded
rebuff
rebuffed
rebuild
rebuilt
rebuke
rebuked
rebukingly
rebus
rebut
rebuttal
rebutted
rebutter
recalcitrance
recalcitrant
recall
recalled
recant
recantation
recanted
recapitalize
recapitulate
recapitulated
recapitulation
recapitulatory
recapture
recast
recede
receded
receipt
receipted
receivable
receivables

receive
received
receiver
receivership
recent
recently
receptacle
reception
receptionist
receptive
receptively
receptiveness
receptivity
receptor
recess
recessed
recesses
recession
recessional
recessionary
recessive
recharge
recharged
recherché
recidivism
recidivist
recipe
recipient
reciprocal
reciprocally
reciprocate
reciprocated
reciprocation
reciprocative
reciprocator
reciprocity
recital
recitalist
recitation
recitative
recite
recited
reck
reckless
recklessly
recklessness
reckon
reckoned
reckoner
reckonings
reclaim
reclaimable
reclaimed
reclamation
recline
reclined
recluse
recognition
recognizable
recognizance
recognize
recognized
recoil
recoiled
recollect
recollected
recollection
recommence
recommend
recommendation
recommendatory
recommended
recommit
recompensable
recompense
recompensed
reconcilable
reconcile
reconciled
reconcilement
reconciliation
reconciliatory
recondite
reconnaissance
reconnoiter
reconnoitered
reconquer
reconsider
reconstitute
reconstruct
reconstructed
reconstruction
reconstructive
reconvert
reconvey
record
recorded
recorder
recordings

recount
recounted
recoup
recouped
recoupment
recourse
recover
recoverable
recovery
recreant
recreate
recreation
recreational
recriminate
recrimination
recriminative
recriminatory
recrudescence
recrudescent
recruit
recruited
recruitment
recrystallization
recrystallize
rectangle
rectangular
rectangularity
rectifiable
rectification
rectified
rectifier
rectify
rectilinear

rectitude
rector
rectorate
rectorial
rectory
recumbency
recumbent
recuperate
recuperated
recuperation
recuperative
recuperatory
recur
recurred
recurrence
recurrent
recurrently
recycle
red
redbird
redbreast
redbud
redden
reddened
redder
reddest
reddish
redeal
redeem
redeemability
redeemable
redeemed
redeemer

redemption
Redemptorist
redemptory
redetermine
redevelop
redirect
redirected
rediscount
rediscover
redistribute
redistribution
redistrict
redness
redolence
redolent
redouble
redoubt
redoubtable
redound
redraft
redress
redressed
reduce
reduced
reducer
reducible
reduction
redundance
redundancy
redundant
redundantly
reduplicate
reduplicated

reduplication
redwood
reecho
reechoed
reed
reedbird
reediness
reedit
reeducate
reeducation
reedy
reef
reefer
reek
reekingly
reel
reelect
reembark
reembarkation
reemploy
reenact
reenforce
reenforcement
reengage
reengrave
reenlist
reenter
reentrance
reentry
reestablish
reexamination
reexamine
reexport

reexportation
refectory
refer
referable
referee
reference
referendum
referred
refigure
refill
refinance
refine
refined
refinement
refiner
refinery
refit
reflect
reflected
reflectingly
reflection
reflective
reflector
reflex
reflexive
reflux
reforestation
reform
reformation
reformative
reformatory
reformed
reformer

refract
refracted
refraction
refractionist
refractive
refractivity
refractor
refractory
refrain
refrained
refresh
refreshed
refresher
refreshingly
refreshment
refrigerant
refrigerate
refrigerated
refrigeration
refrigerative
refrigerator
refuge
refugee
refulgence
refulgent
refund
refunded
refurnish
refusal
refuse
refused
refutation
refute

refuted
regain
regained
regal
regale
regaled
regalement
regalia
regality
regally
regard
regarded
regardful
regardless
regatta
regelation
regency
regeneracy
regenerate
regenerated
regeneration
regenerative
regenerator
regent
regicidal
regicide
regime
regimen
regiment
regimental
regimentals
regimentation
regimented

region
regional
regionalism
regionalize
regionally
register
registered
registrar
registration
registry
regress
regression
regressive
regret
regretful
regretfully
regretfulness
regrettable
regretted
regular
regularity
regularization
regularize
regulate
regulated
regulates
regulation
regulator
regurgitate
regurgitated
regurgitation
rehabilitate
rehabilitated

rehabilitation
rehash
rehearsal
rehearse
rehearsed
reheat
reign
reigned
reimburse
reimbursed
reimport
reimportation
rein
reincarnate
reincarnation
reindeer
reined
reinforce
reinforced
reinsert
reinstall
reinstate
reinstated
reinstatement
reinsurance
reinsure
reintegrate
reintroduce
reinvest
reinvigorate
reissue
reiterate
reiterated

reiteration
reiterative
reject
rejected
rejection
rejoice
rejoiced
rejoices
rejoicingly
rejoin
rejoinder
rejuvenate
rejuvenated
rejuvenation
rejuvenative
rejuvenescence
rejuvenescent
rekindle
relapse
relapsed
relate
related
relation
relational
relationship
relative
relatively
relativism
relativity
relator
relax
relaxation
relaxed

relaxes
relay
relayed
release
released
relegate
relegated
relegation
relent
relented
relentingly
relentless
relevance
relevancy
relevant
reliability
reliable
reliant
relic
relief
relieve
relieved
religion
religious
religiously
relinquish
relinquished
relinquishment
reliquary
relish
relished
relive
reload

relocate
relocated
relocation
relocator
relucent
reluctance
reluctant
reluctantly
rely
remain
remainder
remained
remake
remand
remanded
remark
remarkable
remarried
remarry
remediable
remedial
remedied
remedy
remember
remembered
remembrance
remind
reminded
reminder
remindful
remindingly
reminiscence
reminiscent

remiss
remission
remit
remittal
remittance
remitted
remittent
remitter
remnant
remodel
remonetization
remonetize
remonstrance
remonstrant
remonstrate
remonstrated
remonstratingly
remonstration
remonstrative
remorse
remorseful
remorsefully
remorseless
remote
remoteness
remoter
remotest
remount
removability
removable
removal
remove
removed

removes
remunerate
remunerated
remuneration
remunerative
renaissance
renal
renascent
rend
render
rendered
renderings
rendezvous
rendition
renegade
renege
rênegotiate
renew
renewable
renewal
renewed
rennet
renominate
renomination
renounce
renounced
renovate
renovated
renovation
renown
renowned
rent
rental

rented
renumber
renunciation
renunciative
renunciatory
reopen
reorder
reorganization
reorganize
reorient
repaid
repaint
repair
repaired
repairer
reparable
reparation
reparative
repartee
repast
repatriate
repay
repayment
repeal
repealed
repealer
repeat
repeatedly
repeater
repel
repelled
repellence
repellency

repellent
repellingly
repent
repentance
repented
repercussion
repercussive
repertoire
repertory
repetend
repetition
repetitious
repetitive
rephrase
repine
repined
replace
replaced
replacement
replant
replenish
replenished
replenishment
replete
repletion
replevin
replica
replicate
replication
replicative
replied
reply
report

reported
reporter
repose
reposed
reposeful
repository
repossess
repossessed
reprehend
reprehensible
reprehension
reprehensive
represent
representation
representative
represented
repress
repression
repressive
reprieve
reprieved
reprimand
reprimanded
reprimandingly
reprint
reprinted
reprisal
reprise
reproach
reproached
reproachful
reproachfully
reproachfulness

reprobate
reprobation
reproduce
reproducer
reproduction
reproductive
reproof
reprove
reproved
reprovingly
reptile
reptilian
republic
republican
republicanism
republicanize
republish
repudiate
repudiation
repugnance
repugnant
repulse
repulsed
repulsion
repulsive
repulsiveness
repurchase
reputable
reputation
repute
reputed
reputedly
request

requiem
require
required
requirement
requisite
requisition
requital
requite
requited
reredos
rerun
resale
rescind
rescinded
rescission
rescore
rescue
rescued
research
researcher
resection
resegregation
resemblance
resemble
resembled
resent
resented
resentful
resentfulness
resentment
reservation
reservationist
reserve
reserved
reservist
reservoir
reset
resettle
resettlement
reship
reshipment
reside
resided
residence
residency
resident
residential
residual
residuary
residue
residuum
resign
resignation
resigned
resignedly
resiliency
resilient
resin
resinous
resist
resistance
resistant
resistible
resistive
resistivity
resistless
resoluble
resolute
resoluteness
resolution
resolvable
resolve
resolved
resolvent
resonance
resonant
resonate
resonator
resort
resorted
resound
resounded
resoundingly
resource
resourceful
resourcefulness
respect
respectability
respectable
respected
respecter
respectful
respective
respectively
respell
respirable
respiration
respirator
respiratory

respire
respired
respite
resplendence
resplendency
resplendent
respond
responded
respondent
response
responsibilities
responsibility
responsible
responsive
responsiveness
rest
restate
restatement
restaurant
restaurateur
rested
restful
restfully
restfulness
restitution
restive
restively
restiveness
restless
restlessness
restock
restoration
restorative

restore
restored
restrain
restrained
restrainedly
restrainingly
restraint
restrict
restricted
restriction
restrictive
result
resultant
resumable
resume
resumed
resumption
resurgence
resurgent
resurrect
resurrected
resurrection
resuscitate
resuscitated
resuscitation
resuscitative
resuscitator
retail
retailed
retailer
retain
retained
retainer

retake
retaliate
retaliated
retaliation
retaliationist
retaliative
retaliatory
retard
retardation
retarded
retarder
retch
retched
retell
retellings
retention
retentive
retentivity
rethink
reticence
reticent
reticently
reticle
reticular
reticulate
reticulated
reticulation
reticule
retina
retinal
retinitis
retinue
retire

retired
retirement
retiringly
retold
retort
retorted
retouch
retoucher
retrace
retraceable
retract
retracted
retractile
retraction
retractive
retractor
retread
retreat
retreated
retrench
retrenched
retrenchment
retrial
retribalization
retribalize
retribution
retributive
retrieval
retrieve
retrieved
retriever
retroactive
retroactivity

retrocede
retrocession
retrocessive
retroflex
retroflexion
retrograde
retrograded
retrogress
retrogression
retrogressive
retroreflective
retroreflector
retrospect
retrospection
retrospective
retroversion
return
returnable
returned
reunion
reunite
reuse
reused
rev
revaccinate
revalidate
revalorize
revaluation
revalue
revamp
revascularization
revascularize
reveal

revealed
revealingly
revealment
reveille
revel
revelation
revelatory
reveled
reveler
revelry
revenge
revenged
revengeful
revenue
reverberant
reverberate
reverberated
reverberation
reverberative
reverberator
reverberatory
revere
revered
reverence
reverend
reverent
reverential
reverie
reversal
reverse
reversed
reversibility
reversible

reversion
reversionary
revert
reverted
revertible
revest
revet
revetment
revictual
review
reviewed
reviewer
revile
reviled
revilement
revilingly
revindicate
revise
revised
reviser
revision
revisionism
revisionist
revisit
revival
revivalism
revivalist
revive
revived
revivification
revivifier
revivify
revocation

revokable
revoke
revoked
revolt
revolted
revoltingly
revolution
revolutionary
revolutionist
revolutionize
revolutionized
revolve
revolved
revolver
revue
revulsion
revulsive
reward
rewarded
rewardingly
rewind
rewire
reword
reworked
rewrite
rewritten
rhapsodic
rhapsodist
rhapsodize
rhapsodized
rhapsody
rhenium
rheostat

rhesus
rhetoric
rhetorical
rhetorician
rheum
rheumatic
rheumatism
rheumatoid
rheumy
rhinestone
rhinitis
rhinoceros
rhinology
rhinoscope
rhinoscopy
rhizome
rhodium
rhomboid
rhombus
rhubarb
rhyme
rhymed
rhythm
rhythmic
rhythmical
rialto
riant
rib
ribald
ribaldry
ribbed
ribbon
rice

rich
richer
riches
richest
richly
richness
richweed
rickets
ricochet
riddance
ridden
riddle
ride
rider
riderless
ridge
ridged
ridicule
ridiculed
ridiculous
ridiculously
ridotto
rife
riffle
riffled
riffraff
rifle
rifled
rifleman
riflings
rift
rig
rigadoon

rigged
rigger
right
righted
righteous
righteously
righteousness
rightful
rightfully
rightly
rightness
rigid
rigidity
rigidly
rigidness
rigor
rigorous
rigorously
rile
riled
rill
rim
rime
rind
ring
ringbolt
ringbone
ringed
ringer
ringingly
ringleader
ringlet
ringleted

ringmaster
ringside
ringworm
rink
rinse
rinsed
riot
rioted
rioter
riotous
riotously
riotousness
rip
riparian
ripe
ripely
ripen
ripened
riper
ripest
ripoff
riposte
ripple
rippled
ripplingly
ripply
riprap
rise
risen
riser
risibility
risible
risings

risk
risked
risky
rite
ritual
ritualism
ritualist
ritualistic
ritually
rival
rivaled
rivalry
rive
river
riverside
rivet
riveted
riveter
rivulet
roach
road
roadability
roadbed
roadhouse
roadman
roadside
roadstead
roadster
roadway
roadweed
roam
roamed
roamer
roamings
roar
roared
roarings
roast
roasted
roaster
rob
robbed
robber
robbery
robe
robed
robin
robot
robust
robustly
robustness
rock
rocker
rocket
rockfish
rockweed
rockshaft
rocky
rococo
rod
rodent
rodeo
rodman
roe
roentgen
rogue
roguery
roguish
roguishly
roguishness
roil
roiled
roister
roll
rollbar
rolled
roller
rollmop
romaine
Roman
romance
Romanesque
romantic
romantically
romanticism
romanticist
romanticize
romp
rompers
rondeau
rondo
roof
roofer
roofless
rooftree
rookery
room
roomed
roomer

roomful
roominess
roommate
roomy
roost
rooster
root
rooted
rooter
rootlet
rootworm
rope
ropedancer
ropemaker
ropework
roque
rosaceous
rosary
rose
roseate
rosemary
rosette
rosewood
rosily
rosin
rosiness
roster
rostrum
rosy
rot
Rotarian
rotary
rotate
rotated
rotation
rotational
rotative
rotator
rotatory
rote
rotenone
rotogravure
rotor
rotten
rottenness
rotter
rotund
rotunda
rotundity
rouge
rouged
rough
roughage
roughcast
roughdry
roughen
roughened
rougher
roughest
roughhew
roughhewn
roughhouse
roughish
roughly
roughneck
roughness
roughrider
roulade
rouleau
roulette
round
roundabout
rounded
roundelay
rounder
roundest
roundfish
roundhouse
roundish
roundly
roundness
roundsman
roundworm
rouse
roused
rousingly
roustabout
rout
route
routed
routed
routine
routinization
routinize
rover
rovingly
rovings
row
row

rowboat
rowdy
rowed
rowel
roweled
rowen
rower
rowlock
royal
royalism
royalist
royally
royalty
rub
rubbed
rubber
rubberize
rubberized
rubbery
rubbings
rubbish
rubble
rubdown
rubefacient
rubefaction
rubeola
rubicund
rubidium
ruble
rubric
rubricator
ruby
ruching

rucksack
ruckus
rudder
rudderpost
ruddier
ruddiest
ruddily
ruddiness
ruddy
rude
rudely
rudeness
ruder
rudest
rudiment
rudimental
rudimentary
rue
rued
rueful
ruff
ruffian
ruffianism
ruffle
ruffled
rugby
rugged
ruggedness
rugose
rugosity
ruin
ruination
ruined

ruinous
rule
ruled
ruler
rulings
rum
rumble
rumbled
rumblingly
rumblings
ruminant
ruminate
ruminated
ruminatingly
rumination
ruminative
rummage
rummaged
rummy
rumor
rumored
rump
rumple
rumpled
rumpus
run
runabout
runagate
rune
rung
runic
runner
runoff

runt
runway
rupee
rupture
ruptured
rural
ruralism
ruralization
ruralize
rurally
ruse
rush
rushingly
rushlight

rusk
russet
Russian
rust
rusted
rustic
rusticate
rusticated
rustication
rusticism
rusticity
rusticly
rustier
rustiest

rustle
rustled
rustler
rustlingly
rustlings
rustproof
rusty
rut
rutabaga
ruth
ruthenium
ruthless
rya
rye

S

Sabbatarian
Sabbath
sabbatical
sabbatine
saber
sable
sabotage
saccharine
sacerdotal
sachem
sachet
sackbut
sackcloth
sacked
sackful
sacral
sacrament
sacramental
sacramentalism
sacramentalist
sacramentally
Sacramentarian
sacred
sacredly
sacredness
sacrifice
sacrificed
sacrificial
sacrilege
sacrilegious
sacristan
sacristy
sacrosanct
sacrum
sad
sadder
saddest
saddle
saddleback
saddlebag
saddled
saddler
saddlery
sadiron
sadly
sadness
safari
safe
safeguard
safekeeping
safely
safeness
safer
safest
safety
saffron
sag
saga
sagacious
sagaciously
sagacity
sagamore
sage
sagged
sagittal
sago
sahib
said
sail

sailboat
sailed
sailfish
sailings
sailor
saint
sainted
sainthood
saintliness
saintly
sake
saker
salaam
salability
salable
salacious
salaciously
salaciousness
salad
salamander
salaried
salary
sale
saleratus
salesman
salesmanship
salespeople
salesperson
salesroom
saleswoman
salicylic
salience
salient
saliferous
saline
saliva
salivant
salivate
salivation
sallow
sallower
sallowest
sally
salmon
saloon
salsify
salt
saltatory
saltcellar
salted
saltier
saltiest
saltpeter
salty
salubrious
salubrity
salutary
salutation
salutatorian
salutatory
salute
saluted
salvage
salvaged
salvation
salve
salved
salver
salvo
Samaritan
samarium
same
sameness
samite
Samoan
samovar
sampan
sample
sampled
sampler
samplings
samurai
sanative
sanatorium
sanatory
sanctification
sanctified
sanctify
sanctimonious
sanctimoniously
sanctimoniousness
sanction
sanctioned
sanctitude
sanctity
sanctuary
sanctum
sand
sandal

sandalwood
sandbag
sandbank
sandblast
sandbox
sandbur
sanded
sander
sandfish
sandflower
sandiness
sandman
sandpaper
sandpiper
sandstone
sandstorm
sandwich
sandwiched
sandworm
sandy
sane
sanely
saner
sanest
sang
sanguinary
sanguine
sanitarium
sanitary
sanitation
sanitize
sanity
sank

Sanskrit
sap
sapience
sapient
saplings
saponification
saponify
sapper
sapphire
sappier
sappiest
sappy
sapwood
saraband
Saracen
sarcasm
sarcastic
sarcastically
sarcoma
sarcomata
sarcophagic
sarcophagus
sardine
Sardinian
sardonic
sardonically
sardonyx
sargasso
sari
sarong
sarsaparilla
sartorial
sash

sassafras
sat
Satan
satanic
satchel
sate
sated
sateen
satellite
satellization
satiate
satiated
satiation
satiety
satin
satinette
satire
satiric
satirical
satirically
satirist
satirize
satirized
satisfaction
satisfactorily
satisfactory
satisfied
satisfy
satisfyingly
satrap
saturate
saturated
saturation

Saturday
Saturn
saturnine
satyr
satyresque
sauce
sauceboat
saucedish
saucepan
saucer
saucerlike
saucier
sauciest
saucily
saucy
saunter
sauntered
saunterer
saunteringly
saunterings
saurian
sausage
sauté
sautéed
sauterne
savable
savage
savagely
savagery
savanna
savant
save
saved

savings
savior
savor
savorless
savory
saw
sawdust
sawed
sawfish
sawfly
sawhorse
sawmill
sawyer
Saxon
say
sayings
says
scab
scabbard
scabby
scabies
scabious
scabrous
scaffold
scalar
scald
scalded
scale
scaled
scalene
scaler
scallion
scallop

scalp
scalped
scalpel
scalper
scaly
scamp
scamped
scamper
scampered
scan
scandal
scandalization
scandalize
scandalized
scandalous
scandalously
Scandinavia
scandium
scanned
scanner
scansion
scansorial
scant
scanted
scantily
scantiness
scantlings
scanty
scapegoat
scapegrace
scapula
scapular
scar

scarab
scarce
scarcely
scarcer
scarcest
scarcity
scare
scared
scarf
scarification
scarified
scarifier
scarify
scarlatina
scarlet
scarred
scathed
scatheless
scathing
scathingly
scatter
scatterbrain
scattered
scatteringly
scatterings
scattersite
scavenger
scenario
scenery
sceneshifter
scenic
scenical
scent

scented
scentless
scentwood
scepter
sceptered
schedule
scheduled
schematic
schematically
schematize
schematized
scheme
schemed
schemer
schemingly
scherzando
scherzo
schism
schismatic
schismatical
schist
schizoid
schizophrenia
schizophrenic
schlock
schnapps
schnauzer
schnitzel
scholar
scholarly
scholarship
scholastic
scholastical

scholastically
scholasticism
scholiast
scholium
school
schoolbook
schooled
schoolhouse
schoolman
schoolmaster
schooner
schottische
sciatic
sciatica
science
scientific
scientifically
scientist
scientologist
scientology
scimitar
scintilla
scintillant
scintillate
scintillated
scintillatingly
scintillation
scion
scissors
scleritis
sclerosis
sclerotic
sclerotitis

sclerotomy
scoff
scoffed
scoffer
scoffingly
scofflaw
scold
scolded
scoldingly
scoldings
scoliosis
sconce
scone
scoop
scooped
scoopingly
scoot
scooter
scope
scorch
scorched
scorcher
scorchingly
score
scored
scorer
scorings
scorn
scorned
scorner
scornful
scornfully
scorpion

Scot
Scotch
Scotchman
Scotsman
Scottish
scoundrel
scoundrelly
scour
scoured
scourer
scourge
scourged
scourgingly
scourings
scout
scouted
scow
scowl
scowled
scowlingly
scrabble
scrabbled
scrabblings
scraggy
scramble
scrambled
scramblings
scrap
scrapbook
scrape
scraped
scraper
scrapingly

scrapings
scrapman
scrappier
scrappiest
scrapple
scrappy
scratch
scratched
scratchiness
scratchings
scratchy
scrawl
scrawled
scrawlings
scrawnily
scrawniness
scrawny
scream
screamed
screamingly
screech
screeched
screechier
screechiest
screechy
screed
screen
screened
screenings
screenplay
screw
screwdriver
screwed

scribble
scribbled
scribbler
scribblingly
scribblings
scribe
scriber
scrim
scrimmage
scrimp
scrimped
scrimpily
scrimpiness
scrimpingly
scrimshaw
scrip
script
scriptural
scripturalism
scripturalist
scripture
scrivener
scrod
scrofula
scrofulous
scroll
scrolled
scrollwork
scrouger
scrounge
scrub
scrubbed
scrubbier

scrubbiest
scrubbings
scrubby
scrubland
scruff
scrummage
scrumptious
scrunch
scrunched
scruple
scrupled
scrupulosity
scrupulous
scrupulously
scrupulousness
scrutinization
scrutinize
scrutinized
scrutinizingly
scrutiny
scud
scudded
scuff
scuffed
scuffle
scuffled
scufflingly
scufflings
scull
sculled
sculler
scullery
scullion

sculpin
sculptor
sculptural
sculpture
sculpturesque
scum
scummy
scupper
scuppernong
scurf
scurrility
scurrilous
scurrilously
scurrilousness
scurry
scurvy
scuttle
scuttled
scuttleful
scutum
scythe
sea
seaboard
seacoast
seafarer
seafowl
seagoing
seal
sealed
sealer
sealskin
seam
seaman

seamanlike
seamanship
seamed
seamstress
seamy
seaplane
seaport
sear
search
searched
searcher
searchingly
searchlight
seared
seascape
seashore
seasick
seasickness
seaside
season
seasonable
seasonal
seasonally
seasoned
seasonings
seat
seated
seaward
seaworthiness
seaworthy
sebaceous
secant
secede
seceded
secession
secessionism
secessionist
seclude
secluded
seclusion
second
secondarily
secondary
seconded
seconder
secondhand
secondly
secrecy
secret
secretarial
secretariat
secretary
secrete
secreted
secretion
secretive
secretively
secretiveness
secretly
secretory
sect
sectarian
sectarianism
sectary
section
sectional
sectionalism
sectionalize
sectionalized
sectionally
sector
secular
secularism
secularist
secularity
secularization
secularize
secularized
secularizer
secure
secured
securely
security
sedan
sedate
sedately
sedateness
sedation
sedative
sedentary
sedge
sediment
sedimental
sedimentary
sedimentation
sedition
seditious
seditiously
seditiousness

seduce
seduced
seducer
seducible
seduction
seductive
seductively
seductiveness
sedulous
sedulously
sedulousness
sedum
see
seed
seeded
seedier
seediest
seediness
seedless
seedlessness
seedlings
seedy
seek
seeker
seem
seemed
seemingly
seemly
seen
seep
seepage
seepweed
seer

seeress
seersucker
seesaw
seethe
seethed
segment
segmental
segmentary
segmentation
segregate
segregated
segregation
segregationist
seguidilla
seine
seismic
seismograph
seismology
seizable
seize
seized
seizure
seldom
select
selected
selection
selective
selectivity
selectman
selectmen
selector
selenate
selenic

selenide
selenite
selenium
self
self-actualization
self-assertion
self-assertive
self-assured
self-centered
self-colored
self-command
self-complacent
self-composed
self-conceit
self-concern
self-confidence
self-conscious
self-consciousness
self-contained
self-contradiction
self-control
self-covered
self-deceit
self-defense
self-denial
self-destruct
self-destruction
self-determination
self-determined
self-discipline
self-distrust
self-educated
self-effacement

self-effacingly
self-esteem
self-evident
self-examination
self-executing
self-explaining
self-explanatory
self-expression
self-forgetful
self-governed
self-government
self-help
self-importance
self-improvement
self-induced
self-inductance
self-indulgent
self-interest
selfish
selfishly
selfishness
self-knowledge
selfless
self-limited
self-liquidating
self-love
self-made
self-mastery
self-opinionated
self-possessed
self-possession
self-preservation
self-propelling
self-rating
self-reading
self-realization
self-regard
self-registering
self-reliance
self-reliant
self-renunciation
self-replication
self-reproach
self-reproachful
self-reproachingly
self-respect
self-restraint
self-righteous
self-righteousness
self-sacrifice
self-sacrificingly
selfsame
self-satisfied
self-seeker
self-service
self-starter
self-study
self-styled
self-sufficiency
self-sufficient
self-support
self-surrender
self-sustaining
self-understanding
self-will
self-willed
self-winding
sell
seller
sellout
seltzer
selvage
semantic
semaphore
semblance
semester
semiannual
semicircle
semicivilized
semicolon
semiconscious
semidetached
semifinal
semifinalist
semifinished
semiliteracy
semiliterate
semimonthly
seminar
seminarian
seminary
Seminole
semipermeable
semiprecious
semiserious
semiskilled
Semite
Semitic
Semitism

semitone
semiweekly
semolina
sempiternal
senate
senator
senatorial
senatorially
senatorship
send
sender
Seneca
senescence
senescent
seneschal
senile
senility
senior
seniority
senna
sennit
sensate
sensation
sensational
sensationalism
sensationally
sense
senseless
senselessly
senselessness
sensibility
sensible
sensitive
sensitively
sensitiveness
sensitivity
sensitization
sensitize
sensitized
sensitizer
sensitometer
sensorium
sensory
sensual
sensualism
sensualist
sensualistic
sensuality
sensualization
sensualize
sensualized
sensually
sensuous
sensuously
sensuousness
sentence
sentenced
sententious
sententiously
sententiousness
sentience
sentiency
sentiment
sentimental
sentimentalism
sentimentalist
sentimentality
sentimentalize
sentimentalized
sentinel
sentry
separability
separable
separate
separated
separately
separation
separationist
separatism
separatist
separative
separator
separatory
sepia
sepoy
sepsis
September
septennial
septet
septic
septicemia
Septuagint
septum
sepulcher
sepulchral
sepultural
sepulture
sequel
sequela

sequence
sequencer
sequential
sequentially
sequester
sequestered
sequestrate
sequestrated
sequestration
sequin
Sequoia
seraglio
serape
seraph
seraphic
seraphical
seraphim
Serbian
sere
serenade
serenaded
serenader
serenata
serendipity
serene
serenely
sereneness
serenity
serf
serfdom
serge
sergeant
serial
serialization
serialize
serially
seriatim
sericulture
series
serif
serious
seriously
seriousness
sermon
sermonize
sermonized
serous
serpent
serpentine
serpiginous
serrate
serration
serried
serum
servant
serve
served
server
service
serviceability
serviceable
serviceably
serviced
Servidor
servile
servility
servings
servitor
servitude
servomechanism
servomotor
sesame
sesquisulphide
session
sesterce
sestet
set
setback
setoff
settee
setter
settings
settle
settled
settlement
settler
sever
severable
several
severally
severalty
severance
severation
severe
severed
severely
severer
severest
severity

sew
sewage
sewed
sewer
sewerage
sewn
sex
sexist
sextant
sextet
sexton
sextuple
sextuplicate
sexual
shabbily
shabbiness
shabby
shack
shackle
shackled
shade
shaded
shadier
shadiest
shadily
shadiness
shadings
shadow
shadowed
shadowless
shadowy
shady
shaft

shag
shagbark
shaggier
shaggiest
shaggily
shaggy
shagreen
shake
shakedown
shaken
shaker
Shakespearean
shake-up
shakier
shakiest
shakily
shakiness
shako
shaky
shale
shall
shallop
shallot
shallow
shallowed
shallower
shallowest
shallowly
shallowness
sham
shaman
shamble
shambled

shamblingly
shame
shamed
shamefaced
shamefacedly
shameful
shamefulness
shamelessly
shamelessness
shammed
shammer
shampoo
shampooed
shamrock
shandygaff
shanghai
shanghaied
shank
shan't
shanty
shape
shaped
shapeless
shapelessly
shapelessness
shapeliness
shapely
shard
share
shared
shareholder
shark
sharp

sharpen
sharpened
sharpener
sharper
sharpest
sharply
sharpness
sharpshooter
sharp-witted
shastra
shatter
shattered
shatteringly
shatterproof
shave
shaved
shaver
shavetail
shavings
shaw
shawl
she
sheaf
shear
sheared
shearings
shears
sheathe
sheathed
sheaves
shed
sheen
sheep

sheepherder
sheepish
sheepishly
sheepishness
sheepman
sheepskin
sheer
sheerer
sheerest
sheerly
sheet
sheeted
sheetings
sheetways
sheetwise
sheetwork
shekel
sheldrake
shelf
shell
shellac
shellback
shellburst
shelled
shellfish
shellproof
shellwork
shelter
sheltered
shelteringly
shelterless
shelve
shelved

shelves
shepherd
shepherded
shepherdess
Sheraton
sherbet
sheriff
Sherpa
sherry
Shetland
shewbread
shibboleth
shied
shield
shielded
shift
shifted
shiftier
shiftiest
shiftily
shiftiness
shiftless
shifty
shillelagh
shillings
shim
shimmed
shimmer
shimmered
shimmeringly
shimmery
shin
shinbone

shine
shiner
shingle
shingled
shinily
shininess
shiningly
shinny
shinplaster
Shinto
Shintoism
Shintoist
Shintoistic
shiny
ship
shipboard
shipbuilder
shipload
shipmaster
shipmate
shipment
shipowner
shipper
shipshape
shipworm
shipwreck
shipwright
shipyard
shire
shirk
shirked
shirker
shirr

shirred
shirt
shirtings
shirtless
shiver
shivered
shiveringly
shiverings
shoal
shoalness
shock
shocked
shockingly
shod
shoddier
shoddiest
shoddy
shoe
shoehorn
shoelace
shoeless
shoemaker
shoeman
shoes
shoestring
shogun
shook
shoot
shooter
shootings
shop
shopkeeper
shoplifter

shopman
shopper
shopwork
shopworn
shore
shored
shorn
short
shortage
shortbread
shortcake
shortchange
shortcomings
shorten
shortened
shortening
shorter
shortest
shortfall
shorthand
shorthanded
shorthorn
shortish
shortleaf
short-lived
shortly
shortness
short-range
shortsighted
short-time
shot
shotgun
shotted

should
shoulder
shouldered
shout
shouted
shove
shoved
shovel
shoveled
shovelhead
show
showboat
showcase
showdown
showed
shower
showered
showier
showiest
showily
showiness
showings
showman
showmanship
shown
showroom
showy
shrank
shrapnel
shred
shredded
shredder
shrew
shrewd
shrewder
shrewdest
shrewdly
shrewdness
shriek
shrieked
shrift
shrike
shrill
shrilled
shriller
shrillest
shrillness
shrilly
shrimp
shrimper
shrine
Shriner
shrink
shrinkage
shrinker
shrinkingly
shrink-wrap
shrive
shrivel
shriveled
shriven
shroud
shrouded
shrub
shrubbery
shrubwood
shrug
shrugged
shrunk
shrunken
shuck
shucked
shudder
shuddered
shudderingly
shudderings
shuffle
shuffled
shufflingly
shufflings
shun
shunt
shunted
shut
shutoff
shutter
shuttered
shuttle
shuttled
shy
shyly
shyness
shyster
Siamese
sibilance
sibilant
sibilate
sibling
sibyl

sibylline
Sicilian
sick
sickbed
sicken
sickened
sickeningly
sicker
sickest
sickle
sicklier
sickliest
sickliness
sickly
sickness
sick-out
sickroom
side
sideboard
sidecar
sided
sidelong
sidepiece
sidereal
siderite
sidesplitting
sidewalk
sideways
sidewise
sidings
sidle
sidled
siege

sienna
sierra
siesta
sieve
sift
siftage
sifted
siftings
sigh
sighed
sighingly
sighings
sight
sighted
sightings
sightless
sightliness
sightly
sigma
sign
signal
signaled
signalize
signalized
signally
signatory
signature
signboard
signed
signer
signet
significance
significant

significantly
signification
signified
signify
signpost
signwriter
silage
silence
silenced
silencer
silent
silently
silentness
silex
silhouette
silica
silicate
silicon
silicosis
silk
silken
silkier
silkiest
silkily
silkiness
silkweed
silkworm
silky
sillabub
sillier
silliest
silliness
silly

silo
silt
siltation
silted
silvan
silver
silvered
silversmith
silverware
silvery
simian
similar
similarity
similarly
simile
similitude
simmer
simmered
simmeringly
simony
simoon
simper
simpered
simperingly
simple
simpler
simplest
simpleton
simplex
simplicity
simplification
simplified
simplify

simply
simulacrum
simulate
simulation
simulator
simultaneous
sin
since
sincere
sincerely
sincereness
sincerer
sincerest
sincerity
sine
sinecure
sinew
sinewy
sinful
sinfully
sinfulness
sing
singable
singe
singed
singer
single
singled
singleness
singleton
singly
singular
singularity

singularly
sinister
sinistral
sink
sinkage
sinker
sinkhole
sinkings
sinkless
sinless
sinlessly
sinlessness
sinned
sinner
sinological
sinologist
sinologue
sinophile
sinter
sinuosity
sinuous
sinusitis
Sioux
sip
siphon
siphoned
sipped
sipper
sir
sirdar
sire
sired
siren

sirloin
sirocco
sirup
sirupy
sisal
siskin
sissified
sissy
sister
sisterhood
sister-in-law
sisterly
Sistine
sistrum
sit
site
sitter
sittings
situate
situated
situation
sixth
sizable
size
sized
sizer
sizes
sizings
sizzle
sizzled
sizzlingly
skate
skated
skater
skein
skeletal
skeleton
skeletonize
skeletonized
skeptic
skeptical
skeptically
skepticism
sketch
sketched
sketchily
sketchiness
sketchy
skew
skewed
skewer
skewered
skewings
ski
skiagram
skiagraph
skiametry
skid
skidded
skied
skiff
skijoring
skill
skilled
skillet
skillful
skillfully
skillfulness
skim
skimmed
skimmer
skimmingly
skimp
skimped
skimpiness
skimpy
skin
skinflint
skinker
skinned
skinner
skinnier
skinniest
skinny
skinworm
skip
skipped
skipper
skippingly
skirmish
skirmished
skirmisher
skirmishingly
skirt
skirted
skirtings
skit
skitter
skittish

skittishly
skittishness
skittles
skive
skived
skiver
skivings
skoal
skulk
skulked
skull
skunk
skunkweed
sky
skydive
skyjacker
skyjacking
skylarked
skylight
skyrocket
skyscape
skyscraper
skyshine
skyward
skywriter
skywriting
slab
slack
slacked
slacken
slackened
slacker
slackest

slackness
slag
slain
slake
slaked
slam
slammed
slander
slandered
slanderer
slanderingly
slanderous
slanderously
slanderousness
slang
slangy
slank
slant
slanted
slantingly
slantways
slantwise
slap
slapdash
slapstick
slash
slashed
slasher
slashingly
slashings
slate
slater
slatted

slattern
slatternly
slaughter
slaughtered
slaughterer
slaughterhouse
slave
slaved
slaver
slavery
slavish
slavishly
slavishness
slaw
slay
slayer
slayings
sleave
sleaziness
sleazy
sled
sledge
sleek
sleeker
sleekest
sleekly
sleekness
sleep
sleeper
sleepier
sleepiest
sleepily
sleepiness

sleepless
sleeplessness
sleepy
sleet
sleeve
sleigh
sleight
slender
slenderer
slenderest
slenderness
slept
sleuth
sleuthed
sleuthhound
slew
slewed
slice
sliced
slicer
slick
slicker
slickest
slid
slide
slier
sliest
slight
slighted
slighter
slightest
slightingly
slightly
slightness
slim
slime
slimier
slimiest
slimily
sliminess
slimmer
slimmest
slimness
slimy
sling
slink
slinkier
slinkiest
slinky
slip
slipcase
slipknot
slippage
slipped
slipper
slipperiness
slippery
slipshod
slit
slither
slithered
slitter
sliver
slivered
slivery
slob
slobber
sloe
sloeberry
slog
slogan
sloganeer
slogged
sloop
slop
slope
sloped
slopingly
slopped
sloppy
slosh
sloshed
slot
sloth
slothful
solthfully
slothfulness
slotted
slouch
slouched
slouchily
slouchiness
slouchingly
slough
slough
sloughed
sloven
slovenliness
slovenly

slow
slowed
slower
slowest
slowgoing
slowly
slowpoke
sloyd
slub
slubbed
sludge
slug
sluggard
sluggardly
slugged
slugger
sluggish
sluggishly
sluggishness
sluice
sluiced
sluiceway
sluicings
slum
slumber
slumbered
slumberer
slumberingly
slumberland
slumberous
slump
slumped
slung

slur
slurred
slurringly
slurry
slush
slushily
slushiness
slushy
sluttish
sly
slyboots
slyly
slyness
smack
smacked
smackingly
small
smaller
smallest
smallness
smallpox
smart
smarted
smarten
smartened
smarter
smartest
smartingly
smartly
smartness
smash
smashup
smatter

smatterings
smear
smeared
smearier
smeariest
smeariness
smeary
smell
smelled
smelt
smelted
smelter
smeltery
smidgen
smilax
smile
smiled
smilingly
smirch
smirched
smirk
smirked
smirkingly
smirkish
smite
smith
Smithsonian
smithy
smitten
smock
smog
smoke
smoked

smokehouse
smokeless
smokeproof
smoker
smokestack
smokewood
smokier
smokiest
smokiness
smoky
smolder
smoldered
smooth
smoothbore
smoothed
smoother
smoothest
smoothingly
smoothly
smoothness
smote
smother
smothered
smotheringly
smudge
smudged
smudgily
smudginess
smudgy
smug
smuggle
smuggled
smuggler

smugly
smugness
smut
smutted
smuttier
smuttiest
smuttily
smuttiness
smutty
snack
snaffle
snafu
snag
snagged
snaggled
snail
snake
snakebird
snaked
snakelike
snakestone
snakeweed
snakewood
snakier
snakiest
snakily
snakiness
snaky
snap
snapdragon
snapped
snapper
snappier

snappiest
snappingly
snappish
snappy
snapshot
snapweed
snare
snared
snarl
snarled
snarlingly
snarly
snatch
snatched
snatchingly
snatchy
snath
sneak
sneaked
sneaker
sneakier
sneakiest
sneakingly
sneaky
sneer
sneered
sneeringly
sneeze
sneezed
sneezeweed
snicker
snickered
snickeringly

snickerings
sniff
sniffed
sniffily
sniffiness
sniffingly
sniffings
sniffle
sniffled
sniffy
sniggeringly
snip
snipe
snipped
snippet
snippier
snippiest
snippiness
snippy
snivel
sniveled
sniveler
snivelings
snob
snobbery
snobbish
snobbishly
snobbishness
snood
snooker
snoop
snooper
snoot
snooze
snore
snored
snoringly
snorings
snorkel
snort
snortingly
snortings
snout
snow
snowball
snowbell
snowberry
snowbird
snowbound
snowbush
snowcap
snowdrift
snowdrop
snowed
snowfall
snowflake
snowflower
snowier
snowiest
snowmobiler
snowplow
snowshed
snowshoe
snowslide
snowslip
snowstorm
snowworm
snowy
snub
snubbed
snubber
snubbingly
snubbings
snuff
snuffed
snuffer
snuffle
snuffled
snufflingly
snufflings
snug
snugger
snuggery
snuggest
snuggle
snuggled
snugly
snugness
so
soak
soaked
soap
soapbox
soaped
soapiness
soaproot
soapstone
soapsuds
soapy

soar
soared
soaringly
sob
sobbed
sobbingly
sobeit
sober
sobered
soberer
soberest
soberingly
soberly
sobersides
sobriety
sobriquet
socage
soccer
sociability
sociable
sociably
social
socialism
socialist
socialistic
socialization
socialize
socialized
socializer
socially
societal
societarian
societarianism

society
sociolinguistic
sociological
sociologically
sociologist
sociology
socioreligious
sock
socket
socketed
Socratic
sod
soda
sodality
sodden
sodium
sofa
soft
soften
softened
softener
softer
softest
softly
software
softwood
soggily
sogginess
soggy
soil
soilborne
soiled
sojourn

sojourned
sojourner
solace
solaced
solar
solarium
sold
solder
soldered
soldier
soldiered
soldierly
soldiery
sole
solecism
soled
solely
solemn
solemnity
solemnization
solemnize
solemnized
solemnly
solenoid
solenoidal
soleprint
solferino
solicit
solicitation
solicited
solicitor
solicitous
solicitude

solid
solidarity
solidifiableness
solidification
solidify
solidity
solidly
soliloquize
soliloquized
soliloquy
solitaire
solitarily
solitary
solitude
solo
soloed
soloist
solstice
solubility
soluble
solute
solution
solvable
solvate
solvation
solve
solved
solvency
solvent
somatic
somatology
somber
sombrero
some
somebody
somehow
someone
somersault
something
sometime
somewhat
somewhere
somnambulism
somnambulist
somnolent
son
sonant
sonata
sonatina
song
songbird
songbook
songful
songfulness
songster
sonic
son-in-law
sonnet
sonneteer
sonority
sonorous
soon
sooner
soonest
soot
sooted
soothe
soothed
soothingly
soothsayer
sootier
sootiest
sootily
sooty
sop
sophism
sophist
sophistic
sophistical
sophisticate
sophisticated
sophistication
sophistry
sophomore
sophomoric
sophomorical
soporific
sopranino
soprano
sorcerer
sorceress
sorcery
sordid
sordidness
sore
sorehead
sorely
soreness
sorghum

sorority
sorosis
sorrel
sorrier
sorriest
sorrow
sorrowed
sorrowful
sorrowfully
sorry
sort
sorted
sorter
sortie
sortilege
sostenuto
sot
sottish
sottishness
soubrette
soufflé
sought
soul
soulful
soulfully
soulfulness
soulless
soullessly
soullessness
sound
sounded
sounder
soundest
soundingly
soundings
soundless
soundlessly
soundlessness
soundly
soundness
soundproof
soup
soupbone
sour
source
soured
sourer
sourest
souse
soused
soutane
south
southbound
southeast
southeaster
southeasterly
southeastern
southerly
southern
southerner
southernmost
southward
southwest
southwester
southwesterly
souvenir
sovereign
sovereignty
soviet
sovietism
sovietization
sovietize
sovietologist
sow
sow
sowed
sower
sowings
soy
soybean
spa
space
spaceborne
spacecraft
spaceman
spacewalk
spacewoman
spacious
spaciously
spaciousness
spade
spaded
spadefish
spadework
spaghetti
spalpeen
span
spandrel
spangle

spangled
Spaniard
spaniel
Spanish
spank
spanked
spankingly
spankings
spanner
spare
spared
sparerib
sparingly
spark
sparked
sparkle
sparkled
sparkler
sparklingly
sparred
sparringly
sparrow
sparse
sparsely
sparseness
sparser
sparsest
sparsity
Spartan
spasm
spasmodic
spasmodical
spasmodically
spastic
spastically
spasticity
spat
spatter
spattered
spatteringly
spatterings
spatterproof
spatterwork
spatula
spatulate
spavined
spawn
spawned
speak
speaker
spear
speared
spearfish
spearhead
spearmint
spearwood
special
specialist
specialization
specialize
specialized
specially
specialty
specie
species
specific
specifically
specification
specified
specify
specimen
specious
speciously
speciousness
speck
specked
speckle
speckled
spectacle
spectacles
spectacular
spectacularly
spectator
specter
spectral
spectrometer
spectroscope
spectrum
speculate
speculated
speculation
speculative
speculatively
speculativeness
speculator
speculatory
speculum
speech
speechless

speechlessly
speechlessness
speed
speedboat
speeded
speeder
speedier
speediest
speedily
speediness
speedingly
speedometer
speedway
speedy
speleologist
speleology
spell
spellbinder
spellbound
spelled
speller
spellings
spelter
Spencerian
spend
spender
spendings
spendthrift
spent
spermaceti
spew
spewed
sphagnum
sphere
spherical
spherically
sphericity
spheroid
sphinx
spice
spiced
spicily
spiciness
spicy
spider
spidery
spied
spigot
spike
spiked
spiky
spile
spiled
spill
spilled
spillway
spin
spinach
spinal
spindle
spine
spineless
spinet
spinier
spiniest
spinnaker
spinner
spinneret
spinney
spinningly
spinoff
spinster
spinsterhood
spiny
spiral
spiraled
spirally
spire
spired
spirit
spirited
spiritedly
spiritual
spiritualism
spiritualist
spiritualistic
spirituality
spiritualize
spiritualized
spiritually
spirituous
spirochete
spit
spitball
spite
spiteful
spitefully
spitefulness
spitfire

spittoon
splash
splashdown
splashier
splashiest
splashingly
splashings
splashy
splatter
splatterwork
splayed
splayfoot
spleen
splendid
splendidly
splendor
splendorous
splenetic
splenitive
splice
spliced
splicer
splicings
splint
splinted
splinter
splintered
splinterproof
split
splittings
splitworm
splotch
splotched
splotchy
splurge
splurged
splutter
spluttered
spoil
spoilage
spoiled
spoilsman
spoilsport
spoke
spoken
spokeshave
spokesman
spoliation
spoliative
spoliatory
spondee
sponge
spongecake
sponged
sponger
spongier
spongiest
spongings
spongy
sponsor
sponsorship
spontaneity
spontaneous
spontaneously
spontaneousness
spoof
spook
spookiness
spooky
spool
spooled
spoon
spoonbill
spooned
spoonerism
spoonful
spoonfuls
spoor
sporadic
spore
sport
sported
sportive
sportively
sportscaster
sportsman
sportsmanship
sportswear
sporty
spot
spotless
spotlessly
spotlessness
spotlight
spotted
spotter
spottier
spottiest
spotty

spouse
spout
spouted
spoutings
sprain
sprained
sprang
sprat
sprawl
sprawled
sprawlingly
spray
sprayed
sprayer
spread
spreader
spreadingly
spree
sprig
sprightlier
sprightliest
sprightliness
sprightly
spring
springboard
springbok
springfish
springily
springiness
springingly
springtime
springwood
springy

sprinkle
sprinkled
sprinkler
sprinklingly
sprinklings
sprint
sprinter
sprite
spritsail
sprocket
sprout
sprouted
sproutling
spruce
sprucer
sprucest
sprung
spry
spud
spume
spumed
spumone
spun
spunk
spunkier
spunkiest
spunky
spur
spurious
spuriously
spurn
spurned
spurred

spurt
spurted
sputnik
sputter
sputtered
sputteringly
sputterings
sputum
spy
spyglass
squab
squabble
squabbled
squabblingly
squabblings
squad
squadron
squalid
squalidity
squalidly
squall
squalled
squallings
squally
squalor
squander
squandered
square
squared
squarehead
squarely
squareness
squash

squashed
squat
squatted
squatter
squaw
squawfish
squawk
squeak
squeal
squealed
squeamish
squeegee
squeeze
squeezed
squelch
squelched
squelchingly
squib
squid
squiggle
squiggly
squint
squinted
squintingly
squire
squirm
squirmed
squirmingly
squirmings
squirrel
squirrelfish
squirrelproof
squirt

stab
stabbed
stabbingly
stabbings
stability
stabilization
stabilize
stabilized
stabilizer
stable
staccato
stack
stadia
stadium
staff
stag
stage
stagecoach
stagecraft
staged
stagehand
stager
stageworthy
stagger
staggered
staggeringly
staghorn
staghound
staghunt
stagnant
stagnate
stagnated
stagnation

staid
stain
stained
stainless
stair
staircase
stairway
stake
staked
stalactite
stalagmite
stale
stalemate
staler
stalest
stalk
stalked
stalker
stalkingly
stall
stalled
stallion
stalwart
stamen
stamina
stammer
stammered
stammerer
stammeringly
stamp
stamped
stampede
stampeded

stamper
stampings
stance
stanch
stanchion
stand
standard
standardization
standardize
standings
standoff
standpipe
standpoint
standstill
stank
stannate
stannic
stannous
stanza
staple
stapled
stapler
star
starboard
starch
starched
starchy
stare
stared
starfish
stargazer
staringly
stark

starless
starlet
starlight
starlike
starlings
starquake
starred
starrier
starriest
starry
start
started
starter
startle
startled
startlingly
starvation
starve
starved
starveling
state
stated
statehood
statehouse
stateliness
stately
statement
stateroom
statesman
statesmanlike
static
station
stationary

stationed
stationer
stationery
statism
statist
statistical
statistically
statistician
statistics
statuary
statue
statuesque
statuette
stature
status
statute
statutory
stave
stay
stayed
stead
steadfast
steadfastly
steadfastness
steadier
steadiest
steadily
steady
steak
steal
stealth
stealthier
stealthiest

stealthily
steam
steamboat
steamed
steamer
steamier
steamiest
steaminess
steamship
steamy
steatite
steel
steelhead
steelwork
steelyard
steep
steeper
steepest
steeple
steeplechase
steer
steerage
steered
steering
steersman
stein
stellar
stem
stemmed
stench
stencil
stenciled
stenographer
stenographic
stenography
stenosis
stentorian
step
stepchild
stepdaughter
stepladder
stepmother
steppe
stepped
stepsister
stepson
stereo
stereophonic
stereopticon
stereoscope
stereoscopic
sterile
sterility
sterilization
sterilize
sterilized
sterilizer
sterling
stern
sterner
sternest
sternly
sternness
sternpost
sternum
sternutation
stertorous
stet
stethoscope
stevedore
stew
steward
stewardess
stewed
stick
sticker
stickful
stickier
stickiest
stickily
stickiness
stickleback
stickler
stickpin
stickweed
sticky
stiff
stiffen
stiffened
stiffener
stiffer
stiffest
stiffness
stifle
stifled
stiflingly
stigma
stigmata
stigmatic

stigmatism
stigmatization
stigmatize
stigmatized
stile
stiletto
still
stillborn
stilled
stiller
stillest
stillness
stillroom
stilly
stilt
stilted
stimulant
stimulate
stimulated
stimulating
stimulation
stimulus
sting
stinger
stingfish
stingier
stingiest
stingingly
stingy
stink
stinkbug
stinker
stinkingly
stinkpot
stinkweed
stinkwood
stint
stinted
stintingly
stipe
stipend
stipendiary
stipendium
stipple
stippled
stipplings
stipulate
stipulated
stipulates
stipulation
stipulatory
stir
stirpes
stirps
stirred
stirringly
stirrings
stirrup
stitch
stitched
stitcher
stitchings
stitchwork
stiver
stoa
stoat
stock
stockade
stockaded
stockbreeder
stockbroker
stocked
stockfish
stockholder
stockhouse
stockiness
stockinet
stockings
stockjobber
stockkeeper
stockmaker
stockman
stockowner
stockpile
stockpot
stocktaker
stocky
stockyard
stodgier
stodgiest
stodgy
stogy
stoic
stoical
stoically
stoicism
stoke
stoked
stokehold

stoker
stole
stolen
stolid
stolidity
stolidly
stomach
stomachful
stomachic
stone
stoneboat
stoned
stonefish
stonemason
stoneware
stoneweed
stonewood
stonework
stoneyard
stonier
stoniest
stonily
stony
stood
stool
stoop
stooped
stoopingly
stop
stopcock
stope
stopgap
stopover
stoppage
stopped
stopper
stoppered
stopple
storage
store
stored
storehouse
storekeeper
storeroom
storied
stork
storm
stormbound
stormed
stormier
stormiest
stormingly
stormy
story
storyteller
stoup
stout
stouter
stoutest
stouthearted
stoutly
stoutness
stove
stow
stowage
strabismus
straddle
straddled
straddlingly
strafe
straggle
straggled
straggler
stragglingly
straight
straightedge
straighten
straightened
straighter
straightest
straightforward
straightforwardly
straightforwardness
straightway
straightways
strain
strained
strainer
strainingly
strainings
strait
straiten
straitened
straiter
straitest
strake
strand
stranded
strange

strangelings
strangely
strangeness
stranger
strangest
strangle
strangled
strangler
strangles
stranglingly
stranglings
strangulate
strangulated
strangulation
strap
strapless
strappado
strapped
strappings
strata
stratagem
strategic
strategical
strategist
strategy
stratification
stratified
stratify
stratosphere
stratum
straw
strawberry
strawflower
stray
strayed
streak
streaked
streakier
streakiest
streaky
stream
streamed
streamer
streamingly
streamline
streamway
street
strength
strengthen
strengthened
strengthener
strenuous
strenuously
strenuousness
stress
stressed
stressful
stretch
stretched
stretcher
stretcherman
stretch-out
strew
strewed
strewn
striate
striated
striation
stricken
strict
strictly
strictness
stricture
stride
strident
stridently
stridingly
stridulous
strife
strigil
strike
strikebreaker
striker
strikingly
string
stringed
stringency
stringent
stringently
stringer
stringier
stringiest
stringpiece
stringy
strip
stripe
striped
striplings
stripper

strippings
strive
striven
stroboscope
strode
stroke
stroked
strokings
stroll
strolled
stroller
strong
strongbox
stronger
strongest
stronghold
strongly
strontium
strop
strophe
strophic
strove
struck
structural
structurally
structure
structured
structurism
structurist
structurization
structurize
strudel
struggle

struggled
struggler
strugglingly
strugglings
strum
strummed
strung
strut
strutted
strutter
struttingly
struttings
strychnine
stub
stubbed
stubbiness
stubble
stubbly
stubborn
stubby
stucco
stuck
stud
studbook
studded
student
studfish
studhorse
studied
studio
studious
studiously
studiousness

studwork
study
stuff
stuffed
stuffer
stuffings
stuffier
stuffiest
stuffily
stuffiness
stuffy
stultification
stultified
stultify
stumble
stumbled
stumblingly
stump
stumpage
stumped
stumpier
stumpiest
stumpy
stun
stung
stunk
stunned
stunner
stunningly
stunt
stunted
stupefacient
stupefaction

stupefied
stupefy
stupendous
stupid
stupidity
stupidly
stupor
stuporous
sturdily
sturdiness
sturdy
sturgeon
stutter
stuttered
stutterer
stutteringly
sty
stygian
style
stylebook
styled
stylings
stylish
stylishness
stylist
stylistic
stylistically
stylize
stylized
stylograph
stylographic
stylus
stymie

styptic
Styx
suability
suable
suasion
suave
suavely
suaveness
suavity
subacute
subadult
subagent
subaltern
subaquatic
subaqueous
subarctic
subatomic
subcaliber
subcaption
subcellar
subclass
subcommittee
subcompact
subconscious
subconsciously
subconsciousness
subconstellation
subcontinent
subcontract
subcontracted
subcontractor
subcutaneous
subdeacon

subdivide
subdivided
subdivision
subdue
subdued
subduingly
subeditor
subfamily
subfoundation
subgrade
subgroup
subhead
subheadings
subhuman
subject
subjected
subjection
subjective
subjectively
subjectiveness
subjectivism
subjectivity
subjects
subjoin
subjoinder
subjoined
subjugate
subjugated
subjugation
subjunctive
subkingdom
sublapsarian
sublease

sublessee
sublessor
sublet
sublimate
sublimated
sublimation
sublime
sublimed
sublimer
sublimest
subliminal
sublimity
sublunary
subluxation
submarginal
submarine
submariner
submerge
submerged
submergence
submersible
submersion
submetering
submission
submissive
submissively
submissiveness
submit
submittal
submitted
submittingly
subnormal
subnormality

suboceanic
suborder
subordinate
subordinated
subordinatingly
subordination
subordinative
suborn
subornation
suborned
suborner
subphylum
subplinth
subplot
subpoena
subpoenaed
subrogation
subscribe
subscribed
subscriber
subscript
subscription
subsequent
subsequently
subserve
subserved
subservience
subserviency
subservient
subside
subsided
subsidence
subsidiary

subsidize
subsidized
subsidy
subsist
subsisted
subsistence
subsoil
subspecies
substance
substandard
substantial
substantially
substantiate
substantiated
substantiation
substantive
substation
substitute
substituted
substitution
substratum
substructure
subsurface
subtangent
subtenant
subtend
subtended
subterfuge
subterranean
subterraneous
subtitle
subtle
subtler

subtlest
subtlety
subtly
subtract
subtracted
subtraction
subtrahend
subtreasury
subtropical
suburb
suburban
suburbanite
subvention
subversion
subversive
subvert
subverted
subway
succeed
succeeded
succeedingly
success
successful
successfully
succession
successive
successor
succinct
succinctly
succor
succored
succotash
succulence
succulent
succulently
succumb
succumbed
such
suck
sucked
sucker
suckle
suckled
sucklings
suction
sudden
suddenly
suddenness
sudoriferous
sudorific
suds
sue
sued
suède
suet
suffer
sufferable
sufferance
suffered
sufferer
sufferingly
sufferings
suffice
sufficed
sufficiency
sufficient
suffix
suffocate
suffocated
suffocatingly
suffocation
suffocative
suffragan
suffrage
suffragist
suffuse
suffused
suffusion
sugar
sugared
sugarplum
sugary
suggest
suggested
suggestibility
suggestible
suggestion
suggestive
suggestiveness
suicidal
suicidally
suicide
suicidology
suit
suitability
suitable
suitcase
suite
suited

suitingly
suitings
suitor
sulk
sulked
sulkier
sulkiest
sulkily
sulkiness
sulky
sullen
sullenly
sullenness
sullied
sully
sulphate
sulphide
sulphite
sulphur
sulphuric
sulphurous
sultan
sultana
sultanate
sultrier
sultriest
sultry
sum
sumac
summarily
summariness
summarize
summarized
summary
summation
summed
summer
summered
summery
summit
summon
summoned
sump
sumpter
sumptuary
sumptuous
sumptuously
sumptuousness
sun
sunbeam
sunbonnet
sunburn
sunburned
sunburst
sundae
Sunday
sunder
sunderance
sundered
sundial
sundry
sunfish
sunflower
sunglass
sunglow
sunk
sunken
sunless
sunlight
sunlit
sunned
sunniness
sunny
sunproof
sunrise
sunroom
sunseeker
sunset
sunshade
sunshine
sunshiny
sunspot
sunstone
sunstroke
sunward
sup
superable
superabundance
superabundant
superalloy
superannuate
superannuated
superannuation
superb
superbowl
supercalendered
supercargo
supercharger
supercilious

superciliously
superciliousness
supercity
superconductance
superconductivity
superconductor
supercool
superdreadnought
supereminence
supereminent
supererogation
superfamily
superficial
superficiality
superficially
superfine
superfluity
superfluous
superfluously
superfluousness
superheat
superheated
superheterodyne
superhuman
superhumanly
superimpose
superimposed
superimposition
superimposure
superinduce
superinduced
superintend
superintended

superintendence
superintendency
superintendent
superior
superiority
superjet
superlative
superman
supermolecule
supernal
supernally
supernatural
supernaturally
supernaturalism
supernaturalist
supernormal
supernumerary
superplasticity
superposition
supersaturate
supersaturated
supersaturation
superscribe
superscribed
superscription
supersede
superseded
supersession
supersonic
superstar
superstition
superstitious
superstitiously

superstratum
superstructure
supertax
supervene
supervened
supervise
supervised
supervision
supervisor
supervisory
supine
supineness
supper
supplant
supplanted
supple
supplement
supplemental
supplementary
supplementation
supplemented
suppliant
supplicant
supplicate
supplicated
supplicatingly
supplication
supplicatory
supplied
supplier
supply
support
supported

supporter
suppose
supposed
supposedly
supposition
supposititious
supposititiously
suppressant
suppress
suppressed
suppression
suppressive
suppurate
suppurated
suppuration
suppurative
supremacy
supreme
supremely
surbase
surcease
surcharge
surcharged
surcingle
surd
sure
surely
sureness
surety
suretyship
surf
surface
surfaced
surfacings
surfeit
surfeited
surge
surged
surgeon
surgery
surgical
surlier
surliest
surliness
surly
surmise
surmised
surmount
surmounted
surname
surnamed
surpass
surpassed
surpassingly
surplice
surpliced
surplus
surplusage
surprise
surprised
surprisedly
surprisingly
surreal
surrebuttal
surrebutter
surrejoinder
surrender
surrendered
surreptitious
surreptitiously
surreptitiousness
surrey
surrogate
surrogation
surround
surrounded
surroundings
surtax
surtout
surveillance
survey
surveyed
surveyor
survival
survivalism
survive
survived
survivor
survivorship
susceptibility
susceptible
susceptibly
suspect
suspected
suspend
suspended
suspenders
suspense
suspenseful

suspension
suspensive
suspensively
suspensiveness
suspicion
suspicious
suspiciously
suspiciousness
suspire
sustain
sustained
sustainedly
sustainingly
sustenance
sustentacular
sustentation
susurration
sutler
suttee
suture
sutured
suzerain
suzerainty
svelte
swab
swabbed
swaddle
swaddled
swaddling
swaddlings
swag
swage
swaged
swagger
swaggered
swaggeringly
Swahili
swain
swallow
swallowed
swallower
swallow-tailed
swami
swamp
swamped
swan
swanherd
swank
swankier
swankiest
swanky
swansdown
swap
swapped
sward
swarm
swarmed
swart
swarthy
swash
swastika
swat
swatch
swath
swathe
swatter
sway
swayed
swayingly
swear
swearingly
sweat
sweatband
sweatbox
sweater
sweatier
sweatiest
sweatily
sweatiness
sweatshop
sweaty
Swedish
sweep
sweeper
sweepingly
sweepings
sweepstake
sweet
sweetbread
sweetbrier
sweeten
sweetened
sweetener
sweetenings
sweetheart
sweetish
sweetishly
sweetly
sweetmeat

sweetness
sweetroot
sweetshop
sweetwater
sweetweed
sweetwood
swell
swelled
sweller
swellfish
swellings
swelter
sweltered
swelteringly
swept
swerve
swerved
swift
swifter
swiftest
swiftly
swiftness
swig
swigged
swill
swilled
swim
swimmer
swimmingly
swindle
swindled
swindler
swine
swineherd
swing
swingingly
swinish
swink
swipe
swiped
swirl
swirled
swirlingly
swish
swished
Swiss
switch
switchblade
switchboard
switchgear
switchkeeper
switchman
switchtail
switchyard
swivel
swiveled
swollen
swoon
swooned
swooningly
swoop
swooped
sword
swordbill
swordfish
swordplay
swordsman
swordstick
swordtail
swore
sworn
swung
swum
sybarite
sycamore
sycophancy
sycophant
sycophantic
syllabi
syllabic
syllabicate
syllabicated
syllabication
syllabification
syllabify
syllable
syllabus
syllabuses
syllogism
syllogistic
syllogize
sylph
sylvan
symbiosis
symbiotic
symbol
symbolic
symbolical
symbolically

symbolism
symbolist
symbolization
symbolize
symbolized
symmetrical
symmetry
sympathectomy
sympathetic
sympathetically
sympathize
sympathized
sympathizer
sympathizingly
sympathy
symphonic
symphony
symphysis
symposium
symptom
symptomatic
symptomatology
synagogue
synapse
synapsis
synchronism
synchronization
synchronize
synchronized
synchronous
syncopate
syncopated
syncopation
syncope
syncretism
syndic
syndical
syndicalism
syndicalize
syndicate
syndicated
syndication
syndrome
synectics
synergistic
synergistically
synod
synodist
synonym
synonymous
synopses
synopsis
synoptic
synovial
synovitis
syntactical
syntax
syntheses
synthesis
synthesize
synthesized
synthetic
synthetically
syringe
syrup
system
systematic
systematization
systematize
systematized
systematizer
systematology
systemic
systemically
systole
systolic
syzygy

t

tab
tabard
tabasco
tabernacle
tabernacled
tabes
tablature
table
tableau
tablecloth
tabled
tablemaid
tableman
tablespoon
tablet
tableware
tabloid
taboo
tabor
taboret
tabu
tabular
tabulate

tabulated
tabulation
tabulator
tachistoscope
tachometer
tachygrapher
tachygraphy
tacit
tacitly
taciturn
taciturnity
tack
tacked
tackle
tackled
tackler
tacky
tact
tactful
tactfully
tactfulness
tactical
tactician

tactics
tactile
tactless
tactlessly
tactlessness
tadpole
taffeta
taffrail
taffy
tag
tagboard
tagged
Tahitian
tail
tailboard
tailed
tailfirst
tailings
tailless
tailor
tailored
tailpiece
tailrace

tailstock
taint
tainted
take
takedown
taken
takeout
taker
takingly
takingness
takings
talc
talcum
tale
talebearer
talent
talented
talipes
talisman
talismanic
talk
talkative
talked
talker
tall
taller
tallest
tallish
tallness
tallow
tallowed
tallowiness
tallowroot

tallowwood
tallowy
tally
tallyho
tallyman
Talmud
Talmudic
talon
taloned
tamarack
tamarind
tambour
tambourine
tame
tamed
tameness
tamer
tamest
Tamil
Tammany
tamper
tampered
tamperproof
tampon
tan
tanager
tanbark
tandem
tang
tangent
tangential
tangentiality
tangerine

tangible
tangibly
tangle
tangled
tangleroot
tanglingly
tango
tangy
tank
tankage
tankard
tanked
tanker
tannage
tanned
tanner
tannery
tannic
tannin
tannings
tansy
tantalization
tantalize
tantalized
tantalum
tantalus
tantamount
tantrum
tanvat
tanwood
tap
tape
taped

tapeline
tapeman
taper
tapered
taperingly
tapestry
tapeworm
taphole
taphouse
tapioca
tapir
tapper
tappet
tappings
taproom
taproot
tapster
tar
tarantella
tarantula
tarboard
tarboosh
tarbrush
tarbush
tardier
tardiest
tardily
tardiness
tardy
tare
tarflower
targe
target

targetable
tariff
tarlatan
tarnish
tarnished
tarot
tarpaulin
tarpon
tarragon
tarred
tarried
tarry
tarryingly
tart
tartan
tartar
tartlet
tartness
tartrate
tarweed
task
taskmaster
taskmistress
taskwork
Tasmanian
tassel
tasseled
taste
tasted
tasteful
tastefully
tastefulness
tasteless

tastelessly
tastelessness
taster
tastier
tastiest
tastily
tastingly
tastings
tasty
Tatar
tatter
tattered
tatting
tattle
tattled
tattler
tattoo
tattooed
tattooer
taught
taunt
taunted
tauntingly
taupe
taurine
taut
tauten
tautened
tautological
tautology
tavern
tawdrier
tawdriest

tawdrily
tawdriness
tawdry
tawny
tax
taxable
taxation
taxed
taxes
taxi
taxicab
taxidermist
taxidermy
taximeter
taxingly
taxonomy
taxpaid
taxpayer
tea
teaberry
teacart
teach
teachability
teachable
teacher
teacherage
teachingly
teachings
teacup
teak
teakettle
teal
team
teamed
teammate
teamster
teamwork
teapot
tear
tear
tearful
tearfully
tearfulness
tearless
tearlessly
tearoom
tearstain
teary
tease
teased
teaser
teasingly
teaspoon
teaspoonful
teataster
technical
technicality
technically
technician
technique
technocracy
technocrat
technological
technology
tedious
tediously
tediousness
tedium
tee
teed
teem
teemed
teemingly
teeter
teeterboard
teetered
teeth
teetotal
teetotaler
teetotally
telautograph
telecast
telecommunication
telediagnosis
telegram
telegraph
telegrapher
telegraphic
telegraphy
teleology
telepathic
telepathy
telephone
telephonic
telephoto
Tele-Promp-Ter
telescope
telescopic
teletype

teletypesetter
teletypewriter
televise
televised
television
Telex
telford
tell
teller
tellingly
tellings
telltale
tellurium
telpher
Telstar
temerity
temper
temperament
temperamental
temperamentally
temperance
temperate
temperately
temperature
tempered
tempest
tempestuous
tempestuously
tempestuousness
template
temple
templed
tempo
temporal
temporalty
temporarily
temporary
temporization
temporize
temporized
temporizer
temporizingly
tempt
temptation
tempted
tempter
temptingly
temptingness
temptress
tenability
tenable
tenacious
tenaciously
tenaciousness
tenacity
tenancy
tenant
tenantable
tenanted
tenantless
tenantry
tend
tended
tendency
tender
tendered
tenderer
tenderest
tenderfoot
tenderloin
tenderly
tenderness
tendon
tendril
Tenebrae
tenebrous
tenement
tenet
tennis
tenon
tenor
tenpins
tense
tensely
tenseness
tenser
tensest
tensile
tension
tensor
tent
tentacle
tentative
tenterer
tenterhooks
tenuity
tenuous
tenuously
tenure

tepee
tepid
tepidity
tepidly
teratology
tercentenary
teredo
tergiversate
term
termagant
termed
terminable
terminal
terminate
terminated
termination
terminative
terminological
terminologically
terminology
terminus
termite
termless
tern
ternary
terrace
terraced
terrain
terrapin
terrazzo
terrestrial
terrible
terribly
terrier
terrific
terrifically
terrified
terrify
terrifyingly
terrine
territorial
territoriality
territory
terror
terrorism
terrorist
terroristic
terrorization
terrorize
terrorized
terse
terseness
terser
tersest
tertian
tertiary
tessellate
tessellated
tessellation
test
testament
testamentary
testator
tested
tester
testified
testify
testimonial
testimony
testingly
testings
testy
tetanus
tether
tethered
tetragon
tetragonal
tetralogy
tetrameter
tetrarch
tetrigid
Texan
text
textbook
textile
textual
textualism
textualist
textually
textural
texturally
texture
textured
thalassic
thallium
than
thanatopsis
thane
thank

thanked
thankful
thankfully
thankfulness
thankless
thanks
thanksgiving
that
thatch
thatched
thaumaturgist
thaumaturgy
thaw
the
theater
theatrical
theatricalism
theatricality
theatrically
theatricals
thee
theft
their
theirs
theism
theist
theistic
them
thematic
thematical
theme
themselves
then
thence
thenceforth
thenceforward
theocracy
theodolite
theologian
theological
theologically
theology
theorem
theoretic
theoretical
theoretically
theorist
theorize
theorized
theorizer
theory
theosophic
theosophical
theosophically
theosophism
theosophist
theosophy
therapeutic
therapeutical
therapeutically
therapy
there
thereabouts
thereabove
thereafter
thereat
thereby
therefore
therefrom
therein
thereinafter
thereinbefore
thereof
thereon
thereto
theretofore
thereunder
thereunto
thereupon
therewith
thermal
thermion
thermionic
thermite
thermoelectric
thermometer
thermometric
thermometrical
thermometrically
thermophysical
thermostat
thesaurus
these
theses
thesis
thew
they
thick
thicken

thickened
thickener
thicker
thickest
thicket
thicketed
thickheaded
thickly
thickness
thickset
thick-skinned
thick-witted
thief
thievery
thievingly
thievish
thigh
thill
thimble
thimbleful
thimblerigger
thin
thing
things
think
thinkable
thinker
thinkingly
thinks
thinly
thinner
thinness
thinnest

third
thirst
thirsted
thirstily
thirstiness
thirstingly
thirsty
this
thistle
thither
thole
thong
thoracic
thorax
Thor
thorn
thornbush
thorned
thornier
thorniest
thorny
thorough
thoroughbred
thoroughfare
thoroughgoing
thoroughly
thoroughness
those
thou
though
thought
thoughtful
thoughtfully

thoughtfulness
thoughtless
thoughtlessly
thoughtlessness
thousand
thousandfold
thousandth
thrall
thralldom
thrash
thrashed
thrasher
thrashings
thrasonical
thread
threadbare
threaded
threadweed
threadworm
thready
threat
threaten
threatened
threateningly
three
threesome
threnody
threnos
thresh
threshed
thresher
threshold
threw

thrice
thrift
thriftier
thriftiest
thriftily
thriftiness
thriftless
thriftlessly
thriftlessness
thrifty
thrill
thrilled
thrillingly
thrips
thrive
thrivingly
throat
throated
throatier
throatiest
throatily
throatiness
throatroot
throatwort
throaty
throb
throbbed
throbbingly
throes
thrombosis
thrombus
throne
throneless
thronelike
throng
throngingly
throttle
throttled
throttlingly
through
throughout
throw
throwback
thrower
thrown
throwoff
thrum
thrummed
thrush
thrust
thud
thudded
thuddingly
thug
thuggery
thulium
thumb
thumbed
thumbmark
thumbnail
thumbpiece
thumbprint
thump
thumped
thumper
thumpingly
thumpings
thunder
thunderbird
thunderbolt
thundered
thunderfish
thunderhead
thundering
thunderingly
thunderings
thunderous
thundershower
thunderstruck
thundery
thundrous
thurible
Thursday
thus
thwack
thwacked
thwackingly
thwart
thwarted
thwartingly
thy
thyme
thymus
thyroid
thyself
tiara
tibia
tick
ticked

ticker
ticket
ticketed
tickings
tickle
tickled
tickler
ticklingly
ticklish
ticklishly
ticklishness
tidal
tidbit
tide
tided
tiderace
tidewater
tideway
tidied
tidier
tidiest
tidily
tidiness
tidings
tidy
tie
tieback
tied
tie-dye
tier
tiered
tiff
tiffany

tiffed
tiffin
tiger
tigerish
tigerlike
tigerwood
tight
tighten
tightened
tightener
tightening
tighter
tightest
tightfisted
tightly
tightrope
tightwad
tilbury
tilde
tile
tiled
tilefish
tiler
tileroot
till
tillable
tillage
tilled
tiller
tilt
tilted
tilth
tiltyard

timbale
timber
timbered
timberland
timberwood
timberwork
time
timed
timekeeper
timeless
timelessly
timelessness
timeliness
timely
timepiece
timer
timeserving
timetable
timid
timidity
timidly
timings
timorous
timorously
tin
tinct
tincted
tincture
tinctured
tinder
tinderbox
tine
tined

tineweed
tinge
tinged
tingle
tingled
tinglingly
tinglings
tinhorn
tinker
tinkered
tinkle
tinkled
tinklingly
tinklings
tinned
tinnier
tinniest
tinnily
tinniness
tinnitus
tinny
tinsel
tinseled
tinsmith
tint
tinted
tintinnabulation
tintype
tinware
tinwork
tiny
tip
tipped
tippet
tipple
tippled
tippler
tipsier
tipsiest
tipster
tipsy
tiptoe
tiptoed
tiptoeingly
tiptop
tirade
tire
tired
tireless
tirelessly
tirelessness
tiresome
tiresomely
tiresomeness
tiringly
tissue
tissued
tissues
Titan
titanic
titaniferous
titanium
titbit
tithable
tithe
tithed
tithings
titian
titillate
titillated
titillatingly
titillation
titillative
titivate
titivated
titivation
title
titled
titleholder
titmouse
titrate
titrated
titration
titter
tittered
titteringly
titterings
tittle
tittup
titular
titularly
titulary
to
toad
toadfish
toadroot
toadstone
toadstool
toady

toast
toasted
toaster
tobacco
toboggan
tobogganed
toccata
tocsin
today
toddle
toddled
toddler
toddy
toe
toecap
toed
toenail
toeplate
toffee
toga
together
togetherness
toggle
toggled
toil
toiled
toiler
toilet
toiletry
toiletware
toilingly
Tokay
token

tokened
tokenism
told
tolerable
tolerably
tolerance
tolerant
tolerate
tolerated
toleration
tolerationism
tolerative
toll
tolled
tollgate
tollhouse
tomahawk
tomato
tomb
tombed
tombola
tomboy
tombstone
tomcat
tomcod
tome
tomfool
tomfoolery
tomfoolishness
tomorrow
ton
tonal
tonalist

tonality
tone
toned
toneless
tongs
tongue
tongued
tonic
tonically
tonicity
tonight
tonka
tonnage
tonneau
tonsil
tonsillitis
tonsorial
tonsure
tontine
too
took
tool
toolbox
tooled
toolings
toolmaker
toolroom
toolsmith
toot
tooted
tooth
toothache
toothbrush

toothed
toothless
toothlessly
toothlessness
toothpick
toothy
tootle
tootled
top
topaz
topcoat
toper
topiarist
topiary
topic
topical
topknot
topless
toplofty
topman
topmast
topmost
topographer
topographic
topographical
topographically
topography
topped
topper
toppiece
toppingly
toppings
topple

toppled
topsail
topside
topstone
toque
torch
torchlight
torchweed
torchwood
tore
toreador
torment
tormented
tormentingly
tormentor
tornado
torpedo
torpedoed
torpid
torpidity
torpidly
torpor
torque
torrent
torrential
torrentially
torrid
torridity
torridly
torsion
torsional
torso
tort

tortoise
tortuosity
tortuous
tortuously
tortuousness
torture
tortured
torturer
torturingly
torturous
torturously
Tory
toss
tossed
tossingly
tossings
tossup
total
totaled
totalitarian
totalitarianism
totality
totalization
totalizator
totalize
totalized
totalizer
totally
tote
toted
totem
tother
totter

tottered
totteringly
totterings
tottery
toucan
touch
touchable
touchdown
touched
touchhole
touchier
touchiest
touchily
touchiness
touchingly
touchstone
touch-tone
touchwood
touchy
tough
toughen
toughened
tougher
toughest
toupee
tour
toured
tourism
tourist
tourmaline
tournament
tourney
tourniquet
tousle
tousled
tout
touted
tovarish
tow
towage
toward
towards
towboat
towed
towel
towelings
tower
towered
toweringly
towerman
towhead
towline
town
townfolk
township
townsman
townwear
towpath
towrope
toxemia
toxic
toxicity
toxicological
toxicologist
toxicology
toxicosis
toxoid
toy
toyed
toyingly
toyman
toyshop
trace
traceable
traced
tracer
tracery
trachea
tracheal
trachoma
tracings
track
trackage
tracked
tracker
tracklayer
trackless
trackman
trackmaster
tract
tractability
tractable
tractably
tractarian
tractate
tractile
traction
tractive
tractor

tractorize
trade
traded
trademark
trade-off
trader
tradesman
tradition
traditional
traditionalism
traditionally
traduce
traduced
traducer
traducingly
traffic
trafficked
tragacanth
tragedian
tragedienne
tragedy
tragic
tragical
tragically
tragicomedy
tragus
trail
trailed
trailer
trailingly
train
trainband
trained
trainer
trainful
trainload
trainman
trait
traitor
traitorous
traitorously
trajectory
tram
tramcar
trammel
trammeled
trammelingly
tramontane
tramp
tramped
trample
trampled
trampolin
tramroad
tramway
trance
trancelike
tranquil
tranquilization
tranquilize
tranquilized
tranquilizer
tranquilizingly
tranquillity
tranquilly
transact
transacted
transaction
transalpine
transatlantic
transcend
transcended
transcendence
transcendency
transcendent
transcendental
transcendentalism
transcendentalist
transcontinental
transcribe
transcribed
transcriber
transcript
transcription
transducer
transduction
transearth
transept
transfer
transferability
transferable
transferal
transference
transferred
transferrer
transfiguration
transfigure
transfigured
transfigurement

transfix
transfixed
transform
transformation
transformed
transformer
transformingly
transfuse
transfused
transfusion
transfusions
transgress
transgressed
transgressingly
transgression
transgressor
transient
transistor
transistorize
transit
transition
transitional
transitionally
transitive
transitively
transitiveness
transitory
translatable
translate
translated
translation
translator
translatory

transliterate
translucence
translucency
translucent
translucently
transmarine
transmigrant
transmigration
transmissible
transmission
transmit
transmittal
transmitted
transmitter
transmogrification
transmogrified
transmogrify
transmutable
transmutation
transmute
transmuted
transom
transpacific
transparency
transparent
transparently
transpiration
transpire
transpired
transplant
transplantate
transplantation
transplanted

transport
transportation
transported
transportingly
transposal
transpose
transposed
transposition
transracial
transship
transshipment
transubstantiation
transversal
transverse
trap
trapdoor
trapeze
trapezium
trapezoid
trapped
trapper
trappings
Trappist
traprock
trapshooting
trash
trashier
trashiest
trashy
trauma
traumata
traumatic
traumatically

traumatism
traumatize
travail
travel
traveled
traveler
travelogue
traversable
traversal
traverse
traversed
travertine
travesty
trawl
trawler
tray
treacherous
treacherously
treacherousness
treachery
treacle
tread
treadle
treadmill
treason
treasonable
treasure
treasured
treasurer
treasury
treat
treated
treatise

treatment
treaty
treble
trebled
tree
treed
treenail
trek
trekked
trellis
trellised
tremble
trembled
tremblingly
tremblings
tremendous
tremendously
tremolando
tremolo
tremor
tremulous
tremulously
tremulousness
trench
trenchancy
trenchant
trenchantly
trencher
trencherman
trend
trended
trendily
trendiness

trendsetter
trendy
trepan
trephine
trephined
trepidation
trespass
trespassed
trespasser
tress
trestle
trestlework
triad
triadic
trial
triangle
triangular
triangularity
triangulate
triangulated
triangulation
tribal
tribalism
tribasic
tribe
tribesman
tribulation
tribunal
tribune
tributary
tribute
trice
triceps

trichina
trichinosis
trichotomy
trick
tricked
trickery
trickier
trickiest
trickily
trickiness
trickle
trickled
tricklingly
tricklings
trickster
tricksy
tricky
tricolor
tricorn
tricot
tricycle
trident
tried
triennial
triennially
trifle
trifled
trifler
triflingly
triflings
trig
trigger
triggered
triggerfish
triglyph
trigonometric
trigonometrical
trigonometry
trijet
trilemma
trilingual
trill
trilled
trillion
trillium
trilobite
trilogy
trimester
trimmed
trimmer
trimmings
trimness
trimonthly
trinity
trinket
trinomial
trio
triode
triolet
trip
tripartite
tripe
triphthong
triple
tripled
triplet
triplex
triplicate
triplicated
triplication
triply
tripod
tripped
tripper
trippingly
triptych
trireme
trisect
trisected
trisection
trisector
triskelion
trisyllabic
trite
tritely
triteness
triton
tritone
triturate
triturated
trituration
triumph
triumphal
triumphant
triumphed
triumphingly
triumvir
triumvirate
triune

trivalent
trivet
trivia
trivial
triviality
trivially
trochaic
troche
troika
troll
trolled
trolley
trombone
troop
trooped
trooper
troopship
trope
trophy
tropic
tropical
tropically
tropism
tropist
tropology
tropopause
troposphere
trot
troth
trotline
trotted
trotter
troubadour

trouble
troubled
troublesome
troublesomely
troublesomeness
troublingly
troublous
trough
troughlike
trounce
trounced
trouncings
troupe
trouper
trousers
trousseau
trout
troutlet
troutling
trowel
troweled
troy
truancy
truant
truantism
truce
trucial
truck
truckage
trucked
trucker
truckle
truckled

trucklingly
truckman
truculence
truculent
trudge
trudged
trudgen
true
trued
truelove
trueness
truffle
truffled
truism
truly
trump
trumped
trumpery
trumpet
trumpeted
trumpeter
trumpetings
trumpetlike
trumpetweed
trumpetwood
truncate
truncated
truncation
truncheon
trundle
trundled
trunk
trunnion

truss
trussed
trussings
trust
trustee
trusteeship
trustful
trustfully
trustfulness
trustier
trustiest
trustingly
trustworthiness
trustworthy
trusty
truth
truthful
truthfully
truthfulness
try
tryingly
trysail
tryst
trysted
tsetse
tub
tuba
tubbed
tubbier
tubbiest
tubbings
tubby
tube
tuber
tubercle
tubercular
tuberculin
tuberculosis
tuberculous
tuberosity
tuberous
tubings
tubular
tubulation
tuck
tucked
Tudor
Tuesday
tuft
tufted
tuftings
tug
tugboat
tugged
tuggingly
tuggings
tuition
tularemia
tulip
tulipwood
tulle
tumble
tumbled
tumbler
tumbleweed
tumblingly
tumbrel
tumefaction
tumefied
tumefy
tumid
tumidity
tumor
tumorous
tumult
tumultuous
tumultuously
tumultuousness
tumulus
tun
tuna
tundra
tune
tuned
tuneful
tuneless
tunelessly
tunelessness
tuner
tungsten
tunic
tunings
Tunisian
tunnel
tunneled
tunny
tupelo
turban
turbid

turbidity
turbidly
turbinate
turbine
turbot
turbotrain
turbulence
turbulent
turbulently
tureen
turf
turfed
turfman
turgid
turgidity
turgidly
Turk
turkey
Turkish
turmeric
turmoil
turn
turnbuckle
turncoat
turncock
turned
turner
turnings
turnip
turnkey
turnoff
turnout
turnover

turnpike
turnspit
turnstile
turpentine
turpitude
turquoise
turret
turreted
turtle
Tuscan
tusk
tusked
tussle
tussled
tussock
tutelage
tutelary
tutor
tutored
tutorial
tuxedo
twaddle
twaddled
twain
twang
twanged
tweak
tweaked
tweed
tweezers
twice
twiddle
twiddled

twig
twilight
twill
twilled
twin
twinborn
twine
twined
twinge
twinged
twinkle
twinkled
twinklingly
twinklings
twirl
twirled
twist
twisted
twister
twistings
twit
twitch
twitched
twitted
twitter
twittered
twitteringly
twitterings
two
twofold
twosome
tycoon
type

typed
typesetter
typewriter
typewritten
typhoid
typhoidal
typhoon
typhous
typhus
typical
typically
typification
typify
typings
typist
typographer
typographic
typography
typothetae
tyrannical
tyrannicide
tyrannize
tyrannized
tyrannizingly
tyrannous
tyranny
tyrant
tyro

u

ubiquitous
ubiquitously
ubiquity
udder
uglier
ugliest
ugliness
ugly
uhlan
ukase
ukulele
ulcer
ulcerate
ulcerated
ulceration
ulcerative
ulcerous
ulcerously
ulna
ulnar
ulster
ulterior
ultimate

ultimately
ultimatism
ultimatum
ultimo
ultraism
ultraleft
ultraleftist
ultralegality
ultramarine
ultramicroscope
ultramodern
ultramontane
ultranationalism
ultranationalist
ultrared
ultrasonic
ultraviolet
ululate
ululated
ululation
umber
umbra
umbrage

umbrageous
umbrella
umlaut
umpire
umpired
unable
unabridged
unaccented
unacceptable
unaccommodating
unaccompanied
unaccountable
unaccustomed
unacquainted
unadorned
unadulterated
unaffected
unalloyed
unalterable
unaltered
un-American
unamiable
unanimous

unanswerable
unappeasable
unapproachable
unappropriated
unapprovingly
unarmed
unashamed
unasked
unassailable
unassigned
unassimilated
unassisted
unassumingly
unattached
unattainable
unattempted
unattractively
unauthorized
unavailable
unavailingly
unavoidable
unaware
unbalanced
unballasted
unbar
unbarred
unbearably
unbeatable
unbecomingly
unbefittingly
unbeknown
unbeknownst
unbelief
unbelievable
unbeliever
unbelievingly
unbelievingness
unbend
unbendingly
unbiased
unbidden
unbind
unblemished
unblessed
unblocked
unblushingly
unbolt
unbolted
unborn
unbosom
unbosomed
unbound
unbounded
unbowed
unbreakable
unbridled
unbroken
unbuckle
unburden
unburdened
unburned
unbusinesslike
unbutton
unbuttoned
uncage
uncanny
uncaptivated
uncarpeted
uncataloged
unceasingly
unceremonious
uncertain
uncertainly
uncertainness
uncertainty
unchallenged
unchangeable
unchangeably
unchangingly
uncharitable
unchidingly
unchristened
unchristian
uncial
uncivil
uncivilized
unclad
unclaimed
unclasp
uncle
unclean
uncleanly
unclosed
unclothe
uncoil
uncollected
uncolt
uncomfortable
uncomfortableness

uncommon
uncommunicative
uncompanied
uncompromising
unconcerned
unconditional
unconditionality
unconfined
unconfirmed
unconformity
uncongenial
unconquerable
unconquered
unconscionable
unconscious
unconsciously
unconsciousness
unconsecrated
unconsequential
unconsequentially
unconsiderately
unconsidered
unconstitutional
unconstitutionally
unconstrained
unconstrainedly
uncontaminated
uncontradictory
uncontrollable
uncontrolled
unconventional
unconventionally
unconverted

unconvinced
unconvincingly
uncooperative
uncork
uncorked
uncorrected
uncorrupted
uncountable
uncounted
uncouple
uncoupled
uncouth
uncouthness
uncover
uncovered
uncowed
uncreased
uncritical
uncriticizingly
uncrowded
uncrowned
unction
unctuous
uncultivated
uncultured
uncurbed
uncurl
uncut
undamaged
undamped
undashed
undated
undaunted

undeceive
undeceived
undecided
undecipherable
undeciphered
undecorous
undefeated
undefended
undefiled
undefinable
undeliverable
undemocratic
undemonstrative
undeniable
undependable
undeposited
under
underachiever
underarm
underbid
underbody
underbrush
underbuy
undercapitalization
undercapitalize
undercarriage
undercharge
undercharged
underclassman
underclothes
undercoat
underconsumption
undercover

undercurrent
undercut
underdone
underdose
underestimate
underexpose
underfeed
underfoot
undergarment
underglaze
undergo
undergraduate
underground
undergrowth
underhanded
underhandedly
underhandedness
underhung
underlaid
underlay
underlie
underline
underlined
underlings
undermanned
undermine
undermined
underneath
undernourish
undernourished
undernourishment
underpass
underpinnings
underprivileged
underproduction
underproductivity
underquote
underrate
underrated
underreact
underscore
underscored
undersecretary
undersell
undershirt
undershot
undersigned
undersized
underskirt
underslung
undersparred
understand
understandingly
understandings
understate
understatement
understood
understudy
undertake
undertaken
undertaker
undertakings
underthings
undertone
undertook
undertow
underturn
undervalue
underwater
underwear
underweight
underwhelm
underworld
underwrite
underwriter
undescribable
undeserved
undesirable
undesired
undestroyed
undetected
undetermined
undeveloped
undiagnosed
undiapered
undigested
undignified
undiluted
undiminished
undimmed
undirected
undisciplined
undisclosed
undiscovered
undiscriminatingly
undisguised
undisputed
undistinguished
undistributed

undivided
undo
undock
undomesticated
undone
undoubted
undoubtedly
undramatically
undraped
undrawn
undress
undressed
undrinkable
undue
undulant
undulate
undulated
undulation
unduly
undutiful
undyingly
unearned
unearth
unearthed
unearthly
uneasier
uneasiest
uneasily
uneasiness
uneasy
uneatable
uneducable
uneducated

unembarrassed
unembittered
unembroidered
unemotional
unemployable
unemployableness
unemployed
unemployment
unencumbered
unendangered
unending
unendorsed
unendurable
unenforceable
unengaged
unengraved
unengrossed
unenlarged
unenlightened
unenslaved
unentered
unenterprising
unentertaining
unenthusiastic
unenthusiastically
unenviable
unenviably
unenvied
unequal
unequalable
unequaled
unequalize
unequalized

unequally
unequipped
unequivocal
uneradicated
unerasable
unerased
unerring
unerringly
unessential
unestimated
unethical
unethically
uneven
unevenly
uneventful
uneventfully
unexampled
unexcelled
unexceptionable
unexceptional
unexcitable
unexciting
unexcused
unexecuted
unexhausted
unexpected
unexpectedly
unexpectedness
unexplainable
unexplained
unexploited
unexposed
unexpressed

unexpressible
unexpurgated
unextinguished
unextricated
unfaded
unfadingly
unfailingly
unfair
unfairly
unfairness
unfaithful
unfaithfully
unfaithfulness
unfaltering
unfamiliar
unfarmed
unfashionable
unfashionably
unfasten
unfastened
unfatherly
unfathomable
unfathomed
unfatigued
unfavorable
unfavorably
unfearingly
unfeasible
unfeasibly
unfed
unfeelingly
unfeigned
unfelt
unfeminine
unfenced
unfenestrated
unfermented
unfertilized
unfetter
unfettered
unfiled
unfilial
unfilially
unfillable
unfiltered
unfinished
unfit
unfittingly
unflaggingly
unflappable
unflatteringly
unflickeringly
unflinchingly
unflinchingness
unflooded
unflurried
unflustered
unfocused
unfold
unfolded
unforced
unforeseeable
unforeseen
unforetellable
unforfeited
unforgettable
unforgettingly
unforgivable
unforgiven
unforgivingly
unforgivingness
unforgotten
unformalized
unformed
unfortified
unfortunate
unfortunately
unfounded
unfrayed
unfrequented
unfriended
unfriendliness
unfriendly
unfrock
unfrocked
unfrugal
unfruitful
unfueled
unfulfilled
unfunded
unfunny
unfurbished
unfurl
unfurled
unfurnished
ungainliness
ungainly
ungallant
ungarlanded

ungarnished
ungenerous
ungentle
ungentlemanly
ungerminated
ungifted
ungirt
unglazed
unglorious
ungloved
ungodliness
ungodly
ungovernable
ungovernably
ungracious
ungraciously
ungraded
ungrammatical
ungrateful
ungratefully
ungratefulness
ungrounded
ungrudgingly
unguarded
unguardedly
unguent
unguided
ungummed
unhackneyed
unhallowed
unhampered
unhandiness
unhandsome

unhandy
unhanged
unhappier
unhappiest
unhappily
unhappiness
unhappy
unhardened
unharmed
unharness
unharnessed
unharvested
unhatched
unhealed
unhealthful
unhealthfulness
unhealthy
unheard
unheated
unheeded
unheedfully
unheedingly
unhelpful
unheralded
unheroic
unhesitating
unhesitatingly
unhindered
unhinge
unhinged
unhitch
unhitched
unholiness

unholy
unhomelike
unhonored
unhook
unhooked
unhoped
unhorse
unhumbled
unhumorous
unhurt
unhygienic
unhyphenated
unicorn
unicycle
unidentifiable
unidentified
unification
unified
uniform
uniformed
uniformity
unify
unilateral
unilaterally
unilluminating
unimaginable
unimaginative
unimpaired
unimpeachable
unimpeded
unimportant
unimportantly
unimposing

unimpressed
unimpressionable
unimpressive
unimproved
unincorporated
unindemnified
unindexed
unindicted
uninfluenced
uninformed
uninhabitable
uninhabited
uninhibited
uninjured
uninked
uninscribed
uninspired
uninspiringly
uninstructed
uninstructive
uninsulated
uninsurable
uninsured
unintegrated
unintelligent
unintelligible
unintended
unintentional
unintentionally
uninterested
uninterestedly
uninterestingly
unintermittingly

uninterruptedly
unintimated
unintimidated
unintoxicated
uninvaded
uninventive
uninvigorated
uninvitingly
union
unionism
unionist
unionization
unionize
unionized
unique
uniquely
uniqueness
unirradiated
unisex
unison
unissued
unit
unitarian
unitarianism
unitary
unite
united
unitedly
unity
universal
universalist
universality
universally

universe
university
unjokingly
unjust
unjustifiable
unjustifiably
unjustified
unjustly
unkempt
unkilled
unkind
unkindliness
unkindly
unknowable
unknowingly
unknown
unlabeled
unlace
unlaced
unladylike
unlamented
unlashed
unlatch
unlawful
unlawfully
unlawfulness
unleaded
unlearn
unleash
unleashed
unleavened
unless
unlettered

unliberated
unlicensed
unlighted
unlikable
unlike
unlikelihood
unlikely
unlimber
unlimbered
unlimited
unlined
unlisted
unload
unloaded
unlocalized
unlock
unlocked
unlooked
unloosen
unloved
unlovingly
unluckily
unlucky
unmade
unmagnified
unmaidenly
unmailable
unmake
unman
unmanageable
unmanliness
unmanly
unmanned

unmannerliness
unmannerly
unmarked
unmarriageable
unmarried
unmask
unmasked
unmatched
unmeasurable
unmeasured
unmentionable
unmentioned
unmerciful
unmercifully
unmerited
unmetered
unmindful
unmistakable
unmitigated
unmixed
unmolested
unmoored
unmortgaged
unmotivated
unmounted
unmoved
unmovingly
unnamed
unnatural
unnaturally
unnavigable
unnecessarily
unnecessary

unneeded
unneighborly
unnerve
unnoticeable
unnoticed
unnumbered
unobservant
unobserved
unobtainable
unoccupied
unofficial
unopened
unopinionated
unopposed
unorchestrated
unorganized
unorthodox
unostentatious
unpacified
unpack
unpaged
unpaid
unpainted
unpalatable
unparalleled
unpardonable
unpardoned
unparliamentary
unpasteurized
unpatentable
unpatented
unpatriotic
unpatriotically

unpatrolled
unpaved
unperceived
unperforated
unperformed
unperson
unperturbed
unpitying
unpityingly
unplanned
unplastered
unplayable
unpleasable
unpleasant
unpleasantly
unpleasantness
unpleasingly
unpledged
unplowed
unplugged
unplumbed
unpoetic
unpoliced
unpolished
unpolluted
unpopular
unpopulated
unpopulous
unpracticed
unprecedented
unprecedentedly
unpredictable
unprejudiced

unpremeditated
unprepared
unpreparedness
unprepossessing
unpresentable
unpretendingly
unpretentious
unpretentiously
unpretentiousness
unprincipled
unprintable
unprinted
unproduced
unproductive
unprofessional
unprofitable
unprogressive
unpromising
unprompted
unpronounceable
unpropitious
unprotected
unprovable
unproved
unprovided
unprovoked
unpublished
unpunctual
unpunctuality
unpunctually
unpunished
unqualified
unquelled

unquenchably
unquestionable
unquestionably
unquestioned
unquestioningly
unransomed
unravel
unraveled
unreachable
unread
unreadable
unreal
unrealistic
unreality
unrealized
unreasonable
unreasonably
unreasoned
unreasoningly
unrebuked
unreceipted
unreceptive
unreclaimable
unrecognizable
unrecognized
unrecognizingly
unreconcilable
unrecorded
unredeemable
unredeemed
unrefillable
unrefined
unrefrigerated

unrefuted
unregenerate
unregulated
unrehearsed
unrelated
unrelentingly
unreliability
unreliable
unremitting
unremunerative
unremuneratively
unrentable
unrented
unrepented
unreportable
unreported
unrepresentative
unreproachingly
unreproved
unrequited
unreserved
unreservedly
unresistingly
unresolved
unresourceful
unresponsive
unrest
unrested
unrestrained
unrestricted
unrevealingly
unrewarded
unrhymed

unrighteous
unrighteously
unrightfully
unripe
unripened
unrivaled
unroll
unrolled
unruffle
unruffled
unruled
unruly
unsaddened
unsaddle
unsaddled
unsafe
unsaid
unsalable
unsalaried
unsanctified
unsatiated
unsatisfactorily
unsatisfactory
unsatisfied
unsatisfyingly
unsaturated
unsavorily
unsavory
unscathed
unscented
unschooled
unscientific
unscramble

unscrew
unscrewed
unscrupulous
unscrupulously
unseal
unsealed
unseasonable
unseasoned
unseated
unseaworthy
unseconded
unsecured
unseeingly
unseemingly
unseemly
unseen
unselected
unselfish
unselfishly
unsensitized
unsentimental
unseparated
unserviceable
unsettle
unsettled
unshackle
unshackled
unshaded
unshakable
unshaken
unsharpened
unshaven
unsheathe

unshed
unsheltered
unshielded
unship
unshipped
unshrinkable
unshuffled
unsighted
unsightly
unsigned
unsingable
unsinkable
unsisterly
unsized
unskilled
unskillful
unskimmed
unsmilingly
unsmirched
unsmoked
unsmudged
unsnarl
unsociable
unsoftened
unsoil
unsoiled
unsold
unsoldierly
unsolicited
unsophisticated
unsought
unsound
unsoundly

unspeakable
unspecialized
unspecified
unspoiled
unspoken
unsportsmanlike
unspotted
unsprinkled
unstable
unstained
unstamped
unsteadily
unsteady
unsterilized
unstinted
unstintingly
unstrained
unstressed
unstrikable
unstrung
unsubstantial
unsubstantiated
unsuccessful
unsufferable
unsuitable
unsullied
unsummoned
unsung
unsupervised
unsure
unsurpassable
unsurpassed
unsuspected

unsuspecting
unsuspectingly
unswayed
unsweetened
unswervingly
unsworn
unsympathetic
unsympathizingly
unsystematic
unsystematized
untainted
untalented
untamed
untangle
untanned
untasted
untaught
untaxable
untaxed
unteachable
untechnical
untempted
untenantable
untenanted
untended
unterrified
unthickened
unthinkable
unthinking
unthinkingly
untidily
untidy
untie

untied
until
untimely
untinted
untiringly
untitled
unto
untold
untouchable
untouched
untoward
untraceable
untraded
untrained
untrammeled
untranslatable
untraveled
untried
untrimmed
untrodden
untroubled
untrue
untrussed
untrustworthy
untruth
untruthful
untuned
unturned
untutored
untwine
untwist
ununderstandable
unupbraidingly

unusable
unused
unusual
unusually
unutterable
unutterably
unuttered
unvalidated
unvalued
unvanquished
unvaried
unvarnished
unvaryingly
unvauntingly
unveil
unveiled
unverbalized
unverified
unversed
unvisited
unvoiced
unwalled
unwarily
unwarned
unwarrantable
unwarranted
unwary
unwashed
unwatered
unwaveringly
unwearied
unwearyingly
unwed

unwedded
unwelcome
unwell
unwept
unwholesome
unwholesomely
unwieldiness
unwieldy
unwilling
unwillingly
unwillingness
unwincingly
unwind
unwindingly
unwinkingly
unwise
unwitnessed
unwittingly
unwomanly
unwonted
unworkable
unworkmanlike
unworldliness
unworldly
unworn
unworried
unworthily
unworthiness
unworthy
unwound
unwounded
unwrap
unwrapped

unwreathe
unwrinkled
unwritten
unyieldingly
unyoked
up
upas
upbeat
upbraid
upbraided
upbraidingly
upbringing
up-country
update
updraft
upgrade
upgrowth
upheaval
upheld
uphill
uphold
upholder
upholster
upholstered
upholsterer
upholstery
upkeep
upland
uplift
uplifted
upliftingly
upmanship
upmost

upon
upper
uppermost
uppers
upraise
upraised
upright
uprightly
uprightness
uprisings
uproar
uproarious
uproariousness
uproot
uprooted
upset
upsettingly
upshot
upside
upstairs
upstart
upstate
upstream
upstroke
uptake
uptight
up-to-date
uptown
upturn
upturned
upward
upwind
uranium

urban
urbane
urbanely
urbanite
urbanity
urbanization
urbanize
urbanized
urbanoid
urbanologist
urchin
urge
urged
urgency
urgent
urgently
urgings
urn
us
usability
usable
usage
use
used
useful
usefully
usefulness
useless
uselessly
uselessness
user
uses
usher

ushered
usual
usually
usufruct
usurer
usurious
usurp
usurpation
usurper
usury

utensil
utilitarian
utilitarianism
utilities
utility
utilizable
utilization
utilize
utilized
utmost

utopia
utopian
utopianism
utter
utterance
uttered
utterly
uttermost
uvula
uvular

vacancy
vacant
vacate
vacated
vacation
vacationed
vacationist
vaccinate
vaccinated
vaccination
vaccinator
vaccine
vacillate
vacillated
vacillation
vacillatingly
vacillatory
vacuity
vacuous
vacuum
vagabond
vagabondage
vagabondia
vagabondism
vagabondize
vagary
vagrancy
vagrant
vague
vaguer
vaguest
vagus
vain
vainglorious
vainglory
vainly
vainness
valance
vale
valediction
valedictorian
valedictory
valence
valentine
valerian
valet
valetudinarian
Valhalla
valiant
valid
validate
validated
validation
validity
validly
valise
Valium
valley
valor
valorization
valorize
valorous
valuable
valuation
value
valued
valueless
valve
valvular

vamp
vampire
vanadium
vandal
vandalism
vandalize
vane
vanguard
vanilla
vanillin
vanish
vanished
vanishingly
vanity
vanquish
vanquished
vantage
vapid
vapidly
vapor
vaporings
vaporization
vaporize
vaporized
vaporizer
vaporous
variability
variable
variance
variant
variation
varicolored
varicose
varicosity
varied
variegate
variegated
variegation
varietal
variety
variola
variorum
various
variously
varlet
varnish
varnished
varnishings
varsity
vary
varyingly
vascular
vase
Vaseline
vassal
vassalage
vast
vaster
vastest
vastly
vat
Vatican
vaudeville
vault
vaulted
vaunt
vaunted
vauntingly
veal
vector
vedette
veer
veered
vegetable
vegetarian
vegetarianism
vegetate
vegetated
vegetation
vegetative
vehemence
vehement
vehemently
vehicle
vehicles
vehicular
veil
veiled
vein
veined
veinings
veinlet
vellum
velocipede
velocity
velodrome
velours
velvet
velveteen

velvety
venal
venality
venalization
venalize
venation
vend
vended
vendee
vendetta
vendible
vendor
veneer
veneered
venerable
venerate
venerated
veneration
venerative
Venetian
vengeance
vengeful
vengefulness
venial
veniality
venially
venison
venom
venomous
venomously
vent
vented
venthole

ventilate
ventilated
ventilation
ventilator
ventral
ventricle
ventricular
ventriloquism
ventriloquist
venture
ventured
venturesome
venue
veracious
veraciously
veracity
veranda
verbal
verbalism
verbalist
verbalization
verbalize
verbalized
verbally
verbatim
verbena
verbiage
verbose
verbosity
verdant
verdict
verdigris
verdure

verge
verged
verger
veriest
verifiable
verification
verified
verify
verily
verisimilitude
verism
veritable
veritably
verities
verity
vermeil
vermicelli
vermicide
vermiculate
vermiculation
vermiculite
vermiform
vermifuge
vermilion
vermin
verminous
vernacular
vernal
vernier
versatile
versatility
verse
versicle

versification
versified
versifier
versify
version
verso
versus
vertebra
vertebrae
vertebrate
vertex
vertical
vertically
vertiginous
vertigo
vervain
verve
very
vesicle
vesper
vessel
vest
vestal
vested
vestibular
vestibule
vestige
vestigial
vestment
vestry
vesture
vetch
veteran

veterinarian
veterinary
veto
vetoed
vex
vexation
vexatious
vexed
via
viability
viable
viaduct
vial
viand
viaticum
vibrancy
vibrant
vibrate
vibrated
vibratingly
vibration
vibrationless
vibrato
vibrator
vibratory
vicar
vicarage
vicariate
vicarious
vicariously
vice
vicegeral
vicegerent

vice president
vicereine
viceroy
vicinage
vicinities
vicinity
vicious
viciously
viciousness
vicissitude
victim
victimize
victimized
victimologist
victimology
victor
Victorian
victorious
victoriously
victory
Victrola
victual
vicuña
video
videophone
videotape
vie
view
viewed
vigil
vigilance
vigilant
vigilante

vigilantly
vignette
vignetted
vigor
vigorous
vigorously
Vikings
vile
viler
vilest
vilification
vilifier
vilify
villa
village
villager
villain
villainous
villainously
villainy
villanelle
vinaigrette
vinculum
vindicable
vindicate
vindicated
vindication
vindictive
vine
vinegar
vineyard
vinification
vinify

vinous
vintage
vintner
vinyl
viol
viola
violate
violated
violation
violative
violator
violence
violent
violently
violet
violin
violinist
violoncellist
violoncello
viper
viperous
virago
vireo
virgin
virginal
virginity
virile
virility
virtual
virtually
virtue
virtuosity
virtuoso

virtuous
virtuously
virtuousness
virulence
virulency
virulent
virus
visa
visage
vis-à-vis
viscera
visceral
viscid
viscidity
viscidly
viscose
viscosity
viscount
viscous
vise
visibility
visible
visibly
vision
visionary
visit
visitation
visited
visitor
vista
visual
visualization
visualize

visualized
visually
vital
vitality
vitalize
vitalized
vitally
vitamin
vitiate
vitiated
vitiation
vitreous
vitrifaction
vitrification
vitrified
vitrify
vitriol
vitriolic
vituperate
vituperated
vituperation
vituperative
vituperatively
vivacious
vivaciously
vivacity
vivarium
vivid
vividly
vivify
viviparous
vivisect
vivisection

vivisectionist
vixen
vixenish
vizard
vizier
vocable
vocabulary
vocal
vocalism
vocalist
vocalization
vocalize
vocalized
vocally
vocation
vocational
vocationally
vocative
vociferate
vociferated
vociferation
vociferous
vodka
vogue
voice
voiced
voiceless
voicelessly
voicelessness
voiceprint
void
voidable
voided

volatile
volatility
volatilization
volatilize
volatilized
volcanic
volcano
volcanology
volition
volitional
volitionally
volley
volleyball
volleyed
volt
voltage
voltaic
voltameter
voltammeter
voltmeter
volubility
voluble
volubly
volume
volumetric
voluminous
voluminously
voluminousness
voluntarily
voluntary
volunteer
volunteered
voluptuary

voluptuous
voluptuously
voluptuousness
volute
volvulus
vomit
vomited
vomitory
voodoo
voodooism
voracious
voracity
vortex
vortical
vortically
votary
vote

voted
voter
votive
vouch
vouched
voucher
vouchsafe
vouchsafed
vow
vowed
vowel
vowelization
vowelize
voyage
voyaged
voyager
vulcanization

vulcanize
vulcanized
vulcanizer
vulgar
vulgarian
vulgarism
vulgarity
vulgarization
vulgarize
vulgarized
vulgarizer
vulgarly
vulgate
vulnerability
vulnerable
vulnerably
vulture

W

wad
wadded
waddings
waddle
waddlingly
wade
waded
wader
wafer
waffle
waffling
waft
wag
wage
waged
wager
wagered
wagerings
wages
wagged
waggish
waggle
waggled

wagglingly
Wagnerian
wagon
wagtail
waif
wail
wailed
wailingly
wailings
wain
wainscot
waist
waistband
waistcoat
waistline
wait
waited
waiter
waitress
waive
waived
waiver
wake

waked
wakeful
wakefully
wakefulness
waken
wakened
wakingly
wale
waled
walk
walked
walker
walkover
walk-up
walkway
wall
wallboard
walled
wallet
walleyed
walkout
Walloon
wallop

wallow
wallowed
wallpaper
walnut
walrus
waltz
waltzed
wampum
wan
wand
wander
wandered
wanderer
wanderingly
wanderings
wane
waned
wangle
wangled
Wankel
want
wantable
wanted
wantingly
wanton
war
warble
warbled
warbler
warblingly
warblings
ward
warded

warden
warder
wardrobe
wardroom
warehouse
warehouseman
wareroom
wares
warfare
warily
wariness
warlike
warlock
warm
warmed
warmer
warmest
warmhearted
warmly
warmness
warmonger
warmth
warn
warned
warningly
warnings
warp
warpage
warpath
warped
warplane
warrant
warrantable

warranted
warrantor
warranty
warred
warren
warship
wart
wartime
wartless
wary
was
wash
washable
washboard
washbowl
washcloth
washed
washer
washhouse
washings
washout
washroom
washstand
wash-up
washwoman
wasn't
wasp
waspish
wassail
wastage
waste
wastebasket
wasted

wasteful
wastefully
wastefulness
wasteland
wastepaper
waster
wastingly
wastrel
watch
watchcase
watchdog
watched
watcher
watchful
watchfully
watchfulness
watchhouse
watchkeeper
watchmaker
watchman
watchtower
watchword
water
watered
waterfall
waterfinder
waterfowl
wateriness
waterings
waterline
waterlog
waterlogged
waterloo

waterman
watermark
watermelon
waterproof
waterproofed
watershed
waterside
waterspout
waterway
waterweed
waterworks
watery
watt
wattage
wattle
wattled
wattmeter
wave
waved
wavemeter
waver
wavered
waveringly
waverings
waviness
wavy
wax
waxed
waxen
waxiness
waxingly
waxwing
waxwork

waxy
way
waybill
wayfarer
wayfellow
waylaid
waylay
wayside
wayward
we
weak
weaken
weakened
weaker
weakest
weakling
weakly
weakness
weal
wealth
wealthier
wealthiest
wealthy
wean
weaned
weapon
weaponless
wear
wearability
wearable
wearer
wearied
wearier

weariest
wearily
weariness
wearings
wearisome
wearisomeness
weary
weasel
weather
weatherboard
weathercock
weathered
weatherproof
weatherproofed
weave
weaver
web
webbed
webbings
wed
wedded
weddings
wedge
wedged
wedlock
Wednesday
weed
weeded
weedier
weediest
weedy
week
weekday
weekend
weeklies
weekly
weep
weepingly
weevil
weft
weigh
weighed
weighmaster
weight
weighted
weightier
weightiest
weightings
weightlessness
weighty
weir
weird
weirdly
weirdness
welcome
welcomed
welcomingly
weld
welded
welfare
welkin
well
wellborn
welled
wellhead
wellhole
wellspring
welt
welted
welter
weltered
wen
wench
wend
wended
went
wept
were
werewolf
west
westerly
western
westerner
westward
wet
wetness
wettability
wettable
wetted
wetter
wettest
wettings
we've
whack
whacked
whale
whaleback
whalebone
whaleman

whaler
wharf
wharfage
wharfinger
what
whatever
whatnot
whatsoever
wheat
wheaten
wheatworm
wheedle
wheedled
wheedlingly
wheel
wheelbarrow
wheeled
wheelhouse
wheelwright
wheeze
wheezed
wheezier
wheeziest
wheezily
wheezingly
wheezy
whelk
whelp
whelped
when
whence
whenceforth
whenever
whensoever
where
whereabouts
whereafter
whereas
whereat
whereby
wherefore
wherefrom
wherein
whereof
whereon
wheresoever
whereupon
wherever
wherewith
wherewithal
wherry
whet
whether
whetted
whetstone
whey
which
whichever
whichsoever
whiff
whiffed
whiffle
whiffleball
whiffled
Whig
while
whiled
whilom
whim
whimper
whimpered
whimperingly
whimperings
whimsey
whimsical
whine
whined
whiningly
whinings
whinnied
whinny
whip
whipcord
whipped
whippersnapper
whippet
whippingly
whippings
whippoorwill
whipsaw
whipstitch
whipstock
whipworm
whir
whirl
whirled
whirligig
whirlingly
whirlpool

whirlwind
whirred
whisk
whisked
whisker
whiskered
whisky
whisper
whispered
whisperer
whisperingly
whisperings
whist
whistle
whistled
whistlingly
whistlings
whit
white
whitecap
whited
whitefish
whiten
whitened
whiteness
whitewash
whitewashed
whitewing
whitewood
whither
whitings
whitish
whitlow
whittle
whittled
whittlings
who
whoever
whole
wholehearted
wholeheartedly
wholesale
wholesaler
wholesome
wholesomely
wholly
whom
whomever
whomsoever
whoop
whooped
whoopingly
whose
whosoever
why
wick
wicked
wickedly
wickedness
wicker
wickerwork
wicket
wide
widely
widen
widened
wideness
wider
widespread
widest
widow
widowed
widower
widowhood
width
wield
wielded
wife
wifehood
wifeless
wifely
wig
wiggle
wiggled
wiggler
wigglings
wight
wiglet
wigmaker
wigwag
wigwam
wild
wilder
wilderness
wildest
wildfire
wildlifer
wildness
wile

wilier
wiliest
will
willed
willful
willfully
willfulness
willingly
willingness
willow
wilt
wilted
wily
win
wince
winced
wincingly
wind
wind
windage
windbag
windbreak
winded
winder
windfall
windily
windiness
windingly
windings
windjammer
windlass
windmill
window

windowed
windowpane
windpipe
windrow
windrowed
windshield
windstorm
windward
windwardly
windway
windy
wine
wineberry
wined
wineglass
wineskin
wing
winged
wingfish
wingless
wingspread
wink
winked
winkingly
winkle
winner
winningly
winnings
winnow
winnowed
winsome
winter
wintered

winterize
wipe
wiped
wiper
wire
wired
wireless
wirepuller
wirepulling
wireway
wirework
wireworker
wireworm
wiry
wisdom
wise
wiseacre
wisecrack
wisecracker
wisely
wiseness
wiser
wisest
wish
wishbone
wished
wishful
wishfully
wishfulness
wishingly
wisp
wispier
wispiest

wispy
wisteria
wistful
wistfully
wistfulness
wit
witch
witchcraft
witchery
witchingly
witchweed
with
withal
withdraw
withdrawal
withdrawn
withdrew
wither
withered
witheringly
withheld
withhold
withholdings
within
without
withstand
withstood
witless
witlessly
witlessness
witness
witnessed
witticism
wittier
wittiest
wittingly
witty
wived
wives
wizard
wizardly
wizardry
wizened
woad
wobble
wobbled
wobbliness
wobblingly
wobbly
woe
woebegone
woeful
woefully
woefulness
wok
wolf
wolfed
wolfhound
wolfish
wolverine
wolves
woman
womanhood
womanish
womankind
womanlike
womanliness
womanly
women
won
wonder
wondered
wonderful
wonderfully
wonderingly
wonderland
wonderment
wonderwork
wondrous
wondrously
won't
wont
woo
wood
woodbin
woodbine
woodchuck
woodcraft
woodcut
wooded
wooden
woodenhead
woodfish
woodland
woodman
woodpecker
woodpile
woodshop
woodsman

woodwork
woodworker
woodworm
wooed
wooer
woof
wool
woolen
woollier
woolliest
woolliness
woolly
woolwork
woolworker
woozy
word
wordage
wordbuilding
worded
wordier
wordiest
wordily
wordiness
wordless
wordplay
wordy
wore
work
workability
workable
workaholic
workbag
workbasket
workbench
workbook
workbox
workday
worked
worker
workfare
workhouse
workingman
workings
workless
workman
workmanlike
workmanship
workmen
workout
workpan
workpeople
workplace
workplaces
workshop
worktable
workwoman
workwomen
world
worldliness
worldly
worm
wormed
wormhole
wormier
wormiest
wormlike
wormproof
wormwood
wormy
worn
worried
worriedly
worrier
worriment
worrisome
worrisomeness
worry
worse
worsen
worsened
worship
worshiped
worshiper
worshipful
worshipfully
worst
worsted
worsted
worth
worthier
worthiest
worthily
worthiness
worthwhile
worthy
would
wouldn't
wound
wound

wounded
woundingly
woundless
wove
woven
wrack
wraith
wraithlike
wrangle
wrangled
wrap
wraparound
wrapped
wrapper
wrappings
wrath
wrathful
wrathfully
wrathfulness
wreak
wreaked
wreath
wreathed
wreck
wreckage
wrecked
wrecker
wren
wrench
wrenched
wrest
wrested
wrestle
wrestled
wrestler
wretch
wretched
wretchedly
wretchedness
wriggle
wriggled
wrigglingly
wriggly
wring
wringer
wrinkle
wrinkled
wrinklier
wrinkliest
wrinkly
wrist
wristband
wristbone
wristlet
wristlock
writ
writable
write
writer
writhe
writhed
writhingly
writings
written
wrong
wrongdoer
wronged
wrongful
wrongfully
wrongheaded
wrongly
wrongness
wrote
wroth
wrought
wrung
wry
wryneck

xyz

xenon
xenophile
xenophobia
xeroderma
xerogram
xerography
xerosis
Xerox
X ray
xylophone

yacht
yachtsman
yak
Yale
yam
yammer
yank
yanked
Yankee
yard
yardage
yardarm
yardman
yardmaster
yardstick
yarn
yarrow
yataghan
yaw
yawl
yawn
yawned
yawningly
ye
yea
year
yearbook
yearling
yearly
yearn
yearned
yearningly
yearnings
yeast
yeasty
yell
yelled
yellow
yellowed
yellower
yellowest
yellowish
yellowishness
yelp
yelped
yeoman
yeomanry
yes
yesterday
yet
yew
Yiddish
yield
yielded
yieldingly
yieldingness
yodel
yodeled

yodeler
yoga
yoghurt
yoke
yoked
yokefellow
yokel
yokelry
yolk
yon
yonder
yore
you
young
younger
youngest
youngish
youngster
your
yours
yourself
yourselves
youth
youthful
youthfully
youthfulness
youths
ytterbium
yttrium
Yucca
yule
yuletide

zany
zeal
zealot
zealotry
zealous
zealously
zealousness
zebra
zebroid
zebu
zenith
zeolite
zephyr
zeppelin
zero
zest
zestful
zigzag
zinc
Zion
Zionism
ZIP
zipper
zircon
zirconium
zither
zodiac
zone
zoned
zoo
zoological
zoologist
zoology
zoom
zoomed
zoomer
Zulu
zymase
zymology

part two

Part Two is devoted to the writing of names in shorthand. It contains:

177 common names of women.

189 common names of men.

1,015 most common surnames in the United States taken from a list compiled by the Social Security Administration.

In general, it is wise to write names as fully as possible because context is of no assistance in transcribing. If a name occurs several times during dictation and it appears that it may be used several times more, the writer might improvise a shortcut for it. For example, if the dictator uses the name *Mr. Baldwin* several times, the writer might abbreviate it to the brief form *Mr.* with an intersected *b*. However, when the name ***Baldwin*** comes up again in dictation sometime later, the writer would be wise to write it again in full.

People are proud of their names, and they are understandably annoyed when their names are misspelled. Therefore, check carefully when the name *Brown*, for example, is dictated to determine whether it is spelled *Brown or Browne*—the shorthand outline is the same.

names

Common Names of Women

Abby	Camilla	Eileen
Adelaide	Carmen	Elaine
Adele	Carmelita	Eleanor
Agnes	Carol	Elizabeth
Alberta	Catherine	Ellen
Alexandria	Cecilia	Elsa
Alice	Charlotte	Emily
Amelia	Christine	Emma
Amy	Claire	Estelle
Angela	Clara	Esther
Ann	Clementine	Ethel
Anita	Constance	Eunice
Annabelle	Cynthia	Eve
Antoinette	Daphne	Evelyn
Arlene	Deborah	Felicita
Barbara	Della	Florence
Bertha	Diana	Frances
Bessie	Dolores	Francesca
Beth	Donna	Gail
Betsy	Doris	Gertrude
Betty	Dorothy	Gloria
Blanche	Edith	Grace
Bonnie	Edna	Harriet

Helen
Inez
Irene
Iris
Isabel
Jane
Janice
Jean
Jennifer
Jill
Jo
Joan
Jody
Juanita
Judith
Judy
Julie
Juliet
Karen
Kathleen
Kathy
Katie
Laura
Lillian
Linda
Lisa
Lois
Loretta
Lorraine
Louella
Louise
Lucretia
Lucy
Luz
Lydia
Mabel
Madeline
Madge
Marcy
Margaret
Margarita
Maria
Marian
Marilyn
Marion
Marjorie
Marsha
Martha
Mary
Maureen
Meg
Melissa
Mercedes
Michelle
Mildred
Miranda
Molly
Monica
Muriel
Myra
Nancy
Nannette
Nellie
Norma
Olga
Pamela
Pat
Patricia
Patsy
Paula
Pearl
Peggy
Phyllis
Polly
Priscilla
Rachel
Ramona
Rebecca
Rita
Roberta
Robin
Rosa
Rosalie
Rosario
Rosita
Roxanne
Ruby
Ruth
Sally
Sarah
Shirley
Sue
Susan
Sylvia
Terry
Thelma
Theresa
Tina
Toby

Trudy
Valerie
Victoria
Violet
Vivian
Wanda
Wendy
Wilma
Zelda

Common Names of Men

Aaron
Abraham
Adam
Albert
Alexander
Alfonso
Alfred
Allen
Andrew
Angelo
Anthony
Antonio
Arnold
Arthur
Barry
Benjamin
Bernard
Bill
Bob
Boris
Boyd
Bradley
Brian
Caesar
Camilo
Carl
Carlos
Charles
Chester
Christopher
Clarence
Claude
Clyde
Craig
Daniel
David
Dennis
Dick
Dominic
Donald
Douglas
Dudley
Duncan
Dwight
Edgar
Edmund
Edward
Edwin
Elliott
Emerson
Emil
Emmanuel
Enrique
Eric
Ernest
Eugene
Everett
Felix
Felipe
Fernando
Foster
Francis
Frank
Franklin
Frederick
Gabriel
Gary
Geoffrey
George
Gerald
Gilbert
Glenn
Gordon
Graham
Gregory
Guillermo
Harold
Harry

Harvey
Hector
Henry
Herbert
Herman
Hernandez
Horace
Howard
Hubert
Hugh
Ignacio
Irving
Isaac
Jack
Jacob
James
Jay
Jerome
Jerry
Jesus
Jim
Joe
John
Jonathan
Jose
Joseph
Juan
Julio
Keith
Kelly
Kenneth
Kevin
Larry

Lawrence
Lee
Leo
Leon
Leonard
Leroy
Leslie
Lester
Louis
Manuel
Marco
Marcus
Mario
Mark
Martin
Matthew
Melvin
Michael
Miguel
Milton
Mitchell
Morris
Murray
Nathan
Nicholas
Nolan
Norman
Oliver
Oscar
Otto
Owen
Patrick
Paul

Pedro
Perry
Peter
Philip
Rafael
Ralph
Randolph
Raymond
Ricardo
Richard
Robert
Robin
Roland
Ronald
Roy
Rudolph
Rufus
Russell
Samuel
Scott
Seth
Sherman
Sherwood
Sidney
Simon
Solomon
Stanley
Stephen
Stuart
Theodore
Thomas
Timothy
Vernon

Victor	Walter	William
Vincent	Warren	Winston
Virgil	Wilbur	Woodrow
Wallace	Wilfred	Zeke

Most Common Surnames in the United States As Compiled by the Social Security Administration

Abbott	Bailey	Beard
Abrams	Baird	Beasley
Adams	Baker	Beatty
Adkinson	Baldwin	Beck
Alberts	Ball	Becker
Albright	Ballard	Belcher
Alexander	Banks	Bell
Alford	Barber	Bender
Allen	Barker	Benjamin
Allison	Barlow	Bennett
Alvarez	Barnes	Benson
Anderson	Barnett	Bentley
Andrews	Barr	Benton
Anthony	Barrett	Berg
Archer	Barron	Berger
Armstrong	Barry	Bernard
Arnold	Bartlett	Bernstein
Arthur	Barton	Berry
Ashley	Bass	Best
Atkins	Bates	Billings
Austin	Bauer	Bird
Avery	Baxter	Bishop
Ayers	Beach	Black
Bacon	Bean	Blackburn

Blackman
Blackwell
Blair
Blake
Blanchard
Blevins
Bloom
Bolton
Bond
Bonner
Boone
Booth
Bowen
Bowers
Bowman
Boyd
Boyer
Boyle
Bradford
Bradley
Bradshaw
Brady
Branch
Brandt
Braun
Bray
Brennan
Brenner
Brewer
Bridges
Briggs
Bright
Britt

Britton
Brock
Brooks
Brown
Brownell
Browning
Bruce
Bruno
Bryant
Buchanan
Buck
Buckley
Bullock
Burch
Burgess
Burke
Burnett
Burns
Burris
Burt
Burton
Bush
Butler
Byers
Byrd
Byrne
Cain
Caldwell
Calhoun
Callahan
Camero
Camp
Campbell

Cannon
Cantrell
Carey
Carlson
Carney
Carpenter
Carr
Carson
Carter
Carver
Case
Casey
Cash
Castello
Castro
Chamberlain
Chandler
Chaney
Chapman
Chappell
Charles
Chase
Cherry
Childers
Childs
Christian
Christiansen
Churchill
Clark
Clay
Clayton
Clemens
Clements

Cline
Cobb
Cochran
Coffey
Cohen
Cole
Coleman
Collier
Collins
Colon
Colton
Combs
Compton
Conklin
Connelly
Connor
Connors
Conrad
Conway
Cook
Cooley
Cooper
Corbett
Cornell
Costa
Costello
Courtney
Cowan
Cox
Craft
Craig
Cramer
Crane
Crawford
Crockett
Crosby
Cross
Crowley
Cruz
Cummings
Cunningham
Curran
Currier
Curry
Curtis
Dailey
Dale
Dalton
Daniels
Daugherty
Davenport
Davids
Davis
Dawson
Day
Dean
Decker
Delaney
Delgado
Dempsey
Dennis
Denton
Diaz
Dick
Dickerson
Dickinson
Dickson
Dillard
Dillon
Dixon
Dodd
Dodson
Doherty
Dolan
Domingo
Donahue
Donald
Donnell
Donovan
Dorsey
Dougherty
Douglas
Downey
Downing
Downs
Doyle
Drake
Driscoll
Dudley
Duffy
Duncan
Dunlop
Dunn
Durham
Dwyer
Dyer
Eaton
Edmonds
Edwards

Elder
Elliott
Ellis
Ellison
Emerson
Emery
England
English
Erickson
Espinosa
Estes
Evans
Everett
Ewing
Farley
Farmer
Farrell
Farris
Faulkner
Feldman
Ferguson
Fernandez
Ferrell
Field
Fields
Figueroa
Finch
Fink
Finley
Fisher
Fitzgerald
Fitzpatrick
Flanagan

Fleming
Fletcher
Flores
Flowers
Flynn
Forbes
Ford
Foster
Fowler
Fox
Francis
Frank
Franklin
Franks
Frazier
Frederick
Freeman
French
Frey
Friedman
Fritz
Frost
Fry
Fullerton
Fulton
Gaines
Gallagher
Galloway
Gamble
Garcia
Gardner
Garner
Garrett

Garrison
Garza
Gay
Gentry
George
Gibbons
Gibbs
Gibson
Gilbert
Giles
Gill
Gillespie
Gilliam
Gilmore
Glass
Gleason
Glenn
Glover
Godfrey
Goff
Goldberg
Golden
Goldman
Goldstein
Gomez
Gonzales
Good
Goodman
Goodwin
Gordon
Gorman
Gould
Grady

Graham
Grant
Graves
Green
Greenberg
Greer
Gregg
Gregory
Griffin
Griffith
Grimes
Gross
Gustafson
Guthrie
Gutierrez
Guzman
Haas
Hahn
Haines
Hale
Haley
Hall
Hamilton
Hammond
Hampton
Hancock
Hanna
Hanson
Harder
Harding
Hardy
Harmon
Harper
Harrell
Harrington
Harris
Harrison
Hart
Hartley
Hartman
Harvey
Hastings
Hatfield
Hawkins
Hayden
Hayes
Haynes
Head
Heath
Hebert
Heller
Helms
Henderson
Hendricks
Hendrickson
Henning
Henry
Hensen
Hensley
Herbert
Herman
Hernandez
Herrera
Herring
Hess
Hester
Hewitt
Hickman
Hicks
Higgins
Hill
Hilton
Hines
Hinkle
Hinton
Hobbs
Hodge
Hodges
Hoffmann
Hogan
Holcomb
Holden
Holland
Holley
Holloway
Holman
Holmes
Holt
Hood
Hooper
Hoover
Hopper
Horne
Horton
Hoskins
House
Houston
Howard
Howell

Hubbard
Huber
Hudson
Huff
Huffman
Hughes
Hull
Humphrey
Hunt
Hunter
Hurley
Hurst
Hutchinson
Hyde
Ingram
Irwin
Jackson
Jacobs
Jacobson
James
Jarvis
Jefferson
Jenkins
Jennings
Jensen
Jiminez
Johnson
Johnston
Jones
Jordan
Joseph
Joyce
Justice

Kaiser
Kaplan
Katz
Kaufman
Keith
Keller
Kelly
Kemp
Kendall
Kennedy
Kent
Kern
Kerr
Kessler
Key
Kidd
King
Kinney
Kirby
Kirk
Kirkland
Kirkpatrick
Klein
Knapp
Knight
Knowles
Knox
Koch
Kramer
Krause
Krueger
Kuhn
Lake

Lamb
Lambert
Lancaster
Landry
Lane
Lang
Larkin
Larson
Law
Lawrence
Lawson
Leach
LeBlanc
Lee
Leonard
Lester
Levine
Levy
Lewis
Lindsey
Little
Livingston
Lloyd
Locke
Logan
Long
Lopez
Love
Lowe
Lowery
Lund
Lutz
Lynch

Lynn
Lyon
Lyons
Mack
Mackey
Madden
Maddox
Mahoney
Maldonado
Malone
Maloney
Mann
Manning
Marino
Marks
Marsh
Marshall
Martin
Martinez
Mason
Massey
Mathis
Matthews
Maxwell
May
Mayer
Mayfield
Maynard
Mayo
Mays
McBride
McCabe
McCall
McCann
McCarthy
McCauley
McClain
McClure
McCollum
McConnell
McCormack
McCoy
McCullum
McDaniels
McDermott
McDonald
McDowell
McFadden
McFarland
McGee
McGill
McGinnis
McGowan
McGrath
McGuire
McIntosh
McIntyre
McKay
McKee
McKenna
McKenzie
McKinnon
McKnight
McLaughlin
McLean
McLeod
McMahon
McMillan
McNamara
McNeil
McPherson
Meadows
Medina
Melton
Mendez
Mendoza
Mercer
Merrill
Merritt
Metcalf
Meyers
Middleton
Michaels
Milendez
Miles
Miller
Mills
Minor
Mitchell
Molinar
Monroe
Montgomery
Moody
Moon
Mooney
Moore
Morales
Moran
Moreno

Morgan
Morris
Morrison
Morrow
Morse
Morton
Moser
Moses
Mosley
Moss
Moyer
Mueller
Mullen
Munoz
Murphy
Murray
Myer
Myers
Nash
Neal
Nelson
Newell
Newman
Newton
Nichols
Nicholson
Nielsen
Nixon
Noble
Nolan
Norman
Norris
Norton

Novak
O'Brien
O'Connell
O'Connor
Odell
Odom
O'Donnell
Oliver
Olson
O'Neal
Orr
Ortiz
Osborne
Ott
Owen
Owens
Pace
Padilla
Page
Palmer
Park
Parker
Parks
Parrish
Parsons
Pate
Patrick
Patterson
Patton
Paul
Payne
Pearce
Pearson

Peck
Pedersen
Pena
Pennington
Perez
Perkins
Perry
Peters
Petersen
Peterson
Petty
Phillips
Pickett
Pierce
Pierson
Pike
Pittman
Pitts
Pollard
Pool
Pope
Potter
Potts
Powell
Powers
Preston
Price
Prichard
Prince
Proctor
Pruitt
Pryor
Pugh

Quinn
Ramirez
Ramos
Ramsey
Randall
Randolph
Rankin
Rasmussen
Ray
Raymond
Reed
Reese
Reeves
Reilly
Reyes
Reynolds
Rhodes
Rice
Rich
Richard
Richards
Richardson
Richmond
Richter
Riddle
Riggs
Riley
Rios
Ritchie
Ritter
Rivera
Rivers
Roach

Robbins
Roberson
Roberts
Robertson
Robinson
Robison
Rodriguez
Rogers
Rollins
Roman
Romero
Rose
Rosen
Rosenberg
Ross
Rossi
Roth
Rowe
Rowland
Roy
Rubin
Ruiz
Rush
Russell
Russo
Rutherford
Ryan
Salazar
Sampson
Sanchez
Sanders
Sanford
Santiago

Santos
Sargent
Saunders
Savage
Sawyer
Schaefer
Schiller
Schmitt
Schneider
Schoemaker
Schreiber
Schroeder
Schultz
Schwartz
Scott
Sears
Sellers
Sexton
Shaffer
Shannon
Shapiro
Sharpe
Shaw
Shea
Sheehan
Shelton
Shepard
Shepherd
Sherman
Shield
Short
Siegel
Silva

Silver
Silverman
Simmons
Simon
Simpson
Sims
Singer
Single
Skinner
Slater
Slaughter
Sloan
Small
Smith
Snow
Snyder
Solomon
Sorensen
Soto
Sparks
Spears
Spencer
Springer
Stafford
Stanley
Stanton
Stark
Starr
Steele
Stein
Steinberg
Steiner
Stern

Stevens
Stevenson
Steward
Stewart
Stokes
Stone
Stout
Streeter
Strickland
Strong
Stuart
Sullivan
Summers
Sutherland
Sutton
Swanson
Sweeney
Sweet
Talley
Tate
Taylor
Temple
Terrell
Terry
Thompson
Thornton
Todd
Torres
Townsend
Tracy
Travis
Tucker
Turner

Tuttle
Tyler
Underwood
Valdez
Valentine
Vance
Vandermeer
Vargos
Vasquez
Vaughan
Vega
Velez
Vincent
Vogel
Wade
Wagner
Waldron
Walker
Wall
Wallace
Waller
Walls
Walsh
Walter
Walters
Walton
Ward
Ware
Warner
Warren
Washington
Waters
Watkins

Watson
Watts
Webb
Weber
Webster
Weeks
Weiss
Welch
Wells
Welsh
Werner
West
Whalen
Wheeler
Whitaker
White
Whitehead
Whitfield
Whitney
Whitten
Wiggins
Wilcox
Wilder
Wiley
Wilkins
Wilkinson
Williams
Williamson
Willis
Wills
Wilson
Winkler
Winters
Wise
Witt
Wolfe
Wong
Wood
Woodard
Woodruff
Woods
Woodward
Wooten
Workman
Wright
Wyatt
Wynn
Yates
Yong
York
Ziegler
Zimmerman

part three

Part Three is devoted to the writing of geographical names. It is divided into three sections: (1) The United States; (2) Principal Cities of the United States; and (3) Foreign geographical expressions. It contains:

51 States

90 American cities

382 Foreign geographical expressions

In writing American geographical expressions, it is usually safe to use abbreviated forms such as *n-e-b* for *Nebraska* and *n-a-r-k* for *Newark*. However, there are occasions when the writer must be careful when transcribing an abbreviated form. Is it *Pittsburgh* (with the *h*), *Pennsylvania*; or is it *Pittsburg* (without the *h*), *Kansas*? Is it *Worcester, Massachusetts*, or *Wooster, Ohio*?

Some of the foreign geographical expressions may safely be abbreviated, such as *e-ing* for *England* and *k-a-n* for *Canada*. The writer would be wise, however, to write most foreign cities and countries as fully as possible.

geographical expressions

United States

Alabama [AL]	Louisiana [LA]	Ohio [OH]
Alaska [AK]	Maine [ME]	Oklahoma [OK]
Arizona [AZ]	Maryland [MD]	Oregon [OR]
Arkansas [AR]	Massachusetts [MA]	Pennsylvania [PA]
California [CA]	Michigan [MI]	Rhode Island [RI]
Colorado [CO]	Minnesota [MN]	South Carolina [SC]
Connecticut [CT]	Mississippi [MS]	South Dakota [SD]
Delaware [DE]	Missouri [MO]	Tennessee [TN]
Florida [FL]	Montana [MT]	Texas [TX]
Georgia [GA]	Nebraska [NE]	United States [U.S.]
Hawaii [HI]	Nevada [NV]	Utah [UT]
Idaho [ID]	New Hampshire [NH]	Vermont [VT]
Illinois [IL]	New Jersey [NJ]	Virginia [VA]
Indiana [IN]	New Mexico [NM]	Washington [WA]
Iowa [IA]	New York [NY]	West Virginia [WV]
Kansas [KS]	North Carolina [NC]	Wisconsin [WI]
Kentucky [KY]	North Dakota [ND]	Wyoming [WY]

Principal Cities of the United States

Akron	Baltimore	Bridgeport
Albany	Birmingham	Buffalo
Atlanta	Boston	Cambridge

Camden
Canton
Charlotte
Chattanooga
Chicago
Cincinnati
Cleveland
Columbus
Dallas
Dayton
Denver
Des Moines
Detroit
Duluth
Elizabeth
Erie
Fall River
Flint
Fort Wayne
Fort Worth
Gary
Grand Rapids
Hartford
Houston
Indianapolis
Jacksonville
Jersey City

Kansas City
Knoxville
Long Beach
Los Angeles
Louisville
Lowell
Memphis
Miami
Milwaukee
Minneapolis
Nashville
Newark
New Bedford
New Haven
New Orleans
New York
Norfolk
Oakland
Oklahoma City
Omaha
Paterson
Philadelphia
Phoenix
Pittsburgh
Portland
Providence
Reading

Richmond
Rochester
Sacramento
St. Louis
St. Paul
Salt Lake City
San Antonio
San Diego
San Francisco
Scranton
Seattle
Somerville
South Bend
Spokane
Springfield
Syracuse
Tacoma
Tampa
Toledo
Trenton
Tulsa
Utica
Washington
Wichita
Wilmington
Worcester
Yonkers

Foreign Geographical Expressions

Acapulco
Accra
Addis Ababa

Adelaide
Afghanistan
Africa

Albania
Alberta
Alexandria

Algiers
Amazon
Amoy
Amsterdam
Angola
Anguilla
Ankara
Antwerp
Arabia
Argentina
Armenia
Aruba
Asia
Assam
Athens
Atlantic
Auckland
Austerlitz
Australia
Austria
Avalon
Azores
Baalbek
Baden
Baghdad
Bahamas
Baku
Bangkok
Bangladesh
Bataan
Bayreuth
Beirut
Belfast

Belgian
Belgium
Belgrade
Belize
Bengal
Berlin
Bermuda
Biafra
Bikini
Bismarck
Bizerte
Blenheim
Bohemia
Bolivia
Bombay
Bonn
Bosporus
Brandenburg
Brazil
Bremen
Brindisi
Brisbane
Bristol
Brittany
Bucharest
Buchenwald
Buckingham
Budapest
Buenos Aires
Burma
Cádiz
Cairo
Calais

Cambodia
Canada
Canadian
Canberra
Canton
Cape Town
Capri
Cardiff
Caspian
Cebu
Ceylon
Chatham
Cherbourg
Chesterfield
Chile
China
Cologne
Colombia
Congo
Costa Rica
Crete
Cuba
Cyprus
Czechoslovakia
Dacca
Damascus
Danube
Danzig
Delhi
Denmark
Devon
Dnieper
Dover

Dresden
Dublin
Dumbarton
Dundee
Dunkirk
Ecuador
Edinburgh
Edmonton
Egypt
Eifel
Eire
England
Equator
Eritrea
Estonia
Ethiopia
Europe
Finland
France
Frankfurt
Galata
Galilee
Ganges
Gascony
Gaza
Germany
Ghana
Ghent
Gibraltar
Ginza
Glasgow
Goa
Gobi

Granada
Great Britain
Guatemala
Guinea
Haiti
Hamburg
Hangchow
Hanoi
Heidelberg
Helsinki
Hispania
Holland
Honan
Honduras
Hong Kong
Iceland
India
Indies
Indochina
Indonesia
Ipswich
Iran
Iraq
Ireland
Israel
Istanbul
Italy
Jamaica
Japan
Java
Johannesburg
Jordan
Jutland

Kashmir
Kenya
Khartoum
Kiel
Kimberley
Klondike
Kobe
Korea
Kowloon
Kuwait
Labrador
Laconia
Lagos
Lahore
Lancaster
Laos
La Paz
Latvia
Lebanon
Leipzig
Leyte
Liberia
Libya
Lisbon
Lithuania
Liverpool
London
Lucerne
Luxembourg
Luzon
Lyons
Madagascar
Madrid

Maidenhead
Majorca
Malay
Malta
Manchester
Manchuria
Manila
Manitoba
Martinique
Mediterranean
Mekong
Mexico
Milan
Mindanao
Minsk
Mongolia
Montenegro
Monterrey
Montreal
Murmansk
Nanking
Naples
Nassau
Natal
Nepal
Netherlands
Nevis
Newcastle
Newfoundland
Nigeria
Nile
Nippon
Norway

Norwegian
Nottingham
Nova Scotia
Nuremberg
Odessa
Olympus
Oman
Ontario
Oran
Oslo
Ottawa
Oxford
Pakistan
Palermo
Palestine
Panama
Paraguay
Paris
Parma
Persia
Perth
Peru
Pisa
Poland
Pompeii
Portugal
Portuguese
Prague
Prussia
Puerto Rico
Punjab
Pyrenees
Queensland

Quemoy
Rabat
Ramsgate
Rangoon
Rhine
Rhineland
Rhodes
Riga
Rio de Janeiro
Riviera
Rome
Rotterdam
Ruhr
Rumania
Russia
Saar
Sahara
Saigon
Salerno
Salonika
Salvador
Salzburg
Samoa
Samos
San Jose
San Juan
Santiago
São Paulo
Sardinia
Saskatchewan
Saskatoon
Saudi Arabia
Scandinavia

Scotland
Seine
Seoul
Serbia
Seville
Sfax
Shanghai
Shetland
Siam
Siberia
Sicily
Sinai
Singapore
Southampton
Spain
Spanish
Strasbourg
Sudan
Suez
Sumatra
Sweden
Switzerland
Sydney
Syria
Tabriz
Tahiti

Tallinn
Tehran
Tel Aviv
Thailand
Thames
The Hague
Tibet
Timor
Tonkin
Toronto
Transvaal
Trieste
Trinidad
Tripoli
Tunis
Tunisia
Turin
Turkey
Tyre
Ukraine
Ulm
Ural
Uruguay
Valencia
Valletta

Valparaiso
Vancouver
Vatican
Venezuela
Venice
Versailles
Vichy
Vienna
Vietnam
Volga
Wales
Warsaw
West Indies
Westphalia
Yalu
Yangtze
Yarmouth
Yemen
Yugoslavia
Yukon
Zagreb
Zanzibar
Zeeland
Zion
Zurich

part four

Part Four consists of a compilation of 1,396 useful business phrases presented in alphabetical order. The phrases were selected from a phrase study made by the authors of the phrasing content of 1,500 business letters representing 50 types of businesses. In all, the letters contained 250,143 running words.

The phrases in this compilation are useful to every shorthand writer, no matter in which field he or she uses shorthand. However, the phrases must be so well learned that they come to the writer's mind automatically. If the writer must pause for even the slightest fraction of a second in composing or recalling the outline for a phrase, that phrase becomes a handicap rather than a help.

Occasionally, writers may find it helpful to devise a phrase or shortcut of their own to represent an expression that occurs again and again in their dictation. For example, if a writer finds that the book title *Gregg Shorthand Dictionary* occurs again and again in the dictation (as it would occur in the dictation of a stenographer working for one of the authors of this book), he or she might abbreviate the title to *gay*-intersected *ish-d*.

This expedient, however, should be used with caution. A few such shortcuts will be helpful; too many can be a handicap.

frequently used phrases

able to say
about it
about my
about that
about that time
about the
about the matter
about the time
about them
about this
about this time
about which
about your
after that
after that time
after the
after these
after this
along this
among the
among these
and are
and have

and his
and hope
and I will
and I will be
and is
and let us
and let us know
and our
and see
and the
any one
any one of our
any one of the
any one of them
any other
any time
any way
are not
are sure
are you
as a result
as if
as it has been

as it is
as it will
as it will be
as many
as much
as soon as
as soon as possible
as soon as the
as soon as you can
as that
as that is not
as the
as there was
as there will be
as these
as they
as they are
as they can
as they can be
as they cannot
as they did
as they have
as they will
as this
as this is
as this may
as this may be
as though
as to
as to that
as to the
as to these
as to this

as we
as we are
as we are not
as we can
as we cannot
as well
as yet
as you
as you are
as you can
as you cannot
as you did
as you do
as you do not
as you have
as you know
as you may
as you may be
as you may have
as you might
as you might be
as you might have
as you must
as you must be
as you must have
as you will
as you will be
as you will find
as you will have
as you will not
as you will not be
as you will see
as you would

as you would be
as you would be able
as you would have
as you would not
as your
ask the
ask you
at a loss
at a time
at last
at least
at length
at that
at that time
at the
at the time
at these
at this
at this time
at which time
be able
be done
be sure
been able
before it is
before many
before that
before that time
before the
before they
before us
before you
before you are

before you can
before your
being able
being sure
business world
by it
by mail
by means
by myself
by that
by that time
by the
by the time
by the way
by them
by themselves
by these
by this
by this time
by us
by which
by which it is
by which time
by which you can
by which you may
by you
can be
can be done
can be sure
can have
can say
can see
can you

can you give
can you give us
cannot be
cannot be done
cannot be sure
cannot have
cannot pay
cannot say
cannot see
can't be
centuries ago
check up
Cordially yours
could be
could be done
could be sure
could have
could have been
could not
could not be
could not say
could not see
could say
could see
day or two
day or two ago
days ago
Dear Madam
Dear Miss
Dear Mr.
Dear Mrs.
Dear Ms.
Dear Sir
did not
do it
do not
do not have
do not pay
do not say
do not see
do so
do that
do the
do this
do you
do you know
do you mean
do you think
do you want
does not
does not have
doing so
each case
each day
each month
each morning
each one
each other
each time
ever since
every minute
every month
every one
every one of the
every one of them
every one of these

every other
face to face
few days
few days ago
few minutes
few minutes ago
few moments
few moments ago
few months
few months ago
few times
for a few days
for a few minutes
for a few months
for a long time
for his
for it
for me
for Mr.
for Mrs.
for Ms.
for my
for myself
for next month
for next year
for one
for one thing
for our
for so long a time
for some years
for that
for the
for the last

for the present
for the time
for them
for these
for this
for us
for which
for whom
for you
for your convenience
for your information
for yourself
from him
from his
from it
from our
from that
from that time
from the
from them
from these
from this
from time
from us
from which
from you
gave me
gave us
gave you
give me
give us
give you
glad to have

glad to hear
glad to know
glad to receive
glad to say
glad to see
glad to send
glad to send you
good deal
good many
good many of the
good many of them
good many of these
good time
had been
had not
had not been
has been
has been able
has been done
has come
has done
has given
has made
has not
has not been
has not been able
has not yet
has not yet been
has that
has the
has this
has to
has written

have been
have been able
have done
have had
have made
have not
have not been
have not been able
have not yet
have not yet been
have you
have you made
he called
he came
he can
he can be
he can be sure
he can have
he can make
he cannot
he cannot be
he cannot have
he can't
he could
he could not
he did
he did not
he did not pay
he did not say
he did not see
he didn't
he does
he does not

he felt
he found
he gave
he gives
he is
he is not
he knew
he knows
he lost
he made
he may
he may be
he may be able
he may be sure
he may have
he mentioned
he might be
he might have
he might have been
he might not
he must
he must be
he must have
he needed
he needs
he said
he saw
he says
he seemed
he should
he should be
he should be able
he should have
he should not
he told
he took
he wanted
he wants
he was
he will
he will be
he will be able
he will be glad
he will find
he will have
he will not
he will not be able
he will see
he wished
he would
he would be
he would be able
he would be glad
he would have
he would not
he would not be
hear from him
hear from you
help us
help you
here are
here is
here is the
hope that
hope you will
hours ago

how many
how many of the
how many of them
how many of these
how many times
how much
I am
I am glad
I am of the opinion
I am sure
I came
I can
I can be
I can have
I can say
I can see
I cannot
I cannot be
I cannot be sure
I cannot have
I can't
I could
I could be
I could have
I could not
I desire
I did
I did not
I did not say
I do
I do not
I do not say
I do not see

I do not think
I doubt
I enclose
I fear
I feel
I feel sure
I felt
I find
I found
I gave
I give
I have
I have been
I have been able
I have done
I have given
I have had
I have made
I have not
I have not been able
I have not had
I have not yet
I have seen
I have tried
I hope
I hope it will
I hope it will be
I hope that
I hope you will
I knew
I know
I made
I may

I may be
I may have
I might
I might be
I might have
I must
I must be
I must have
I need
I notice
I read
I realize
I regret
I said
I saw
I say
I see
I sent
I should
I should be
I should have
I suggest
I talked
I thank you
I thank you for the
I think
I thought
I told
I took
I want
I want to see
I wanted
I was

I will
I will be
I will be able
I will have
I will not
I will not be
I will not be able
I will see
I wish
I would
I would be
I would have
I would not
I wrote
I wrote you
if it
if it is
if it was
if it will
if it will be
if my
if not
if so
if that
if the
if there are
if there is
if they
if they are
if they are not
if they can
if they cannot
if they may

if they would
if this
if this is
if we
if we are
if we can
if we can be
if we cannot
if we could
if we do
if we have
if you
if you are
if you are sure
if you can
if you can be
if you cannot
if you could
if you did not
if you do
if you do not
if you give
if you have
if you know
if you may
if you must
if you need
if you think
if you want
if you will
if you will be
if you will have
if you wish

if you would
if you would be
if you would have
in a few days
in a few minutes
in a few months
in a position
in addition
in addition to the
in behalf
in case
in fact
in his
in it
in order
in order that
in order to be
in order to be able
in order to obtain
in order to see
in our
in our opinion
in part
in particular
in question
in relation
in spite
in that
in the
in the future
in the past
in the world
in them

in these
in this
in this matter
in this way
in time
in which
in which case
in which it is
in which the
in which you
in which you are
into it
into the
into this
is it
is not
is not yet
is that
is the
is there
is this
is to be
it has been
it is
it is the
it isn't
it was
it will
it will be
it will have
it will not
it will not be
left hand

less and less
less than
less than the
let me
let us
let us have
let us know
let us make
let us say
let us see
letting me
letting us
line of business
line of goods
long ago
long time
long time ago
make the
many of the
many of them
many of these
many other
many times
may be
may be able
may be done
may be sure
may have
men and women
might be
might be able
might have
might have been

might not
might not be
might not be able
months ago
more than
must be
must be able
must be done
must have
my time
need not be
next day
next day or two
next month
next time
next year
next year's
no doubt
none of the
none of them
not only
now and then
of course
of course it is
of his
of its
of mine
of my
of our
of that
of that time
of the
of their

of them
of these
of this
of time
of which
on behalf
on his
on it
on our
on our part
on request
on sale
on that
on that day
on the
on the part
on the question
on the subject
on these
on this
on this case
on time
on which
on your
once a month
once or twice
one of our
one of the
one of the best
one of the most
one of them
one of these
one or two

one thing
one time
one way
only one
only one of these
other than
ought to be
ought to be able
ought to be done
ought to have
out of date
out of the
out of the question
out of them
question of time
quite sure
reach us
reach you
realize that
relation to the
Respectfully yours
safe deposit
seem to be
seems to be
send him
send them
send this
send us
send you
several days
several days ago
several months
several months ago

several other
several times
she can
she cannot
she could
she could not
she could not be
she is
she is not
she may be
she must
she would
should be
should be done
should be made
should have
should have been
should not
should not be
should see
since that time
since the
since this
Sincerely yours
so far
so long
so long a time
so many
so many of the
so many of them
so many times
so much
so that

so well
some of our
some of that
some of the
some of them
some of these
some of this
some time
some time ago
some years
some years ago
suggest that
take the
than the
thank you
thank you for
thank you for your
thank you for your order
that are
that are not
that can
that can be
that do
that do not
that does not
that have
that is
that is not
that is the
that is to say
that it
that it is
that it was
that it will
that it will be
that may
that may be
that must
that our
that this is
that the
that there are
that there is
that these
that they
that they are
that this
that those
that time
that will
that will be
that will not
that would
that would be
that would have
the only thing
there are
there has been
there have
there is
there may
there may be
there might be
there was
there will
there will be

they are
they are not
they can
they can be
they can have
they cannot
they cannot be
they cannot have
they can't
they come
they could
they could not
they did
they did not
they do
they do not
they have
they may
they may be
they may be able
they might
they might be
they might not
they must
they must be
they must be able
they must have
they think
they want
they will
they will be
they will be able
they will have

they will not
they would
they would be
they would be able
they would be glad
they would have
this can
this can be
this cannot
this cannot be
this case
this did not
this information
this is
this is not
this is the
this matter
this may
this may be
this means
this month
this morning
this one
this time
this was
this way
this will
this will be
this would
this would be
through its
through that
through the

through this
to be
to be able
to be done
to be sure
to become
to begin
to believe
to buy
to call
to change
to charge
to check
to choose
to come
to continue
to convince
to cover
to do
to do it
to do so
to do the
to face
to fall
to feel
to fill
to find
to follow
to form
to forward
to furnish
to get
to give

to give me
to give you
to go
to have
to have been
to have you
to his
to it
to keep
to know
to make
to me
to participate
to pass
to pay
to persuade
to place
to plan
to please
to prepare
to present
to prevent
to print
to proceed
to produce
to prove
to provide
to publish
to purchase
to put
to say
to see
to sell

to serve
to serve you
to ship
to speak
to spend
to surprise
to take
to talk
to tell
to thank you
to thank you for
to that
to the
to their
to them
to these
to think
to this
to time
to try
to turn
to us
to verify
to which
to which the
to whom
to you
too much
twice as much
two months ago
two or three
up to
up to date

up to the
up to the minute
up to this time
upon the
upon the subject
upon this
upon which
Very cordially yours
very glad
very glad to hear
very good
very important
very many
very much
Very sincerely yours
very small
very soon
Very truly yours
very well
want to see
was done
was it
was made
was that
was the
was this
we are
we are not
we are not yet
we are of the opinion
we are sending
we are sure
we can

we can be
we can have
we cannot
we cannot be
we cannot say
we can see
we can't
we could
we could be
we could have
we could not
we desire
we did
we did not
we do
we do not
we do not say
we do not see
we do not think
we enclose
we feel
we feel sure
we felt
we find
we found
we give
we have
we have been
we have been able
we have done
we have had
we have made
we have not

we have not been
we have not yet
we have your order
we hope
we hope it will
we hope that
we hope that the
we hope this will
we hope to have
we hope you will
we hope you will not
we knew
we know
we made
we mailed
we make
we may
we may be
we may be able
we may have
we might
we might be
we might be able
we might have
we must
we must be
we must have
we need
we realize that
we should
we should be
we should be glad
we should have

we should not be able
we thank you
we thank you for
we thank you for the
we think
we tried
we try
we want
we will
we will be
we will be able
we will have
we will not
we will not be
we will see
we will send you
we wish
we would
we would be
we would be glad
we would have
we would not
we would not be
we would not be able
we wrote
week or two
week or two ago
weeks ago
were not
were sure
what are
what has been
what is

what our
what was
what will
when that
when the
when they
when this
when you
when you are
which does
which has
which have
which is
which may
which may be
which means
which must
which they have
which was
which way
which we are
which you can
which you cannot
who are
who are not
who can
who can be
who cannot
who could
who could be
who could not
who desire
who do not

who have
who have done
who have had
who have not
who is
who is not
who know
who made
who may
who may be
who might
who might be
who might have
who must
who need
who should
who should be
who should have
who want
who will
who will be
who will be able
who will have
who will not
who will not be
who would
who would be
who would have
who would have been
who would not
why not
will be
will be able
will be done
will be glad
will find
will have
will not be
will not be able
will you
will you please
wish to say
with him
with his
with our
with ours
with that
with the
with them
with these
with this
with us
with which
with whom
with you
within the
would be
would be able
would be done
would be glad
would have
would have been
would not
would not be
would not have been
written you

years ago
years of age
you are
you are not
you are sure
you can
you can be
you can be sure
you can get
you can give
you can have
you can make
you cannot
you cannot have
you cannot pay
you cannot see
you could
you could be
you could have
you could have been
you could see
you could not
you could not have
you couldn't
you desire
you did
you did not
you did not say
you did not see
you do
you do not
you don't
you gave

you have
you have been
you have had
you have not
you have not been
you have not been able
you knew
you know
you made
you may
you may be
you may be able
you may be sure
you may have
you might
you might be
you must
you must be
you must be able
you must have
you need
you order
you ordered
you see
you should
you should be
you should be able
you should have
you should not
you think
you want
you wanted
you will

you will be
you will be able
you will be glad
you will be sure
you will find
you will have
you will not
you will not be
you will not be able
you will not have
you will see
you would
you would be
you would be able
you would be glad

you would be sure
you would have
you would have been
you would not
you would not be
you would not be able
you would not have
your inquiry
your name
your order
your orders
Yours cordially
Yours sincerely
Yours very sincerely
Yours very truly

part five

Part Five contains abbreviations for 126 expressions, with a suggested shorthand outline given for each expression.

Some expressions are dictated and transcribed almost exclusively in the abbreviated form—*FOB* (*free on board*). Others may be dictated and transcribed either in full or in the form of initials—*AV* (*audiovisual*).

There are many acceptable variations in the use of periods and capitals in abbreviations. For example, the expression *revolutions per minute* may be expressed *rpm, r.p.m.,* or *RPM*.

abbreviations

AA	Alcoholics Anonymous
ABC	American Broadcasting Company
ACE	American Council on Education
ACTH	adrenocorticotropic hormone
AEC	Atomic Energy Commission
AFL-CIO	American Federation of Labor and Congress of Industrial Organizations
a.m.	*ante meridiem*
AMA	American Medical Association
AP	Associated Press
ARC	American Red Cross
ASAP	as soon as possible
AV	audiovisual
AVA	American Vocational Association
B.A.	bachelor of arts

B.C.	before Christ
B.S.	bachelor of science
Btu	British thermal unit
C	Celsius
CAB	Civil Aeronautics Board
CBS	Columbia Broadcasting System
CIA	Central Intelligence Agency
CIF	cost, insurance, and freight
CNO	chief of naval operations
COD	cash on delivery
CPA	certified public accountant
CPO	chief petty officer
cu cm	cubic centimeter
DA	district attorney
DAR	Daughters of the American Revolution
D.C.	District of Columbia
DDD	direct distance dialing
D.D.S.	doctor of dental surgery
DOA	dead on arrival
e.g.	*exempli gratia* (for example)
EKG	electrocardiogram
ESP	extrasensory perception
EST	eastern standard time
ETA	estimated time of arrival
et al.	*et alii* (and others)
etc.	*et cetera* (and so forth)
FAA	Federal Aviation Agency
FBI	Federal Bureau of Investigation

FCC	Federal Communications Commission
FDA	Food and Drug Administration
FM	frequency modulation
FOB	free on board
G.B.	Great Britain
GI	general issue
GM	general manager
GNP	gross national product
GOP	Grand Old Party (Republican)
GP	general practitioner
HEW	Health, Education, and Welfare
HQ	headquarters
IBM	International Business Machines
ID	identification
i.e.	*id est* (that is)
ILA	International Longshoremen's Association
IQ	intelligence quotient
IRS	Internal Revenue Service
LIFO	last in, first out
LL.B.	bachelor of laws
LL.M.	master of laws
M.A.	master of arts
MC	master of ceremonies
M.D.	doctor of medicine
mm	millimeter
MP	member of parliament
mph	miles per hour
ms	manuscript

mss	manuscripts
MST	mountain standard time
n/30	net in 30 days
NA	not applicable, not available
NAACP	National Association for the Advancement of Colored People
NASA	National Aeronautics and Space Administration
NATO	North Atlantic Treaty Organization
N.B.	*nota bene* (note well)
NBC	National Broadcasting Company
NLRB	National Labor Relations Board
NOW	National Organization for Women
OAS	Organization of American States
OK	okay
PAL	Police Athletic League
PBX	private branch exchange
PGA	Professional Golfers' Association
PHA	Public Housing Administration
Ph.D.	doctor of philosophy
PHS	Public Health Service
PL	profit and loss
p.m.	*post meridiem*
P.O.	post office
POW	prisoner of war
PR	public relations
PS	*postscriptum* (postscript)
PST	Pacific standard time
PTA	Parent-Teacher Association
PX	post exchange

RAF	Royal Air Force
R&D	research and development
RBI	runs batted in
REA	Rural Electrification Administration
ROTC	Reserve Officers' Training Corps
rpm	revolutions per minute
R.S.V.P.	*répondez s'il vous plaît* (please reply)
SBA	Small Business Administration
SEATO	Southeast Asia Treaty Organization
SEC	Securities and Exchange Commission
SRO	standing room only
SSA	Social Security Administration
TV	television
TVA	Tennessee Valley Authority
U.K.	United Kingdom
UN	United Nations
UP	United Press
UPI	United Press International
U.S.	United States
U.S.A.	United States of America
U.S.S.R.	Union of Soviet Socialist Republics
V.I.	Virgin Islands
VIP	very important person
V.P.	vice president
W.I.	West Indies
wpm	words per minute
YMCA	Young Men's Christian Association
ZIP	Zone Improvement Plan

part six
the metric system

Part Six contains 48 suggested shortcuts for common metric terms. If you take dictation in which there are many occurrences of metric measurements, you will have frequent use for the abbreviated forms given below. It is not wise to attempt to learn these forms until you know you will have use for them.

The metric system was devised by France and adopted there by law in 1799. Since that time its use has become almost universal except in Great Britain and the United States. It is rapidly coming into use in those two countries and, therefore, it is possible that you will need these special outlines. If the terms occur only infrequently in your dictation, it is better to write them in full.

The following abbreviations will be useful to those who must frequently take metric measurements in dictation.

		meter	**liter**	**gram**
kilo-	1,000			
hekto-	100			
deka-	10			
deci-	1/10			
centi-	1/100			
milli-	1/1,000			
micro-	1/1,000,000			
nano-	1/1,000,000,000			

Additional Metric Measurements

Celsius		kilowatt		micron	
centigrade		kilowatt-hour		microsecond	
cubic centimeter		megabit		milliampere	
kilobit		megahertz		millibar	
kilocalorie		megaton		millifarad	
kilocycle		megawatt		millivolt	
kilohertz		megohm		milliwatt	
kilovolt		micromicron		nanosecond	